STRIP CLUB HEIRESS

STRIP CLUB HEIRESS

The Jet Strip, My Father's Conviction, and the Murder of Mac McKenna

Laurel Woods

BLOOMSBURY ACADEMIC
NEW YORK • LONDON • OXFORD • NEW DELHI • SYDNEY

BLOOMSBURY ACADEMIC
Bloomsbury Publishing Inc, 1359 Broadway, New York, NY 10018, USA
Bloomsbury Publishing Plc, 50 Bedford Square, London, WC1B 3DP, UK
Bloomsbury Publishing Ireland, 29 Earlsfort Terrace, Dublin 2, D02 AY28, Ireland

First published in the United States of America 2026

Cover design: (c) iStock.com/EyeOfPaul
Cover image by Sally Rinehart

Library of Congress Cataloging-in-Publication Data

ISBN: HB: 979-8-216-37218-9
ePDF: 979-8-216-37219-6
eBook: 979-8-216-37220-2

Typeset by Integra Software Services Pvt. Ltd.
Printed and bound in the United States of America

For product safety related questions contact productsafety@bloomsbury.com.

For Anne Hurley Obot, my partner in crime, who accepted and loved me unconditionally. You are so incredibly missed.

CONTENTS

ACKNOWLEDGMENTS

First off to Dr. Pearson, my New York therapist, who said I needed to write this shit down. Shahnaz Habib, my memoir instructor at Gotham Writers Workshop, who believed in my Huey story. Rebecca Weston, my fantastic editor who worked on early drafts of my story, was more of a therapist, and a great listener. Roger Browning, Janet, and Lena Munoz, the best attorney and paralegal team who helped us pick up the many pieces after the dust settled. Patty, Stanley, and Dustin Zahn, who called to check on us often, took us out to dinner after Dad's arrest. Ron and Sandy Shaw for Thanksgiving and making us laugh when all seemed impossible.

The following people offered endless amounts of love, support, meals, and tissues throughout my dad's ordeal, and the writing of this book, which was just as traumatizing …

The Hurley family, Jim and Connor Obot, Nicole Adams, Alyn Topper, Ben Roussel, Josh Kossack, *Moonlighting* buddies Carolyn Gandy, Ana Morino, Mary Costill Fullum, John Osborn, Shawna Saari and Danielle LaBue, Gemma Dempsey, Kendra Howe, Sandy and Linda Dee, Justin and Ferris, David Matezanz, Leigh Kunis, Laura Germida, Lee Chamel, Martha Norton, Mindy Romero, Shama Alexander, Mark Anderson, Carrie Prince, Bobby Cheslin and Chris Aurit, Genevieve Morgan, Heather Jones, Cutter Hodierne, Kyle Spaulding, Marc Olson, Alireza, Amanda Anderson, Curtis Armstrong, Georgia Gruber, Miki Garcia and Renée Mason.

Westlake High School friends Tom Cull, Nicki Swafford, Terri Bumbarger, Christina Harrison, Cindy O'Brien, Olivia Wright, Lisbet Halverson, Kim Castro, Keisha Gallegos, Leslie Daland, Jill Kitka-Leonard, Heather Maciorski, Debbie Phillips, and Cathleen Cull.

UCSB friends Susan Han, Heather Savelle, Carrie Cassée, Dennis McCauliff, Gus Hoek. Playboy besties Susan Edelist, Carolita Blythe, and Debra Leavitt.

Lucasfilm family Nagisa Yamamoto, Adrienne Biggs, Erin West, Kimberly Lashbrook, Amy Shepard, Huck Wirtz, Jack Haye, David Tanaka, Nancy Luckoff, Jiri Jacknowitz, John Ellis, Zoe Hare, Ken Maruyama, Suzy McLaughlin, Matt Wallin, Ronn Brown, Heidi Zabit, Joanne Hafner, Jon Alexander, Jack Mongovan,

Susan Kelly, Katherine Tate, John Stillman, Ed Chin and Coya Elliot, Amy and Bill Tiller, Tony Burquez, Tim Schafer, Mike Gallo, Wayne Cline, Dave Harris, Heather Philipps, Vince Clark, James and Lamona Wood, Joan Amberg, Jessica Forys, Melanie Lamoureux, Rachel Hardwick, Catherine Durand, Kristen Becht, Neena Bonetti, Emily Duval, Kari Zanotto, David and Lani Gershik.

MTV crew Stefanie Malachi, Matt Anderson and Thaddeus Delonis, Scotty Albrecht, Jimmy McCain, Rory Rockmore, Tim Haldeen, Kerstin Recker, Amanda Havey, Brian Wong, Bradley Hatfield, Paul DeGeorges, and Jason Cipriano.

American Airlines flight attendants Kelly Morrison, Kathy Piombo, Cindy O'Shea, Jill Sanders, Chiriya Harding, Dominique Stewart, Tony Cataldo, and Masie Comtois.

Connie and Paul Kniss, Beth and Brett Kniss, Aunt Deanie, Uncle Derrick and Vance Bluschke, and Kristen LaBaume, my second family.

To all the other visitors at jails and prisons who helped us maneuver the system in the beginning.

My Mom, Dad, and sister for blessing me with one wacky family.

If I forgot anyone, please accept my apologies, and I owe you one!

PHOTOS

Dad and me in Inglewood, circa 1970

Mom, Dad and me in North Bergen, New Jersey, at Uncle Derrick's mom's house, circa 1971.

Dad on the California Highway Patrol, April 1967. He loved that job so much and still talks about it every day.

The Jet Strip, one of Mac and Dad's strip clubs. Located at 10624 Hawthorne Boulevard, Inglewood.

Bobby Cheslin and his best friend Horace "Mac" McKenna, in Vegas. Bobby worked at the strip clubs after Dad's arrest. Bobby and Dad are still in touch.

Visiting Dad for the last time before his release from prison, California Institution for Men, Chino, California. April 22, 2017.

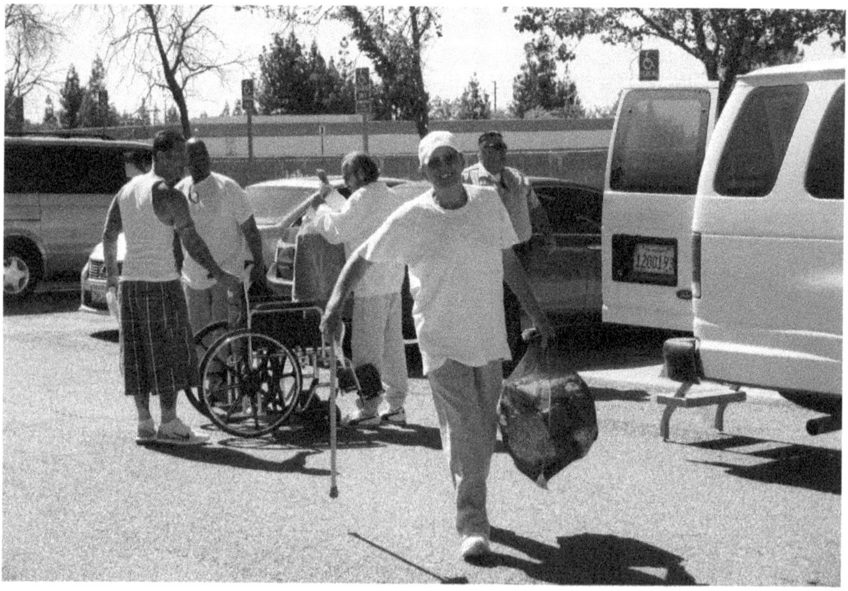

Dad being released from prison at the Montclair Transit Center, June 28, 2017. I hadn't seen that smile in almost 20 years.

Mom brought Dad balloons and flowers to celebrate his release.

Taking Dad out to dinner at one of his favorite restaurants in downtown Los Angeles, The Water Grill, December 2017. He wasn't used to nice meals after 17 years of prison chow.

Dad in his family apartment on Gregory Street prior to being sold to the Thompsons. Jersey City, circa 1946.

PART ONE

INNOCENCE IS OVERRATED

1 Shiny Brass Pole

In the spring of 1977, my life was a version of *CHiPs* meets *Shaft*—the kind of thing happening outside Los Angeles' suburbs when you stay up past 9:00 p.m.

Dad's decision to own and manage the club appalled Mom, a devout Christian, who couldn't imagine how she was going to cover up this horrific embarrassment in our *Stepford Wives* neighborhood. She began giving my father the cold shoulder for months as he began putting his top-secret business plan together. "If you go through with this, I can't guarantee the kids and I will stay around, Michael," she said with her arms crossed.

Mom ran a tight ship at home, dressing up Rachel and me in our cute outfits and making sure our hair was brushed, putting our hair in symmetrical pigtails with the perfect part down the middle before we walked out the front door. We weren't allowed to wear tennis shoes with skirts, like the other girls at our elementary school. Mom knew the Avon and Tupperware ladies, the milk man, and the Hoover vacuum repair guy who'd all say she had angelic little girls. She donated what money they could afford each Sunday to the donation basket at church. Dad's new gig would crush the image she worked so hard to maintain for our family.

"But I'll be bringing in good money," Dad tried to assure her as he went in to hug Mom, stiff as a telephone pole. *A job's a job*, I thought. Why did she care so much if we had what we needed? Dad always dreamed of bigger and more. He wanted a bigger house, more cars, nicer jewelry, and vacations for mom. He wanted to be "the guy".

Anything your dad could do, my dad could do with a cherry on top and extra sprinkles. That Halloween, Dad dressed up like Darth Vader in full gear—helmet, cape, and in black from head to toe. He knocked on the door to the den where Rachel and I were watching television. I started crying, and Dad lifted the helmet from his head. Darth Vader still scared me to death, and I thought he might use the Force to crush my throat. Dad laughed and hugged his girls, before heading to the door to greet trick-or-treaters.

I heard tidbits of Dad's new job he'd just started. Rachel and I weren't sure what the full story was, but we knew two things—it involved something with nudity, and Mom was not happy. "I almost divorced your father over his decision," she later admitted. Dad's friend Mac, an old police buddy, was just released from prison. I thought it was cool that Dad knew someone in the slammer, as Dad called it. I knew Mom didn't like the naked part, but I mean Adam and Eve walked around naked in the Bible. Mom was sure Dad's new job would lead to things like the mafia. "What's the mafia?" I asked her. "Laurel, remember those *Godfather* movies you watched with us where everyone dies?" I mostly remembered them eating lots of spaghetti and meatballs in those movies and something about taking a cannoli.

"What do people do there? Is there dancing? Is there disco?" I asked Dad. It was the seventies, and I was obsessed with disco. I had a pair of satin pants and knew all the words to the *Saturday Night Fever* album. As best he could, Dad described the Jet Strip as a nightclub that served food and drinks where pretty girls danced. I totally pictured it to be like American Bandstand at Bob's Big Boy.

Rachel and I regularly heard Mom and Dad argue in the kitchen while we watched *Bugs Bunny* and *The Flintstones* cartoons in the den. I always felt bad for Dad when Mom yelled at him.

"I don't like you coming home every night at three in the morning smelling of booze and smoke!"

Dad would hug Mom and tell her how much he loved her, with his Pepé Le Pew grin and wooing her over, just like the female cats Pepé chased in the cartoon.

It's my job, blue eyes.

9:00 p.m. was a strict bedtime at our house. No way would Mom let me wait up for Dad, but he always came in to kiss me good night minutes after his headlights flashed in my bedroom window. He loved imitating Elmer Fudd with "I'm gonna get you, you crazy *wabbit*!" when he leaned over, brushed my hair out of my face, kissed me good night on the forehead, and it made me giggle.

One Sunday, when I was 9 and Rachel was 7, a few months after the Jet Strip opened, Mom had to work a weekend shift at the hospital, so Dad decided to take us to his club. "The club? Really Michael? That's just *great*," Mom said, slamming the kitchen cabinets shut. Dad couldn't wait to show off his little girls to his employees, and we were super excited to see not only where he worked but what had caused so much commotion between our parents. It was like going to Disneyland for the first time. I wasn't sure what to expect. I thought about the roller skate nights at my elementary school. I knew there would be music, and I hoped they would play the Bee Gees and ABBA, especially "Dancing Queen". I danced to ABBA at home on our couch when my parents weren't watching. Dad said there would be a DJ, and I could make a request!

I barely slept a wink the night before our trip to the Jet Strip. When I woke up the next morning, John Denver's music played in the kitchen while Mom made us breakfast. Dad made his appearance in a maroon leather jacket with matching ankle boots over gray polyester slacks and a white dress shirt (think Gene Hackman in *The French Connection*). He'd recently had his hair permed, and we were still getting used to it. We were getting used to Dad's whole new look, which was nothing like a cop, except he did still carry a gun with him everywhere. He grabbed Mom in a bear hug and flashed a Cheshire Cat grin. She squirmed away to place the cereal bowls in front of Rachel and me.

"Dad, will you let us dance at the club? Roller skate?" I asked.

He smirked and stared down the floor while Mom grimaced. "I don't like this," she said. But she was distracted and running late and needed us out of the way. She donned her white kitty-print nurse uniform and brushed her Dorothy Hamill bob instead of readying us with a backpack of sandwiches and coloring books. I once asked her why she always had to wear white. "I just do, baby. Those are the rules." She grabbed me by the shoulders, leaned forward, and said, "Don't do anything stupid." Stethoscope and nametag in place, she yelled over her shoulder to us, "Somebody clean Coco's litter box out," as she slammed the front door and left without a kiss goodbye.

We took off for the day in our orange van with mushroom wallpaper on the inside walls and brown shag carpeting. An hour later, we pulled into a gated parking lot. Airplanes flew overhead as a sign appeared, bearing the silhouette of a woman riding atop a plane and the name "Jet Strip." I wanted to look grown-up, so I left Holly Hobbie behind.

Entering the Jet Strip was like walking into a matinee movie, and it took my eyes awhile to adjust to complete darkness, as there were no windows. The whole place smelled like Windex and stale smoke. Dad tossed his keys and gun on the bar and turned on the stage lights to reveal a rotating disco ball. Soon, the Bee Gees' "Night Fever" burst through the speakers. Rachel and I ran toward the stage and danced on brightly lit colored floor panels surrounded by mirrors. Our hands squeaked as we swung around the shiny brass pole in the middle of the stage, a little girl Heaven.

Blinding sun filled the room as pretty women filtered in, one after the other, smiling, laughing, and shooting us puzzled looks as we carried on. I felt awkward, froze in place, and stumbled down off the stage. We ran over to the bar and met a tall, thin woman, Kelly, with perfect blond hair straight out of *Alice in Wonderland*. She played with our pigtails, and asked, "What would you ladies like to drink?" I had no idea what to ask for besides milk. "How about two Shirley Temples?" Kelly suggested, and came back with two drinks, with umbrellas and maraschino cherries.

"What's in it?" Rachel asked. I had already slammed mine down and asked for another cherry. *I could live here*, I thought.

We met other women with names like "Krystal," "Amber," and "Destiny." I can't be sure, but I could swear I met one named Jell-O! "Those are their stage names, not their real names," Dad revealed. Why would anyone want two names? Should I have two names? I thought about another name I'd like to be called, like Leia or Jaime Sommers.

We grabbed our drinks and followed Dad into the back room complete with a cigarette machine, pool tables, and video games. Dad pushed a few buttons so we could play Space Invaders for free. I buzzed from the excitement and the chance to experience the adult world. But what was "adult" about it? In my newly inspired view, it was the perfect place for kids!

The club opened at 11:00 a.m., and customers started to trickle in. Dad barked out orders to the dancers, the DJ, and the cook, and everyone began scurrying around. He was so important, and I felt like his princess. He explained that the women were professional dancers, and while they would each dance to three different songs, we could only watch the first song. This sent my mind racing, wondering what the difference was between each song and each dance. Krystal, wearing a long, red rhinestone dress with slits up the side, appeared from behind the red velvet curtains as a new song came on. She strutted onto the stage, grabbed the pole, and wiggled her hips around like in a hula hoop. She looked like a beauty pageant contestant. Men tossed dollar bills, which fell in a magical motion like leaves from trees all around her. No wonder Dad wanted this business. Money was floating around everywhere!

As another song started, Dad rounded us up and escorted us to a secret door. It led upstairs to an office with wood-paneled walls, beige shag carpeting, a gray metal desk, and a worn-out burgundy leather couch with gold rivets. A television sat on top of a glass coffee table. Along the wall opposite the couch was a series of security monitors with fuzzy black and white views of the parking lot, bar, entrance door, and stage.

Mac was in the office tearing into an almost-raw steak with a large knife. That is, Mac McKenna, Dad's longtime friend and new business partner in this dark, dreamy dwelling. He got up and with all his form, hugged us like a giant bear would if bears hugged people. As was customary when we saw him, he showed us a couple of pictures in his wallet that defied imagination—more real-life safari animals that were his new "pets." I was so amazed that they could be at his house just like my cat Coco, except his cat was a big tiger. That alone made Mac seem larger than life. In his polite way, he asked us how school was going. The topic was totally boring compared to wildlife and wild women, so we brushed it off with a "Good!" in unison.

Dad led Rachel and me up another flight of stairs and opened a door to the roof. He showed us the planes flying overhead as they landed at LAX. The sunlight contrasted with the club's dark interior, and our eyes slowly adjusted. We returned inside, where Dad slipped a bootlegged copy of *Star Wars* into a Betamax video player. We must have watched that same tape over 200 times already, but I couldn't get enough. I liked to daydream that I was Princess Leia's friend, helping her save the galaxy.

Dad called his cook, Carl, over to take our order. He said we could eat anything we wanted. I went straight for the hamburger with extra ketchup, pickles, and Coke. "Don't watch the security monitors," Dad instructed. "I'll come back up to check on you both soon."

We sat on the couch, munched on our burgers, and watched the movie, drinking Cokes garnished with colorful umbrellas. I don't know why Mom was so upset about Dad's new business. This place was amazing. I couldn't wait to tell everyone at school. I was definitely going to be the most popular girl now!

After lunch, Mac came upstairs to greet us in that low Darth Vader voice he had. He then pulled out some Double Bubble gum and handed us each a piece. He petted both our heads. "Your daddy is so proud of you," he cooed, and we uttered a "Thank you, Mac," in unison. Then he headed back downstairs to the floor.

Now alone in the office, we rushed over to the monitors. There was no audio feed, but we heard Journey's "Wheel in the Sky" vibrating through the floor. On the monitor, a dancer, now topless, with high heels and dark hair, appeared and swung around the pole. Our jaws dropped. Our eyes fixed on the stage monitor. The dancer du jour swirled around naked—and not embarrassed at all. How did she do *that*? I looked away in shame, but then turned right around and watched more. She had big boobs. Right then, I decided that when I grew up, I definitely wanted those too.

Carl returned, collected our dishes, and led us back downstairs for a tour of the kitchen. We were mind-blown by the stacks of ice cream and the raw meats stored in the walk-in freezer. When Carl walked away, we glanced through the order window for a peek at the stage. Kelly came on, wearing high-heeled shoes and a sheer nightgown. She shimmied out of her nightgown to reveal bright pink, sparkling underwear that, as she swung around the pole, didn't display a back. How did she get her underwear to stay on? Mom bought our underwear at Sears, and they covered my whole bottom. It annoyed me when they'd creep up, but Kelly's underwear creeping didn't seem to bother her. She performed gymnastic moves on the pole and could do the splits upside down. Her underwear material did not budge.

The customers whistled, and she seemed to be having fun—dancing around, flipping her hair, legs in the air. The song ended. Kelly grabbed her clothes and dollar bills and scurried off the stage. Dad came into the kitchen and found us staring, open-mouthed, at the stage. "I told you not to leave the office. What happened?" Dad sent us back upstairs to watch more *Star Wars*.

Dad drove us back home in time for dinner. I was exhausted from all the excitement, but I felt like I'd been welcomed into Dad's secret club. The naked women didn't faze Dad—it was like being naked was normal.

On the ride home, Dad promised we could visit the club again. "Just don't tell your mother you saw the dancers nude." I eagerly agreed to the small price of being able to return. Emboldened, I asked, "Why do they dance naked in front of people?"

"They make great money, that's why." Dad stepped on the gas, and our orange van merged onto the 101 freeway.

"Are they real dancers, like me? Do they take ballet?"

"Yeah, some have a dance background."

"Do you feel bad about the dancers being naked?"

Rachel was in the back napping with her doll during my inquiry.

"No, sweetheart. The girls make good money, and I make great money, which means I can provide more for our family. Do you understand that?"

"Yes, Dad."

He explained that many of his customers were married but wanted to stare at pretty girls with nice bodies.

"But why, Dad?"

"Not all women have bodies like that, Lip," Dad's pet name for me.

"Why do the men's wives let them come here?"

"Oh, I doubt they tell their wives, honey."

We walked in the front door, and Mom greeted us with dinner. My sister and I shared stories of our day at the club. She responded with a curt *mm-hmm*, but continued listening. "Mommy, don't you want to know who we met?" We told her about Kelly serving Shirley Temples and Carl grilling us burgers. We left out the naked dancing part because we wanted to go again. I didn't say I was full of food I ate at The Jet. I tried to finish dinner. Her face stiffened, but I knew she wouldn't be mad at us if only she knew how much fun we had. Then with an ominous tone, she said, "Girls, I don't think it's a good idea to tell your friends at school about going to the club with Daddy." My sister and I glanced at each other. How could I keep this a secret? I wanted to tell everyone at school and had already made a list of friends to bring the next time. My next birthday party would for sure be at the super cool Jet Strip!

After dinner, we played in the backyard and coordinated two picnic benches together in a T-shape. I played Barry Manilow's "Copacabana" on our cassette tape player, and Dad introduced us with dazzling new stage names, "Holly" and "Coco," as we paraded onto our stage, swaying and swinging.

"Look, Mommy, look!" we shouted to her in the kitchen window as she washed the dishes from dinner. Dad snickered and shrugged his shoulders at her as she studied us like she no longer knew what or who she was seeing.

2 Just a Normal Family

The year 1968 was a turbulent time in America—anti-Vietnam War protests were at their height, Martin Luther King Jr. and Robert Kennedy were both assassinated, the Beatles released their *White* album, and I was born in Inglewood, California.

Dad used to call the Beatles and Jane Fonda "commies." "Daddy, why are they called 'commies' if they're not Russian?" I asked. "Because they're just a bunch of hippies poisoning our country." I pretended to know what he meant, but you can't explain politics to a 6-year-old without some confusion.

We lived in a modest two-bedroom apartment in Baldwin Hills, South Los Angeles, where rapper Ice-T and Duchess of Sussex Megan Markle grew up. My parents managed the twenty-eight-unit apartment complex. Dad also worked as a California Highway Patrol officer and rode a motorcycle, like hunky Erik Estrada in *CHiPs*. That's how he and Mac initially met, riding bikes and patrolling the city on the force together.

After my sister, Rachel, was born in 1970, we got priced out of Los Angeles, and moved to a suburb an hour north called Newbury Park. My parents bought their first house for $26,000 with the help of a VA loan. Newbury Park had small houses, orange groves, and a groovy drive-in. Now the homes are McMansions, the orange groves are terra cotta strip malls, and my old ice rink is a Hampton Inn. The drive-in where I saw *Herbie The Love Bug* is a Kohl's department store.

When I drive through Newbury Park today, old memories flood in. I feel simultaneously lucky to have grown up in such a serene town and outrage over the horrifying incident that stole my serenity when I was 6 years old. That day, the neighborhood kids and I were playing the ultimate game of hide-and-seek. I thought I was clever enough to find the best hiding place in a two-block radius. A crowded patch of bushes and shrubs a little off the beaten path. I even giggled aloud to myself, thinking of my ingenious choice. But the 10-year-old bully on the block heard me. He pulled me deeper into the bushes from behind. It happened so fast. He pulled off my purple bell-bottom pants and my underwear. He laid me on the ground and put his penis inside me, panting heavily. I was terrified … frozen. And then after he was done, he jumped up from the dirt and ran away toward the rest of the kids on the street. It was agonizing, confusing, and quick. I pulled up my pants, ran home, and hid under my bed, my heart pounding as I held my breath. I thought I was in trouble. I stayed under my twin bed until Mom called me to the dinner table. I kept expecting a phone call from his mom next door telling on me, but that never happened. Then for all too long, I would stay in hiding from normal sexual exploration, dating, and love. I didn't tell my parents for forty-eight years.

"Okay, ready? One, two, three, jump!" I screamed at my elementary school classmates, swinging on the swing set. We'd jump into the sandbox to see who could leap the farthest during recess. "What happened to your knees?" Mom would often ask me. We also climbed the trees and ate the walnuts off of them. I figured out all on my own why the school was named Walnut Elementary. We played outside every day because California days were always warm and sunny.

At home, Dad played Mister Fixit on his time off. He mowed the lawn, washed the cars, and dragged the metal trash cans out to the street curb. Mom took care of washing and dressing Rachel and me, plus all the cooking and cleaning. One day, as I sat on Dad's knee, he disclosed, "I never thought I'd live past 21 years old. And I definitely never thought I'd marry someone as pretty and smart as your mother." I thought 21 years old was rather old, but I was happy he thought Mom was cool.

I loved spending time with Mom when it was just us girls. I watched her pack our lunchboxes with tuna fish sandwiches on Wonder Bread, a box of milk, and a piece of fruit each day before school. I envied the kids who had colorful M&M's and chocolate milk in their lunchboxes, but Stepford Moms would never allow Stepford Kids all that sugar. Mom was gentle, with her slim frame, bright blue eyes, and wavy, brown hair, and a longing to nurture us. I think she wanted for us what she never had growing up—parents. She could also dish out the silent treatment if she was mad at you. If you danced on the living room sofa to "Dancing Queen" by ABBA, spilling a can of V8 juice, you could expect the cold shoulder for at least twenty-four hours. I hated it when Mom ignored me, and wished she would just spank me instead. That way the torture was quick.

Mom would make us Mickey Mouse pancakes for breakfast on Saturdays with Bisquick blueberry muffins. Rachel and I would lick the mixer beaters and bowl clean. For supper, Mom usually prepared Swanson TV dinners in the oven. We'd eat them on TV trays while watching *Mash* or *Hogan's Heroes* on the "boob tube," as Dad called it. Dad occasionally enjoyed making us corned beef hash with eggs for dinner, his favorite. Rachel and I thought having breakfast food for dinner was so cool.

Mom dressed Rachel and me up in similar outfits, and most people thought we were twins. I liked our groovy polyester outfits, especially anything with purple and green flower patterns. Sometimes she wound our hair in pigtails with a Mickey Mouse bandana tied around our head. Hand-me-downs were the usual in our house, while Kmart was reserved for special occasions. We did most of our shopping at the Fedco in Los Angeles on La Cienega. Fedco was similar to Costco and offered lifetime memberships to government employees for five dollars. They had everything from food to toys to candy. I wished I could live there! I'd spend hours in the toy gun section, picking them up and aiming at people. I also loved their bakery and drooled at all the colorful cookies and cupcakes. My favorite was their cookie monster cupcake. Mom said it would turn my teeth blue.

In the seventies, Dad was usually outside hosing down or fixing something. Rachel and I hung outside with him, playing on the backyard lawn. I worshipped him. He set up an above-ground Doughboy pool and a Slip 'N Slide in the backyard. The grass glittered with water drops and smelled fresh, and the bright orange California poppies grew wild along the fence. Sometimes Dad chased Rachel and me with the hose as we screeched and ran. "Please be careful!" Mom would yell outside at all three of us. He always declared how much he loved us and how lucky we were to have parents who doted on us.

On Saturdays, we piled into our red Volkswagen bus with red-checkered curtains, and went to the local drive-in. Rachel and I wore our pajamas and had sleeping bags in the back. Dad took us to the snack stand for hot dogs, sodas, and popcorn. We were allowed to watch the cartoons and the first movie, but our folks made us go to sleep once the second movie started. One time, the second movie was *Coming Home*, starring Jon Voight and Jane Fonda. It was about the Vietnam War, and there were several sex scenes. Rachel and I pretended to be asleep but watched the whole movie with our eyes and mouths wide open. My first time seeing nudity and sex on a big screen! Questions chirped in my mind. Why did they do those things to each other? And why were they so sweaty? Had the neighborhood bully wanted to replicate this type of scene with me, a mere child? My mind couldn't reconcile the meaning of this aggression as anything positive or loving.

We went to church every Sunday. Afterward, Rachel and I attended Sunday school with our children's Bibles given to us by Aunt Deanie and Uncle Derrick. If we behaved at Bible study, which was about 70 percent of the time, Mom and Dad took us to IHOP afterward for breakfast. One time in Sunday school, I peed in my underwear while laughing and pointing in my Bible at naked illustrations of Adam and Eve. I couldn't believe my stupid teacher told on me. We did not go to IHOP that Sunday.

On hot summer nights, Dad would set up Mom's green Girl Scout tent in our backyard for a camping night. Rachel and I brought our friends along—Barbie, Cher Barbie, Holly Hobbie, and Raggedy Ann. Dad tucked us in to our sleeping bags and then read us a story with Mom's Girl Scout flashlight. "I do not like green eggs and ham. I do not like them, Sam-I-Am," Dad recited.

“Will you make us *green eggs*, Daddy?” I asked.

“If your mother lets me, sweetheart,” he said. Then Dad would zip Rachel and me up in the tent, leaving us the flashlight in case we got scared. Most times, we’d end up back in the house after hearing a stir in the bushes.

See? We were just a normal family.

3 Living on Tootsie Rolls and Twinkies

My father, Michael, was born in Jersey City in 1942 and grew up in nearby Hoboken, attending the same grade school as Frank Sinatra. His great-great-grandfather came from Ireland, and his mother's family were Irish and English. He was one of nine siblings, but three died of malnutrition in infancy. I didn't understand how his mom could just not feed her kids. To make matters worse, his family lost their rented house because his father, Michael, spent most days in saloons getting drunk. My grandfather took my father and moved into a flophouse, while his mother and other siblings lived with their maternal grandmother, Annie, a few miles away.

Dad's childhood memories were sometimes fuzzy. Data trickled out at random times. He revealed that his parents sold him to a couple his dad met at a saloon in Hoboken. Dad then lived with his new family for six months before his father wanted him back. Ironically, Dad said he didn't want to leave because his living conditions were better. His new family, the Johnsons, provided a car and a heated apartment with a refrigerator, a phone, a television, and hot water. He wore clean clothes and even tasted his first peanut butter and jelly sandwich. After taking Dad back, his mother promised the Johnsons her latest unborn child in return, by checking into the hospital as Mrs. Johnson. After the birth, the real Johnsons brought Dad's younger brother, Cooper, to their home. Dad's mom informed him that Cooper Johnson was his cousin. Only years later did his father admit that Cooper was actually Dad's younger brother. My father's mother remained irate about the transaction, as she wanted more money for the child. After Cooper, she gave birth to fraternal twins named "Martha" and "Chuck." *Why would a mother keep having more babies if she couldn't take care of the ones she had*, I thought.

When Dad was seven, his father, Michael, came home one night drunk from the local saloon and fell down, suffering a seizure and fracturing his skull. An ambulance whisked him away to a county hospital, where they admitted him to an alcoholic ward. When his wife went to pick him up, the hospital administrator said she had to sign paperwork to have him released. With a baby in one hand and a pen in the other, she realized she had an option and decided not to sign, leaving him there. She went back home and with six kids to take care of, she started dating other men to help support her needs. The administrator transferred Michael to Hudson County Mental Hospital in Secaucus, New Jersey, where Dad visited his father until he passed away in 1965.

When we were kids, Dad shared wild tales about breaking into the Tootsie Roll and Twinkie Hostess factories to steal food. He also loitered near the Holland Tunnel entrance because the cops there fed him apple pie and chocolate milk. They also gave him rides through the tunnel during shift changes in the sidecar of their motorcycles.

Two sisters named Deanie and Dodie, living in the same projects, befriended Dad and gifted him his nickname, "Mickey." Deanie and Dodie's mom, Marianne, straightened out Mickey by encouraging him to dress better and attend church. She motivated Dad to enlist in the Army, where he was stationed in Virginia as a supply clerk and reinvented himself. He had his rotten teeth pulled out, got dentures, and completed courses for his GED.

I loved listening to Dad tell stories about his life before us, which always sounded adventurous to me, except for the severe neglect, physical abuse, and homeless parts. Eating Tootsie Rolls and Twinkies and not having to be home by dark sounded like Heaven. His life sounded just like Tom Sawyer's. I even had dad make me my own hobo stick that I'd carry around the backyard.

My mother, Debbie, was an only child, born in Newark, New Jersey. Her ancestors came from Germany and Lithuania. Mom never met her father, and her mother died of cancer when she was 15. Her family hid her mother's illness from her, so Mom found out about the terminal cancer a week before her mother passed away. I can still see the sadness in Mom's eyes when she talks about her mom. I wish I could have been her friend then to help cheer her up.

After that, she lived in her maternal Grandma Bush's house in the countryside of Wayne, New Jersey. Mom remembers driving around town in Grandma's green and white '56 Chevrolet with her relatives. Her family smoked, and in the snowy winters, they kept the car windows up while lighting up, forcing Mom to gasp for fresh air. To this day, she detests smoking, coughing loudly around anyone who does.

After Mom's mother died, her stepfather, Herm, saw the effect her mother's death had on her as a teenager, and suggested she go visit her Aunt June for the summer in California. At Herm's insistence, Mom flew out to Victorville, California and finally had kids her own age, including three cousins, to play with, she had the time of her life smack dab in the Mojave Desert. Aunt June's family lived in a tract home in a safe community so Mom could walk or bicycle everywhere. She decided to stay and finish high school in Victorville. After graduation, Mom landed a job as a carhop at the local A&W Root Beer delivering burgers and milkshakes to eager customers in their cars with an attachable window tray. She didn't wear roller skates like they did at Mel's Diner in *American Graffiti*, unfortunately, but it still seemed like a cool job.

Meanwhile, Dad finished his three-year stint in the Army, and moved to Victorville. He hated his mother, still living in Hoboken, and didn't care if he saw her again. He told Rachel and me that her boyfriends regularly beat Dad up and one shot his puppy. And, well, I guess if my mom tried to sell me, I'd probably hate her too! I never really considered her a grandma. Dad lived with his childhood friend, Aunt Deanie, as we referred to her, and her husband, Uncle Derrick, at George Air Force Base, where Derrick worked as a chaplain. Deanie and Derrick Bluschke were our closest family, even now with their three kids and their extended families. Uncle Derrick baptized Rachel and me, and they became our godparents. It took me a while as a kid to understand that we weren't blood related—we still considered them as our relatives.

After settling into California with the Bluschkes, Dad worked at a local cement factory and then as a mail carrier for the Victorville Post Office. He met Mom one night when she served him at the A&W Root Beer, striking up a conversation about growing up in New Jersey. Giddy and smitten, Dad came back to A&W a few more times before summoning the nerve to ask Mom out. On December 10, 1964, Dad took Mom to see *How the West Was Won*. They married four months later and honeymooned with a road trip to San Francisco and Yosemite in their beat-up but still pretty stylish 1959 Jaguar. Their life seemed so easy and carefree in those days. My parents were hipsters!

They moved one neighborhood over, to the high-desert city of Apple Valley, and Mom got a job at the local post office as a clerk, riding her Suzuki motorcycle fifteen minutes each way across the heated Mojave Desert, passing tumbleweeds and snakes. At night, they both did janitorial work to earn extra money. A year later, inspired by his days hanging out with cops at the Holland Tunnel, Dad accepted a job with the California Highway Patrol. The CHP is still recognized as one of the best in the country, so Mom and Dad relocated to Los Angeles.

4 I Am the Bionic Woman

Dad's final day as an active officer involved popping wheelies in the California Highway Patrol (CHP) parking lot, showing off to his fellow officers. He ended up crashing his bike right there in front of everyone. His leg sported a cast and hinged in a wheelchair for weeks. Following the crash, he received a reprimand from his commander citing that he had deviated from upholding officer safety. As far back as I can remember, Dad always had a rebellious side. After eight years of duty, the last six months of which he was on crutches, Dad retired from the CHP in 1974. Luckily, he received money from his disability insurance policy and retirement from the force.

Dad was home recuperating and had more time for Rachel and me than ever. I cherish a few memories. He'd dance with us in the living room while people picked Juicy Fruit gum off trees in a TV commercial featuring a banjo player singing, "Juicy Fruit's the flavor lover's gum!" My sister and I would grab our dolls as he tucked us in our beds at night and sang Frank Sinatra or Nat King Cole.

In 1975, one morning after a night of Dad's Sinatra serenade, Rachel and I, about 6 and 8 years old, woke up and noticed the drawn dining room curtains. The room was dark. Ominous. I thought maybe someone died. Mom and Dad were drinking coffee at the table and suggested we open the curtains. I was groggy and didn't grasp why they couldn't pull the curtains themselves. But I did what I was told, ran over, and pulled down on the cord as morning light poured into the room, blinding me.

Rachel spotted it. "Oh my God! Look … *look Laurel*!" she screeched.

I joined her jumping up and down, though I wasn't yet sure why. Dad opened the sliding glass door, and we took off running outside, like wind-up toys in our pink nightgowns. Dad had turned our backyard tree into a Juicy Fruit gum tree—like in the commercial! Taped to the leaves were packs of Juicy Fruit. We could only reach those on the lower branches, so Mom and Dad lifted us so we could pluck the higher packs off, too. By the time it was over, I swished about five sticks of gum in my mouth. Mom collected our packs so we couldn't eat them all at once, while Dad reveled in our excitement as one of us, giddy in celebration of a new, impromptu holiday of his own making. Rachel and I were on a sugar high the rest of the day, bragging to the other kids on the block about our special tree.

Every time I see a pack of Juicy Fruit gum, I'm reminded of the tree, our tree, and smile. I think about all the gum I scored for a non-Halloween occasion, how happy we all were, and what a great day we had. Behind the scenes Dad had come home the night before with over fifty packs of gum, put us to bed, snuck outside with Scotch tape and a step ladder, and taped the packs of gum to the tree in the dark, careful not to tape them too high. I imagine it was hard for him to get the tape to stick to the leaves coated with moisture of the nighttime dew. These were the actions of a man who derived immense joy from seeing his daughters happy—and showing off.

My other favorite memory from this time was when I sent away for actress Lindsay Wagner's autograph. I had it displayed on the Pepto Bismol pink wall of my bedroom. I loved pretending that I was *The Bionic Woman* springing from the backyard picnic bench in slow motion, or fake tearing through a phonebook, with the bionic sound effects playing in my head. I wanted to be a strong, independent woman like "Jaime Sommers."

One Saturday morning, we sat down to watch *Bugs Bunny*, when a loud static bang came out of the television. We figured the antennae fell off the roof and the TV was out. I thought little of it until I realized that I might miss my show the next day. "Don't worry, it'll be back on soon," Dad reassured.

The next morning after a sleepless night, I ran to the TV, turned it on, and was shocked to see the screen still full of black and white speckles, laughing in my face. Dad saw my look of despair, went over to the neighbors, and asked if their TV was working. "It's fine," I heard from over the fence. He returned to the TV den, took off the back of the TV, and that saw one of the cathode ray tubes had blown. I had a sobbing meltdown. Dad's own eyes had tears in them as he held my face in his hands. "It'll be okay." He removed the blown tube, and off we went to the hardware store. My future was in his hands.

The technician gave us the replacement tube. I was ecstatic until Dad went to replace it, and it didn't fit our TV. He cursed, making me go outside to lurch back and forth on the swing set to get my mind off this catastrophe. We drove back to the hardware store in silence. The guy promised nothing but gave Dad two different tubes to try. I glanced at my Mickey Mouse watch. My heart sank. The minutes ticked away like time bombs. I watched Dad on his hands and knees, working on our TV while I held my breath and bit my lip, whispering, "I love you, Daddy," in support. Dad turned the TV on and off to see if what he jimmied worked, but it didn't, and I resolved myself to having a non-*Bionic Woman* evening. As a backup,

Dad asked the neighbors if I could watch Jaime Sommers on their TV, but they were watching Sunday Night Football. I hated them.

Then, with only minutes to spare, Dad turned the TV on one more time. A clear, color picture flashed with sound. I ran to Dad, jumping up and down and squeezing him. Mom came into the TV den. "Good job, Michael!" Dad wiped the grease off his hands with a rag. I sat down on the couch to watch the show, beaming ear to ear, Holly Hobbie at my side. Disaster averted.

5 Ronald Reagan's Limo ... and Other Beauties

When Dad policed West Hollywood on the CHP, he'd swing by this exotic car lot on Sunset Strip, owned by a Frenchman named Michel. Ever since he was little, Dad had a thing for cars, admiring Buicks, Oldsmobiles, and fifties Fords. After recuperating from his crash, Dad stopped by Old Time Cars on La Cienega Boulevard, Michel's showroom of bling on wheels: classic Mercedes, Porsche, Ferrari, and Rolls-Royce.

After a few conversations, Michel suggested that Dad enter the car business. So, Dad took his $3,000 in savings and started buying cars starting with an old forties Packard for $300. After cleaning it up and detailing it in our driveway, he sold the Packard for $800. On the weekends, Dad recruited us to help him clean cars. We usually ended up getting into water fights with the garden hose. Over the next year, Dad made more contacts in the car industry, buying cars and putting them for sale on lots on Sunset Strip or advertising in the local papers. An expert in hustling from his days in the projects, Dad quickly became an entrepreneur in the exotic car business. At one point, he purchased Ronald Reagan's famous limousine during his California governor days from a funeral parlor for $1500. After refurbishing Ronnie's old limo, Dad placed it in a car auction at the Disneyland Hotel in Anaheim. Dad knew the guy running the auction, so they featured Dad's limo as the main attraction, leading to a $3,800 sale. He averaged about $1,500 profit per month on flipping cars, which was double his CHP salary.

That same year, Mom enrolled in nursing school in downtown Los Angeles. Her program was demanding, so she was rarely home. When she *was* home, she needed peace and quiet to study, so on the weekends, Dad took Rachel and me with him to the car lots. My favorite lot was on Sunset Boulevard by Carney's Hot Dogs, where we played hide-and-seek in between vintage Model A Fords, Rolls-Royces, and Porsches. We giggled as the customers told Dad how adorable we were, and he loved showing us off. We climbed into cars when no one was looking. "Don't go into the street!" Dad would yell at us. Once Dad let me drive an ATV in the lot. I was 6 so it seemed perfectly normal to me. I lost control and ran over Rachel's foot. She still likes to bring that up.

That year, we drove around Los Angeles visiting Dad's cars on consignment and in repair shops. Dad would pull up in his latest fixer-up he'd found—I loved the El Caminos and Cadillacs best—and he'd shoot the shit with the lot managers while Rachel and I watched TV in their back office, eating hot dogs and drinking sodas. Mom liked Dad taking us to work. It got us out of her hair during the day, and she could relax until we returned, sapped of energy, ready for bed after dinner.

These were simple, carefree days. And to this day, Rachel and I are always equipped with Armor All, a car duster, and a rag in the trunk.

When I turned eight, we stopped driving to car lots around LA. We thought we'd done something wrong. Turns out Dad had gotten a new job. There was lots of whispering going on around our house whenever Dad mentioned his friend, Mac.

6 Big Mac

Horace "Mac" McKenna was a big Black guy—a New Orleans native and a bodybuilder who weighed nearly 300 pounds and stood at 6'6. Dad knew Mac from their days on the California Highway Patrol together, occasionally pairing up when working nights on motorcycles. Dad liked Mac because he was easygoing, and no one fucked with them when Mac was around. Mac possessed a deep Barry White voice, huge muscles bulging under his fitted shirts, and tattoos peeking out. Barely 5'9, Dad was your average white guy with blue eyes and brown hair. At the time, I was a little afraid of Mac, but I liked him, and couldn't take my eyes off him whenever he was present. I never thought his name would come back to haunt me for the rest of my life.

Mac and Dad worked together until Mac was fired by the CHP for using stolen credit cards in Palm Springs. He later spent four years in federal prison after being convicted of passing counterfeit money. A few years later, he returned to prison for violating parole, by getting into a fight with an off-duty police officer. Dad visited Mac when he was at Lompoc Prison.

The first time I met Mac, Dad took Rachel and me to his penthouse in Inglewood. At first, Rachel and I were nervous. I mean, the dude was huge with a powerful voice. But Mac picked us up and squeezed us, offering us beverages and a home tour. His penthouse was lavish, with a private elevator, lots of mirrors, and a pet cockatoo. Mac wore jeans, cowboy boots, a big belt buckle, and a tight tee shirt. He seemed so big. He would have made a fine Darth Vader.

In 1977, Mac and Dad started discussing going into the strip club business together. Mac had cash on hand and the location picked out by LAX Airport. Mac wanted a front man who had street smarts and a clean image. Dad filled in the picture frame as a white, young, married father with two kids and a polished record. You would never associate Dad with pedaling adult entertainment.

PART TWO

GLITTER, G-STRINGS, AND BAD DECISIONS

7 Girl in the Fast Lane

A year after Dad's career change from cars to clubs, we moved from Newbury Park to swanky Westlake Village, ten minutes further south off the 101 Highway. We lived on Cheswick Place, which still sounds uppity to me. I remember clinging to Mom's legs as neighbors stopped by to introduce themselves. They dropped off welcome gift baskets filled with wine, cheese, and flowers, and invited us to stop by anytime. Mom looked forward to a new chapter in life. She enrolled me in my new elementary school, as well as piano, ballet, tap, and jazz classes. We still went to our Presbyterian church every Sunday in Newbury Park. Dad only went because it made Mom happy.

Dad installed a house alarm system and hid guns in every closet. He'd let me hold the guns after he removed the bullets, and I couldn't believe how heavy guns were. I wanted to learn how to shoot, so one weekend, Dad assembled a shooting party with Aunt Martha's Sicilian husband, Sal, along with some strip club managers, in an empty dirt lot out in Valencia, by Magic Mountain. Mom gave both Dad and me the silent treatment as we left. Rachel had no interest and chose to play with her Barbie Dolls instead.

We picked up a bucket of Kentucky Fried Chicken and a six-pack of Coors beer for everyone, met the others at a freeway offramp, then caravanned to the empty lot. Dad set up soda cans far away for targets. He took the first shot with his Smith and Wesson five-shooter, and my ears rang for about half an hour. He even let me shoot his double-barrel shot gun, showing me how to stand with my feet planted into the ground, so the kickback wouldn't knock me on my ass. I wanted to make Dad proud, so I focused really hard, maintaining my stance, just like in ballet. Dad placed headphones over my ears to help with the noise. I attempted to pull the trigger, but it was really hard, and my 10-year-old fingers weren't strong enough. Dad instructed me to try using two fingers, so I held my breath, and pulled the trigger. *BOOM!* I couldn't believe the force of the gun; it all seemed to happen in slow motion. I looked around and everyone clapped because I had successfully hit the soda can target and was still standing. I released a huge sigh and Dad patted me on the back, "That's my girl," he cooed. He handed the shotgun over to Uncle Sal for a go, but he wasn't as lucky when he pulled the trigger. The gun scraped his right shoulder blade through his wife-beater tank top, as he fell back landing in the dirt, his cigarette flying. It was such a fun day and Dad even let me drink his beer. "You'll need to keep practicing, Lip. Someone in this house besides me should know how to use a gun. I know your mother or sister never will," he said, squeezing my knee on the ride home.

A couple of months later, I turned eleven. After NBC cancelled *The Bionic Woman*, I had extra time to kill, so I asked Dad to teach me how to drive. Dad let me sit on his lap behind the wheel as he drove down the block. He had recently purchased a dark blue Subaru Brat truck with plastic seats in the back cargo. It seemed less like a car and more like a life-sized Tonka truck, the perfect kid's car, instead of Dad's Cadillac, to learn on. Dad liked it because it was a stick shift, which he insisted I learn first because, in his words, "Women never learn how to drive a stick." He never permitted me to learn the easy way, but he was right; none of my female friends drive stick ... well, except Mom and Rachel.

One night after dinner with Mom nervous as usual, we hopped in the Brat to practice shifting gears. "Listen to the engine, and when it sounds like it's ready, release your left foot and shift up to the next gear. The car will chug if it's not in the right gear," he coached, and demonstrated the chug as our heads bobbled back and forth in our seats. I didn't want to fail.

He drove to Westlake Elementary School at the end of the street and urged me to switch seats with him. My heart raced as I pushed my right foot on the gas pedal and stalled the truck. He laughed. "Start it up again." After four failed attempts and Dad laughing like a hyena, I successfully started the truck and drove the Brat up the driveway to my school, an incline that seemed as steep as the Matterhorn at Disneyland. Dad beamed with pride as I conquered that hill. I didn't need school; I could be a truck driver! Dad let me drive back home, and even though the Brat chugged, I never stalled once. Little did I know that soon after acquiring my new driving skills, I would be helping get Dad out of a sticky situation with the law.

8 Money!

Changing neighborhoods to Westlake and moving into a two-story house with a real pool and slide seemed fancy to us. But that was just the beginning of our new lavish lifestyle. Even our meals were different—no more TV dinners and chili. On Sundays, we'd go to the Bonaventure Hotel in downtown Los Angeles for brunch. The whole floor rotated, and the city views mesmerized me. Mom dressed Rachel and me up in the same dresses, with black patent leather shoes. Even though I was now taller, people frequently came up to us and screamed "Twins!" Dad also took us to the theme building restaurant at LAX, which also rotated, or the Cock and Bull on Sunset Boulevard, where we'd see English celebrities like actors Richard Harris and Peter O'Toole. Dad always tipped the host for the best available table.

Mom and Dad dressed nicer, and instead of Fedco, they now shopped at Bullocks or The Broadway department stores. Dad bought Mom a rabbit fur coat, and he wore gold pinky rings and a gold bull, the sign of the Taurus, around his neck. He was obsessed with cowboy boots and purchased about thirty customized pairs, ranging in different colors and animal skins. He'd come home at night from the clubs, pulling out envelopes of cash and his gun from his boots. Mom's car got upgraded from a Toyota to a Mercedes. Even our vacations elevated from the camper to Carnival cruises, Hawaii, and Europe editions.

At only 11 years old, I could see Dad using his nouveau riche status to pull in the best hotel room, the best table, and the best view wherever he went, showcasing a wad of bills from his gold money clip. Sometimes I was embarrassed by his flashy behavior and overly thanked servers and hostesses when we went out. These people didn't know about Dad's awful childhood. If they did, I felt sure they'd understand him more. I was just happy to sit down and savor delectable food. "It's nice not having to worry about money, isn't it?" he'd say with his sheepish grin as he raised his eyebrows. You could almost see his false teeth sparkling with pride.

That same year, Mom graduated from nursing school. We got her red roses and took her out to dinner in her uniform. She secured a job at Los Robles Regional Medical Center, the biggest hospital in the area. Dad didn't like Mom working, and they often argued about it. "I make ten times what you make, Debbie, and it offends me that you feel the need to work. You should stay home with the kids." "But Michael, what if something happens to you, then what?"

I felt bad for Mom; it wasn't about the money. She enjoyed nursing and taking care of people. Besides, it was the only thing she had for herself. Dad told her that if she insisted on working, she had to be home with the family during the day. Mom found a night shift at the hospital and switched to working 11:00 p.m. till 7:00 a.m., arriving back home right after Rachel and I woke up. She still filled our lunchboxes and drove us to school, taking naps and doing laundry while we were all out of the house. Dad usually left the house about 11 a.m. and sometimes didn't get home till after 2:00 a.m. I knew he was working hard to support us all and had a lot of responsibility. I constantly thanked him for all he did for us. "Family is everything to me, Lip. Never forget that," he insisted, squeezing me tight in my pink bedroom.

In December 1978, a year after opening the Jet Strip, Dad and Mac bought a second club called New Frontier around the corner from The Jet. Mom rolled her eyes when Dad said they were expanding the business, but I thought it was exciting. I'd become used to visiting Dad at the Jet Strip, and I wanted to expand my horizons. I wanted to go to this roller disco club in West Hollywood named Flippers. In the seventies, Flippers was *the* place to go, like Studio 54 on wheels, especially after the roller skate movie, *Xanadu*, with Olivia Newton-John came out. I asked Dad if he could take me to Flippers, but he said I couldn't go because I was only 11 years old. "But I won't drink, Dad, I only want to skate."

"It doesn't work that way, Lip," he said, patting my head and laughing.

"Oh great," Mom said to Dad. "You've created a monster."

Dad and Mac's second club turned into the strip club version of Flippers. They expanded and remodeled the space, and had a grand opening under its new name, Bare Elegance. Clientele could see it from the 405 freeway, close to LAX, and around the corner from The Jet.

The Bare was their more upscale club. The décor, inspired by *Xanadu*, was comprised of pinks, whites, soft grays, and greens. The bar top was tempered glass with neon lights underneath, and diamond plate aluminum covered the back wall. Dad wanted the club to mimic a sexy girl's bedroom, and the girls really liked working there. Dad and Mac kept the classiest girls dancing at The Bare, only rotating them out to other clubs when necessary. The furniture still smelled like vinyl, the girls smelled like Calvin Klein's Obsession, and the carpet smelled like new, lacking the booze stains and cigarette burn holes the Jet Strip had. The brass poles and stage railings were shiny, the mirrors had no cracks, and the tables were laid out spaciously. Sometimes it felt cold when the A/C was on, but the dancers built up quite a sweat working the stage and needed the air. Outside, bright pink and green neon lights accentuated the establishment, with a red-carpet entrance, a velvet rope, and valet parking. Limo drivers lingered in the parking lot smoking and waiting for their clients to come out. I loved hanging at The Jet with Dad, and he'd let me in early so I could dance on the stage to the *Xanadu* soundtrack before the front doors opened.

Before I could even break the place in, Flippers the roller disco closed, turning into an Esprit Outlet then eventually a CVS pharmacy. The seventies and disco were sadly dying as the eighties took over with new wave, punk, and country music. Dad bought me Charlie perfume by Revlon for my twelfth birthday. The ad for Charlie read, "Charlie's a gorgeous, sexy, young smell. And full of surprises, just like you!" He remembered from when I visited the Jet Strip how much I loved that smell. Spraying from the bottle, he also informed me they were enrolling me in private Catholic School for a better education.

9 Bear Attacks

La Reina High School was a private Catholic school in Thousand Oaks catering to all girls and nuns, in strict uniform, all the time. Mom took me to Sears and bought me training bras to wear underneath my white uniform shirt. I was still waiting for my breasts to sprout, and when I started at La Reina, I couldn't take my eyes off the girls who had ample chests in gym class.

I didn't exactly thrive at La Reina. I dyed the school toilets with food coloring during Easter, put whoopee cushions on my classmates' chairs, and removed the rubber bands from my braces, aiming them at classmates. I laughed out loud when Sister Josella sang the beatitudes with her hands raised up in the air holding a crucifix. I spent more time outside the classroom in the hallway serving detention than I did inside learning. Each student had an honor card that was part of our obedience grade, and if we disobeyed the rules, the nuns would strike points off our card. Points were deducted for too-short skirts, wrong-colored socks, too much makeup, gum, eating in class, talking in class, or wild jewelry. I was usually on the cusp for a parent–teacher conference, and I do recollect having at least a couple with Dad present. He'd just laugh on the way home. "You know when I was in Catholic school, we got the shit beat out of us by the nuns!" he bellowed with pride.

Sister Josella discussed the male species in our religion class. She advised us to only sit on a man's lap if we place a telephone book under our bottom first. I thought of the times I had observed strippers give men lap dances at Dad's strip clubs. I thought of all the times I sat on Santa's lap at the mall and felt bathed in sin. As I settled into a new life of nuns and the Bible, Dad and Mac opened a regular nightclub in Agoura Hills, one community over from Westlake Village. They named the club JR's Place, after JR, the character from the popular TV show *Dallas*. The club had live music with acts like John Cougar Mellencamp, two-step dancing, a restaurant, and a bar. Aunt Martha, Dad's sister, and her Sicilian husband, Sal, had recently moved to Westlake from New Jersey, where they had been working at

Thumann's, a family-run deli and butcher shop. When they moved, Dad hired the pair to run the daily operations of the club, but he was still searching for a general manager.

Through Dad's car buddy, Michel, he met a guy named Dave Smith from the UK, who was big and unpredictable, usually trying to pick a fight with anyone. Dad used him as his driver and muscle man to rough up people on his behalf, usually for not paying back money he lent them or for harassing the girls. I have a feeling other stuff went on too that I didn't know about, mostly because I was 12. Dave had another friend named David Amos, a boxer who had moved from London, seeking employment. David Amos was 6'4, had a sexy English accent, dark hair, and blue eyes, and was a perfect gentleman. I had an instant crush on him. Dad started David out as a bouncer at the clubs and then made him the general manager at JR's Place. Dad told me later that Mac never liked David.

At La Reina, classmates asked me what my parents did for a living.

"My mom's a nurse!" I'd proudly say.

"And what does your dad do?"

"Uhm, he owns a restaurant."

"Which one?"

"Oh, one in LA, it's like a supper club, I don't remember the name." I hated lying, and I wasn't consistent. I had already told some friends he was an investor.

I asked Dad what I should tell my friends. "You can tell them the truth, honey," he said. "I'm not ashamed." And if he wasn't ashamed, why should I be? I told my friends at school that Dad was in the bar and restaurant business and owned JR's. I felt at ease having a legit alibi for Dad's job.

But soon, JR's Place began losing money, so Dad and Aunt Martha added female mud wrestling and male exotic dance shows to boost business. It still wasn't enough, so Dad and Aunt Martha changed the name to The Bear Cabaret and decided to turn it into a topless nightclub.

The city had it out for The Bear. It brought negative publicity to Mac and Dad from the LA County Sheriff's department by associating them with their LA strip clubs. Plus, the sheriff's department was convinced they were involved in organized crime. News reporters nicknamed the place "Sodom and Agoura." Aunt Martha and Dad's names and pictures were now a regular feature of the *Los Angeles Times*.

It wasn't long before my perfect little bubble burst. A doctor at Mom's hospital, who lived down the street, found out what Dad did through the papers, and rumors spread like wildfire on our cul-de-sac. We weren't invited to block parties anymore and people turned away when they saw our Mercedes coming down the street. On the way home from school one day, we came home to our front lawn full of trash. Our "friends" and neighbors shapeshifted into gossiping busy bodies.

I hung out a lot at The Bear, as it was close to home. I played the arcade games for free and drank Shirley Temples. I did homework in the back office when patrons came in. I felt so cool.

The city fought The Bear Cabaret over the topless ordinance, insisting the club had to be farther than 660 feet away from a freeway compared to its "intimate" fifty feet from the freeway. The sheriffs cited the club for operating a five-game video arcade without a permit. Then the city cited the club for exhibiting an illegal sign with a naked girl, saying "Girls, Girls, Girls." Dad talked about it at home. Mom cried because of all the negative publicity. I didn't understand why all these people cared so much. Couldn't they just not go to the club? The ridicule seemed so silly!

After the City of Los Angeles shut down the topless-club feature, Aunt Martha, Dad, and David changed The Bear Cabaret to a gay club. Local sheriffs would park outside the club at night and harass the gay clientele, performing random sobriety tests and asking for their identification. Most of the customers were married men who didn't want people to know they frequented the club. More news articles infiltrated the papers and our neighbors' driveways.

Soon, the heat from the clubs reached me, too, when my very own 13-year-old girlfriends dropped me from the ballet carpool, after their parents found out Dad owned The Bear. It hit me what a big deal this was in our perfectly manicured community. I became afraid to go outside. Were they jealous of Dad's money and cars that he'd worked so hard for? I still didn't understand why people cared so much about someone else's line of work. I felt protective of him but began wishing maybe he had earned a less controversial title, like airline pilot or insurance salesman.

When I was uninvited to a friend's birthday party, I sobbed in my pink bedroom, wondering why I was being punished. My dance buddies ignored me inside and outside of class and whispered behind my back. I didn't feel so cool anymore. "These people have nothing better to do with their lives, Lip," Dad said. He was right, and instead of trying to fit in, beg for forgiveness, or fight, I ignored them.

Dad wasn't exactly a role model for ignoring a confrontation. In fact, he always fueled provocation. He loved a challenge and fed off attention.

Dad and Mac argued from the start of going into business together, mostly over what kind of boss image to project to staff and customers. Dad had issues with Mac's demeanor with people. Mac was known for screaming and smacking people around. Dad said even Mac was overwhelmed by his reputation as a kingpin in the strip club circuit. I heard them argue at the clubs and on the phone, but Mac was always a gentleman to me. He may have screamed his head off at some employee, but he always apologized to me after. One time, Dad had me cover my ears—not from the bad words Mac used but from the high volume.

Then Dad and Mac began having problems with the FBI. Ever since Mac's prison release, the FBI had been after him for organized crime, and as they were making lots of money in a mostly cash business, it didn't look so good. I trusted Dad and knew he would never get involved in anything like that. This is the same father who regularly made large donations to my Catholic school and our church. He got a chuckle out of giving money made by nude women dancing to school nuns without their knowledge. He had a sick sense of humor. Those nuns would have taken the cash either way!

One day, at 4:30 in the morning, we got a call at our house from the Jet Strip's alarm company. The FBI had raided Mac's penthouse when they got tipped off about him running an illegal gambling parlor. They arrested Mac and were raiding the Jet Strip, scouring the place for signs of gambling, prostitution, tax evasion, money laundering, and drugs. Basically, anything to nail them. We were all up with the lights on in the house, super groggy, our hearts pounding. Rachel and I had school that day. Mom just kept repeating as if in a trance, "Michael, Michael, Michael."

The FBI called our house soon after and spoke with Dad. "Do you want me to come down to the club now?" Dad asked.

"No, it's not a good idea for you to come down at this time. My advice to you would be to call an attorney." We all heard what the FBI said on speakerphone.

Dad called his attorney, who told him to get out of the house immediately. We all started scurrying around, asking Dad what we should do. It was still dark out, but Mom made coffee and eggs. Dad didn't have time to eat. He ran around the house, grabbing envelopes of cash from our safe, his gun, and an overnight bag. It was the first time I ever saw Dad scared.

He told me to get dressed and grab a backpack "like" I was going to school. "Dad, I *am* going to school today."

"I know, Lip, I just need you to do something for me before you go."

Dad trusted me. I'd have done anything he asked! The swelling of pride I felt was mildly diminished by Mom crying in the kitchen, still flipping her eggs.

Dad was afraid the FBI was coming out to catch him, and I could help him get away. Dad stuffed about $10,000 in cash, with my school uniform, in my backpack. He handed me the keys to his 1976 red Cadillac El Dorado.

It was dawn, and the neighbors' lights came on one by one. I walked down the driveway as birds chirped in the trees, pretending I was leaving for school with my backpack. No one would suspect a 13-year-old of aiding and abetting, right?

I ducked into his car and drove away. I sat on a phone book to appear taller and to see over the large steering wheel. Dad snuck out the back of the house, walked down the street behind ours, meeting me at my elementary school lot. It was all so exciting. I was doing something grown-up, something sneaky.

I handed him the keys and cash, and he kissed me goodbye. "I love you, Lip." He put his hands around my face and kissed me.

"I love you too, Daddy," I said. I walked back home, wondering the whole way if I was being followed.

Mom drove me to Catholic school that morning. I was still on a high from all the excitement. Her eyes were glassy as she leaned over and kissed me goodbye.

"It's okay Mommy, Daddy's going to be alright."

"I knew something like this was going to happen, I told your father. Mac is involved with scary people, Laurel."

I prayed for Dad that day in school.

Dad checked into the Marriott in Marina Del Rey and called us from random pay phones. "Don't answer the door, no matter who they say it is! Keep a low profile in the house, curtains closed and the TV on low volume in case anyone is watching the house," he instructed Mom. I looked outside the windows at night with the lights off, but I didn't see any secret agent men or government cars on our street.

After five days, Dad received the okay from his attorney to come home, after his attorney spoke with the FBI. They only found a small stash of cash and a bag of white powder that they thought was cocaine, but after testing it determined it was the household cleaner, Comet. Dad said someone had been stealing Mac's cocaine from the back office, so Mac set up a bag of Comet with a camera on it to catch the thief. One of Mac's associates, nicknamed "Chicken Wing," took the fall for the illegal gambling and would spend about two years in prison in exchange for enough money to live on from Dad and Mac when he got out.

10 Happy Hoarding

After the dust settled from the raid, Mac and Dad opened up a fourth club in 1983 called The Odd Ball Cabaret in the San Fernando Valley. The nicest hotel nearby was a Motel 6, and the street behind the club was a known place for drug deals. The Odd Ball was their largest club with the usual "Girls, Girls, Girls" neon lights outside. I was 14 years old when Dad brought me by to check it out. Dark and smoky, The Odd Ball smelled like coconut tanning oil and grilled chicken sandwiches. It was low-lit and full of eager men holding a handful of crinkled dollar bills.

Girls with big, permed hair wore clear-plastic high-heeled shoes that looked like goldfish could live inside. Dad pointed out stretch marks, bad boob jobs, tummies, and C-section scars. I brushed off this crude examination of women's bodies as work-related. After all, they were hired help. "Single mom," he would divide them aloud to me. Wow, I never thought of the dancers as being actual moms. I thought they were beautiful and talented, but I never imagined their lives outside the clubs.

Dad talked about the strippers a lot at home, emphasizing the importance of displaying nice figures for business. With the rise of the industry nationwide, he wanted his clubs to be memorable. I would listen to him tell stories about the strippers in my parents' bathroom while he shaved his face with Old Spice. Sometimes he would dot shaving cream on me and pretend to shave me, then slap some aftershave on my cheeks, professing, "No one will ever love you as much as I do, kiddo!"

One day, I paraded into the kitchen, wearing a blue and red Hang 10 bikini to go swimming in the backyard pool. "Daddy, am I skinny?" I asked, sucking in my stomach, hands on my hips, and pushing back my shoulders.

"Well, you'll always have breeder's hips like your mother," Dad said, sitting at the kitchen table, drinking coffee, and flipping through *The Los Angeles Times.*

"What does that mean?"

"Some women have wide hips, but that helps them with having babies. And hey, some men like a woman with a big ass!"

"I have a big ass?" I had never thought about my butt like that before. It was the second time I felt self-conscious about my body. As if I wasn't already obsessed with having big boobs, now I had to worry about my stupid butt too? I flipped through *Tiger Beat* magazines, checking out other girls to see if they had big hips.

Dad also critiqued the actresses' bodies and female news reporters on TV.

"Oh, she could stand to lose five pounds … "

"Wow, she looks rough … "

"Look at those saddle bags … "

I began solely eating salads coated with lemon juice instead of dressing. Luckily, Rachel was still too young to worry about her weight. Even Mom started cooking "light" meals at home. She bought a cookbook called *Microwaving on a Diet* and made most of our meals in the new microwave Dad brought home. Mom began taking Jazzercise and Jane Fonda aerobics classes around town. Suddenly her cheeks sank in.

While Mom and I were dieting, Dad, with his newfound wealth, continued buying *stuff*. He always had about six cars he shuffled around. Some of my favorites included a DeLorean; a Porsche 928 like the one from the movie, *Risky Business*; a right-drive Bentley; a Silver Cloud Rolls-Royce; an orange Bricklin with gull-wing doors; a black Lincoln Continental with suicide doors; and an El Camino. For a while, he even had a limo that Dave Smith drove him around in, but I think it embarrassed Mom too much with the neighbors, so he sold it. I grew to dislike the neighbors and instead, obnoxiously honked and waved at them as I drove down the street. I enjoyed making them feel uncomfortable.

Besides cars, Dad began collecting random things like a carousel horse on a brass pole that rested in our living room, more guns, and a red English phone booth we had some guy lift up with a crane to place in our front garden as the nosy neighbors watched *The Woods Show* from their driveways. Dad still loved K-Mart and went regularly to buy car supplies and tools for his garage. Mom urged him to stop spending so carelessly.

"But why? It's my money," Dad replied.

Our once minimal house transformed into the kitschy museum of his dreams.

I personally liked all the stuff Dad brought home. I thought it was cool and always a surprise to see what he had in his hands as he walked in through the garage door. But Dad went too far with Mom when he brought home a parrot one night. After meeting Mac's cockatoo at his penthouse, Dad decided he wanted a parrot and told people at the clubs to be on the lookout for one. One day, Big Wally, a Russian thief who had spent more time in prison than on the streets, paid Dad a visit at the Jet Strip. "Hey, I hear you like parrots. You wanna buy one?" Wally opened up his coat and revealed a green Amazon, shaking and lunging with his sharp beak. Story had it, Wally seized the parrot from a guy named Johnny Sanchez, who owed him money. Dad brought the parrot home late that night.

We named the parrot "Huey" because the damn bird kept screaming that name. We later realized it was probably his previous owner's name, but oh well. He bit us and screamed for the first six months before warming up to us. Mom peeled him grapes because he didn't like to eat the skin. He liked me the most, so I took care of him, cleaned his cage, and showered with him. We took Huey to the vet and found out parrots lived a long time, like fifty to eighty years. And Huey was about the same age as me now, 15. "Oh great," Mom griped. Dad laughed his ass off, but Mom knew that once he had that bird, it would only be a matter of time before he moved onto another shiny object.

11 The Prozac Days

In tenth grade, I still felt like a big, flat-chested, Protestant loser at La Reina. If you weren't Catholic, you were labeled as a second-class citizen. Plus, the nuns had their favorites, and, with my mischievous ways, I knew I'd always be in the back of the class. Mom had sent Rachel and me to computer camp at Pepperdine University in Malibu, the summer before. Overlooking the ocean, I learned how to do basic programming and smoke pot with some of the other kids from camp. I confided in Rachel that I had gotten high at the beach, and when Mom picked us up from camp, Rachel squealed on me. She was still under the spell of those damn nuns and wanted to convert to Catholicism to become a nun herself. I had gone through that phase myself two years earlier.

At Pepperdine, I became friends with some cool public-school kids. Between my new crew and watching the TV show, *Square Pegs*, starring Sarah Jessica Parker, I decided I wanted to transfer to public school. I was sick of uniforms, nuns, and church. I talked to two friends I knew from La Reina, who had made the jump to public school. "O-M-G, Laurel. It's the best!" my friend, Kim, exclaimed. "You can wear whatever you want, they have school dances, and there are cute boys!"

I honestly didn't think that my parents would allow me to transfer from the grip of virtuous education but caught in their own conflicting work lives of vice and virtue, they dropped their guard. Before my first day learning alongside boys again, Dad cornered me in the bathroom. "Just tell me, Lip, before you do anything stupid like sex or drugs," Dad said as he covered his face in shaving cream. "You don't want to end up pregnant like some of my dancers."

Mid-tenth grade in 1984, I transferred to Westlake High School, and it's still one of the best decisions I've ever made. However, the week between school semesters, I panicked. I had no idea what to wear to public school, wishing it could still be green plaid uniform and penny loafers. I was wardrobe stunted. I still wore my *Mork and Mindy* rainbow suspenders from Sears on the weekends. But from my *Tiger Beat* magazines, I knew all those name-brand jeans like Chemin De Fer,

Dittos, and Jordache were the rage. I was beyond nervous about fitting in, so I asked Mom to take me to the cool place in the Valley on Ventura Boulevard that everyone shopped at, according to my Pepperdine friends. Mom and the saleslady notified me that my hips were too big for some of the jeans I liked. Even the shop lady was in on this? What the hell?

I lay down on the floor in the shop to zip up the pair of Jordache jeans I fell in love with. Mom watched me with pity in her eyes and shook her head. She thought all these name brands were silly—Izod and Polo shirts, Dolphin shorts, Vans, Camp Beverly Hills. But I managed to fit into some pairs and begged Mom to buy them. With new clothes in hand, I felt ready to say goodbye to Sister Josella, and start the next chapter of my life.

My first week at Westlake High School, I reconnected with friends from Westlake Elementary, like Laura, Tom, Christina, Alice, and Leslie. They asked what had happened to me and I replied, "Well, La Reina happened!" People thought I had moved away. I enrolled in honors classes, received my first straight "A" report card, and had a solid group of friends whose parents were involved in the community. I could wear whatever I wanted, and there was no more praying before class or walking two miles to church once a week.

Every day, I couldn't wait to jump out of bed. I needed extra time in the morning now that I had to pick out an outfit to wear! I tutored geometry and French and joined the French club. My new circle of friends was involved in student government, so I thought, *why not*, and joined them. After my straight "A" report card, I was also accepted into the National Honor Society and California Scholarship Federation. I was on fire! In the back of my head, I continued to wonder if these people knew about my dad's business even though I only emphasized investing and exotic car sales. JR's Place was still open and in the local papers almost daily. I just prayed that nobody put it together that it was my family. Aunt Martha was mostly mentioned, as she was the legal owner, and as she had a Sicilian last name, I figured I might be somewhat safe. Some kids on my block went to Westlake too, and when we crossed paths in the hallways, we'd both look away.

I met my future best friend, Anne Hurley, in student government. We bonded quickly, especially after realizing our birthdays were three days apart. Anne reigned over a group of friends who constantly surrounded her and was perpetually chirpy. Her blue eyes and blond hair gave her that angelic quality. But she loved getting into trouble. Anne and I were most famous in high school for rigging the homecoming king and queen votes. We wanted our friend, Melissa, to win homecoming queen instead of the popular girl with the latest eighties hair trend and expensive boots, so we stuffed the ballots, and our friend won. Our student body director was tipped off that the ballots were tampered with, but we never confessed.

Student body government became my social life. We all hung out together, making posters for football and basketball games, organizing dances and bake sales. At sports games, we'd dress up in our school colors, blue and orange, with orange nail polish and shaking pom poms. I was the one to "spot beer" as we called it, where you waited outside the supermarket asking an adult to buy you alcohol. I would ask a guy and rarely got turned down. We would take our stash and drink beers and wine coolers in the school bushes and then go to the stands to cheer on our school teams.

Meanwhile, Mom was busy running Rachel and me around to two different schools, dance, and music lessons. Plus, she still worked the night shifts at the hospital, in addition to taking care of the housework. Dad was around in the mornings, but would be gone until late at night, often coming home past 2:00 a.m. As I got older, I assessed all the work Mom did while Dad hung out at strip clubs barking out orders, eating up beautiful women (at least with his eyes), and counting cash all day. Mom began taking Prozac, like every movie housewife in the eighties. Dad would give Mom an envelope full of hundred-dollar bills and she would get her retail therapy on at the mall and donate the rest to her church. These observations made me realize I never wanted to be in a relationship like that. I wanted to be strong, like Princess Leia or the Bionic Woman, saving the world and crushing the bad guys. But somehow it never diminished the shining image I had of my dad.

At the end of the year, I obtained my driver's permit, and Dad let me drive him around in his exotic cars, sometimes stopping by the strip clubs or K-Mart. I couldn't wait to get my driver's license and a little freedom of my own.

After driver's ed class and scoring 100 percent on my driving test, I got my license! The instructor was so impressed with my skills that he thought he helped to cultivate—I didn't have the heart to tell him I'd already been driving for nearly six years and passed the ultimate test of facilitating an aiding-and-abetting incident. Dad taught me to check my own oil, air in tires, and to always have at least half a tank full of gas. "You never know what kind of situation you can get yourself into while driving," he said. *Yeah, or the call for another escape or money drop.*

Now a legal driver, I visited Dad at The Odd Ball for dinner, as it was the closest one to home when I was in high school. Sometimes the new managers, who didn't know me, thought I was showing up for my shift. I smiled and took it as a compliment. Dad didn't think it was funny. He'd straighten out the manager by asserting I was his daughter. So? Every dancer was someone's daughter.

The dancers were the clubs' main revenue source, and I held them in high regard. Many of them had a professional dance or gymnastics background. They didn't just swing around a pole but also did flips, backbends, and splits. I liked watching them work the room as the perfect package of grace, charm, and ambition. They were responsible for the care and welfare of their children, supporting the household, getting them to school, doctor appointments, babysitters, and being present during the day. Some women had rough childhoods involving abuse and neglect by their fathers and, later, relationships with abusive boyfriends. It wasn't uncommon for a bouncer to escort a dancer's jealous boyfriend to the parking lot outside after that boyfriend had attacked a patron for flirting with his girl. Some dancers were lesbians and enjoyed watching each other's shows.

One dancer I met attended UCLA law school, paid for by stripping, as cliché as that sounds. She was terrified of being recognized at the clubs by another student or professor. The dancers made very good money if they worked the floor for tips. Some blew their money on expensive cars, plastic surgery, and unemployed boyfriends. Dad brought in financial advisors to talk at employee meetings about how to invest their money and begin saving their earnings. The clubs even offered a 401K plan. Some dancers had cheap boob jobs and needed their breast implants repaired due to a sac leaking, resulting in deformed breasts and scar tissue. Dad invited plastic surgeons to employee meetings to discuss breast implants, tattoo removal, and other procedures.

The Odd Ball started offering shower shows, where patrons could spray shaving cream onto the dancers' bodies as the dancers lathered themselves while dancing in a shower. However, the city's Disabled Access Appeals Commission got word of the show and ruled that The Odd Ball's shower was a stage and, by law, needed to be accessible to able-bodied nude dancers and patrons who required wheelchairs alike. The city was starting to get creative when it came to ways to shut down strip clubs.

In high school, Dad permitted me to watch the strippers dance on stage. One time, I recognized one of the dancers from my ballet school. Her stage name was Destiny. I told Dad I wanted to try stripping. "No daughter of mine is ever going to be a stripper! You're going to college, young lady." If I had the body of a stripper, I'd make money off it too!

Rachel used to say, "You don't need an education if you got big tits."

I couldn't shake Dad's comments about my hips. I wanted a plastic surgeon to simply shave off my hip bones. I tried dieting again by eating 500 calories a day. I had two Diet Cokes for breakfast, Yoplait nonfat yogurt, and rice cakes for lunch, and a cup of milk for dinner, counting the calories of each item. If I felt dizzy, I'd eat a banana or a scoop of peanut butter. But after a few days of headaches and hunger pains, I decided to eat more, like microwave popcorn or fat-free Jell-O. I tried bulimia but I couldn't make myself throw up. I read *Dancing on My Grave*, an autobiography of a New York City Ballet dancer named Gelsey Kirkland. She talked about her eating disorders and her attempt to stay thin by drinking Ipecac, a cough syrup used to induce vomiting. I asked Mom if she would bring me some home from the hospital. Horrified, she declined.

12 Clubbing Intel

As a junior in high school, I was 16 and eager to work. I didn't need the money because Dad gave Rachel and me an ample allowance, but I needed a cover. Occasionally, friends would come over and see stacks of cash lying around the house as if my parents were Pablo Escobar and Griselda Blanco! I wanted desperately to fit in with other teens, so I landed a job working at Penguin's Frozen Yogurt—a prime location and a casual environment where I could chat with customers, making myself very visible.

My friend, Kim, had just transferred to Westlake from La Reina. We were eating lunch in the main quad area, and she told me she went clubbing. In my constant attempt to be cool, I asked if we could go together.

"Yeah, I go dancing at Club 321 in Santa Monica, all the time." She leaned back onto her elbows on the grass.

"You do? Can we go together?" I was electrified by the possibilities. Inside, I still felt like that virginal Catholic schoolgirl. At the same time, how many teenagers got to swing around stripper poles and watch topless dancers up close and personal since they were a child? I was a walking contradiction.

Kim and I created a plan to go to the dance club. You were allowed in at age 18 but couldn't drink. We did the usual teenage move—obtaining fake IDs and dressing trashy with gobs of makeup. I borrowed a leopard-print tank top and leather mini skirt from my friend for the occasion. I had to lie to my parents. They would never let me go to a dance club, which was absurd. I told them we were going to the movies at the mall and came downstairs in my outfit.

"Oh no, you're not leaving the house dressed like that, young lady," my mom huffed.

"Why not?"

"Because I said so, that's why. Michael, get down here and tell your daughter she can't leave the house dressed like that." Dad came downstairs and snickered devilishly. "Your mom's right, go upstairs and change." His words did not sound authoritative. I changed into jeans and a tee shirt and brought the slutty combo with me. Kim picked me up in her white Bronco, and we took off for Santa Monica. I changed in the car.

We arrived at the club, and the bouncer admitted us, no problem. Our outfits had worked! It was my first time going to a nightclub that Dad didn't own. We walked over to the bar, and I ordered an Amaretto and club soda. It was the only alcoholic drink I knew, as Aunt Martha, Uncle Sal, and Dad drank a slew of them at Christmas. Kim brought cigarettes, and we both lit one up. Depeche Mode came on next, and we ran onto the dance floor, my skirt riding up. My curfew was 11:30 p.m. and we only had about half an hour left of indulging. I couldn't wait to tell the kids at school that I had gone clubbing!

On the ride home, I changed back into my jeans and tee shirt and kept the window open to air out the cigarette smoke from my hair. Mom could smell smoke from a mile away, so I popped a couple of mint Lifesavers into my mouth the second Kim dropped me off. The lights were off upstairs, but I could see the TV glare from my parents' bedroom. *Shit!* Feigning fatigue, I stood at their bedroom door and told them I had a nice time and went straight to my room. My ears still rang from the club music as I hit the pillow.

A week later, I came home from school to Dad waiting to talk to me.

"Hey Dad, what's up?" I said standing in our garage, watching him polish his car.

"Did you wear that leather outfit after I told you not to?"

"Uhm, yeah." I was a horrible liar and giggled anytime I tried to fib.

"And were you smoking and drinking on the dance floor at Club 321?" This stunned me. Had he followed us?

"Yes," I said, trembling, avoiding eye contact.

"Okay," was all he said, throwing his car rag on the ground.

The following week, Dad sold my beloved Saab turbo, revoked my off-campus lunch pass at school, and grounded me for six months. I locked myself in my room, blasted Depeche Mode, screamed "I HATE YOU BOTH!" and cried into my pillow.

It turned out the same entertainment law firm that represented Dad's strip clubs represented Club 321. I had visited their offices a few times with Dad, and Jill, the secretary, recognized me at Club 321. My dad stopped by their offices the week after my clubbing and caught up with Jill. *Bitch.*

"Oh, by the way, I think I saw your daughter Laurel at Club 321 last week. Boy, she looks all grown up, dancing and smoking like a chimney."

"Really?" Dad said. "Can you tell me what she wore?"

"Yeah, a tight leather miniskirt and some wild, revealing tank top."

"Yep, that was her, thank you for the info." That was the end of my teenage club-hopping.

13 Excelling at U Can Study Buzzed

I graduated high school in 1986. Dad was so proud, he cried. Mom took pictures of me posing with all my friends and held my lip gloss for me. I was covered in gold tassels and ribbons for the Honors Society and CSF. Anne occasionally removed them and put them on her to take pictures. I was off to UC-Santa Barbara in the fall, about an hour north of Westlake Village. Most of my friends went to Hawaii or took hedonistic cruises to Mexico as their graduation gift.

"You'll get a gift when you graduate from college," Dad said. My protective parents weren't about to let me wander off overseas.

As my first year of college approached, Mom took me shopping for linens, towels, and school supplies, while Dad painted my old Schwinn ten-speed bike pink and green, my two favorite colors. He spent all weekend on it in the garage and pinstriped it for me. Dad excelled at pinstriping, and often pinstriped our cars and boats.

Even though I was an hour away from home, college was going to be a different world where I could reinvent myself.

My first year at UC-Santa Barbara, I lived across the hall from a woman named Julie who was a "wake and baker." Julie was petite, with long, permed hair out of a Van Halen video, and wore black-checkered Vans. She drove a Camaro. Her license plate said *HVYMTLR*. Julie convinced me my mind would be more open to studying if I got stoned beforehand. My mind may have opened up, but nothing stayed inside it. I got my first grades back, and the school placed me on academic probation for the rest of the year. I hadn't declared my major yet and took upper-class courses in modern dance, so I thought that would be as good a major as any. Dad said I wouldn't make any money as a dance teacher. As French was my other passion, I wanted to major in French next. Again, Dad told me I'd never make any money as a French teacher. In the end, I chose a generic degree in communication studies.

I was thrilled that people didn't ask what my parents did. Keg parties and suntans consumed me. I roller skated to calculus class, hung out with friends at the beach, and watched *Moonlighting* in our dorm.

Every other weekend, I visited Anne at her dorm at California Lutheran University in Thousand Oaks. She had a *Top Gun* poster on her side of the room—we saw that movie about eight times when it came out. Even though we were only an hour away, we wrote each other letters, sharing our crazy college adventures with each other. Her school was religious, and Anne was a proud Lutheran. Meanwhile, my school had been dubbed U Can Study Buzzed (UCSB).

After finishing my first year in college, I had gained the "freshman fifteen," as Dad pointed out to me. Liposuction had just come on the scene, and I begged my parents to let me get my thighs and butt sucked. Mom took me for a consultation with a plastic surgeon, Dr. Hayashi. His daughters and I had gone to La Reina and the same ballet school. He explained the procedure—and the complications—emphasizing how much pain I would be in for six weeks afterward. He didn't seem happy about doing the procedure as he gave Mom and me a stern look. But Mom knew how self-conscious I was and supported my decision. I didn't want Dad to criticize my body anymore and felt insecure around him. I knew I would never have large breasts like the strippers, but at least I could be thinner.

After the surgery, purple pen marks and bruises massacred my ass and thighs. I wore a surgical girdle for six weeks. I waddled when I walked and was in excruciating pain. Dad didn't have a problem with the procedure. I didn't dare tell my friends or Rachel, and I wondered how long it would take for the scars to heal and the swelling to go down. I felt thinner, but after a while, I realized it didn't make a difference. I gained more weight in college with my pot-smoking munchies and dorm food. And I still had tiny scars on my thighs and butt from the procedure, but soon, liposuction became the least of my problems.

In the summer of 1988, the Los Angeles District Attorney's office raided our family house and the strip clubs. They were yet again convinced that Dad was involved in tax evasion and organized crime. A judge granted them a search warrant, saying they were certain that the evidence was inside our home. Aunt Deanie, from Dad's Hoboken days, her husband, Uncle Derrick, and their son, Vance, happened to be visiting. Everyone was in the backyard pool, including Rachel and Mom, while Dad took a shower. I was home from college that summer and at work temping for an insurance company in the valley.

According to the family, a police officer rang the doorbell and Mom answered. Six police detectives walked in, displaying the warrant to search the house, and asking if Dad was home. She said no. Eventually, they found him upstairs getting out of the shower. All six officers drew their guns and shouted different orders at Dad, "Turn around, get down, don't move, hands up, freeze!" Dad stood there naked and wet, with his arms raised, and waited. He patiently asked them to make up their minds. They identified him positively as Michael Woods and ordered him to get dressed.

They dragged everyone out of the pool at gunpoint. The armed police detectives corralled everyone into the living room and held them in their wet bathing suits. They sat on the sofa huddled in damp towels for six hours, getting up for bathroom breaks one at a time. Mom, Rachel, and Aunt Deanie cried. Huey squawked so loud that they locked him up in the bathroom. Agents tore the house apart, just like in the movies. They knocked stuff off shelves in our bedrooms, emptied our closets out onto the floor, and pulled everything out from underneath our beds. They strip-searched Mom's Cabbage Patch Dolls and found a bong in Rachel's room. They left finally, taking only a couple of boxes of tax paperwork and our Macintosh Plus computer.

When I came home from work, it looked like a tornado had struck. My family filled me in on the details. Mom's eyes were red and puffy from crying, and she was still sniffling. I gave her a huge hug and started putting things away with Aunt Deanie's help. Mom had a blank look on her face as she went through the motions of making dinner. Dad acted as if it were a big mistake, so I wasn't upset about it.

"Laurel, you don't know how scary it was for us, you weren't here," Rachel murmured.

In the end, the agents had nothing solid on Dad. All they succeeded in doing was putting on quite the show for the neighbors. We were used to that. Mom told Dad he had to get out of the business, and Aunt Deanie and Uncle Derrick concurred, saying he was putting his family at risk.

Dad shrugged his shoulders, "They didn't get anything on me because I haven't done anything wrong."

It was the hardest on Mom. She left the house in disarray, but in the end, she was the one left to clean up the mess.

The coast was clear this time. Still, Dad and Mac's relationship became more strained with the constant heat, Mac's felonious history, David moving up in the ranks of the clubs fueling Mac's jealousy, and Mac's drug use. I heard Dad on the phone with Mac, screaming happening from both ends, coupled with a lot of phone slamming. Mac could easily out-yell Dad on a call. Then Dad promoted David without approval from Mac, who threatened to kick David's ass if he screwed up, as Dad recalled.

I just knew Dad would protect us all. But I also wondered when the police would be back.

PART THREE

EXIT WOUNDS

14 It Could Have Been Anyone

In my junior year at Santa Barbara, I secured a job as a resident assistant. Out of 500 applicants, they only chose fifty, and the university paid for room, board, and spending money. I organized community events like blood drives and movie nights. I surprised my parents with the news, but they only complained that I wouldn't have enough time to study. I kept the job, and my grades improved. I outgrew my freshman party image, and my responsible peers became my new circle of friends. I successfully dodged questions about what Dad did, and it was such a relief after all the stress in junior high and high school.

On March 9, 1989, I was in my resident director's apartment as a bunch of us were finishing up a staff meeting. We sat around chatting and watching TV when the news came on. I wasn't paying attention until I heard Mac's name and saw his photo on the TV screen. "Horace Mac McKenna gunned down and murdered in his limo outside his ranch in Brea," the newscaster said. My heart stopped. He described how Mac had died—execution-style. A shooter had hidden in the bushes outside Mac's ranch gates and hammered his chauffeured limousine with a machine gun, as twenty-seven bullets hit Mac's body. He was only 46 years old. Next, they showed a picture of Dad and Mac from the time they worked together on the California Highway Patrol, posing in uniform on their motorcycles. The reporter described their partnership in the strip clubs, explaining that the authorities were looking into Dad as a "prime suspect."

"Laurel, is that guy related to you?" my friend, Betsy, asked with pure shock on her face.

"Uhm, yeah, that's my dad and his business partner," I replied.

"Why don't we let Laurel leave and contact her family," Cecily, my boss, announced. Everyone staged the kind of sad look when they don't know what to say to someone.

My friend, Dennis, walked me to my dorm room, and I heard my phone ringing. I fumbled for my keys and raced inside to grab it. It was Dad calling me from Aunt Martha's house to announce that Mac had been murdered.

"Dad, I know, I just saw it on the news. What happened?"

"Laurel, I don't want you going anywhere alone. Make sure you have someone escorting you all the time."

Then I talked to Mom. She had come home from work that morning even though Dad asked her not to. He was in panic mode. He thought someone might come after the family.

"Who do you think is involved?" I asked Dad. I could hear Huey squawking in the background.

"Who knows? Mac had an enemy list a mile long," he responded, sighing.

"I just can't believe it. It doesn't seem real. I've never known anyone who was murdered." Mac was such a huge force of nature and had been around the club scene for so long. Why hit him now?

"Yeah, and now business is down because people are afraid to come around the clubs in case they get hit. Even the employees are afraid to come in."

"Who should I be on the lookout for?" I could hear people playing soccer in the dorm hallway.

"Laurel, it could be anyone, with all of Mac's enemies. Just watch your back and try not to go anywhere alone, especially at night. And never walk anywhere at night without streetlights."

I was living in paradise, and now I was suddenly paranoid, afraid to leave my dorm.

The family camped out mostly at Aunt Martha's house before coming up to visit me in Santa Barbara a few days later, taking me out to dinner.

Mom and Dad laid low the next two months, staying at hotels in San Luis Obispo to visit Rachel in college, me in Santa Barbara, or Marina Del Rey so Dad could check out boats. Dad bought Rachel and me tasers to carry around in our backpacks at school, but I felt like whoever attacked me would probably taser me first. Dad was afraid someone would hit their house or come after them, so he had his manager, whom I thought of as "English David," run the businesses in his absence. Dad checked in daily via phone, but he liked David so much, he promoted him to business partner soon after.

When Dad returned to the clubs almost three months later, he now carried two guns—a handgun and a double-barrel shotgun, the same one he taught me to shoot ten years prior. Whenever we went out to dinner, he insisted on facing the entrance so that he could spot who came in. His gun was concealed in his boots at all times. He reiterated not to let our guards down as he had alarms and sensor lights installed in our house. I'd never seen Dad so scared and on edge. Eventually, Mom and Dad moved to a secluded area in Westlake against the mountains, with fewer neighbors. Mom hated living on Cheswick Place anyway, after our life had been exposed by JR's Place and the house raid.

By my senior year at UCSB, Mac's murder investigation had died down. Dad had originally been a prime suspect, but they found no evidence of anything, and the case remained a cold case. Dad said someone from the LAPD Organized Crime Unit came into the clubs, offering the theory of a mafia hit. Maybe they were trying to take over the clubs. People in the clubs exchanged intel that Mac was doing a lot of cocaine, selling cocaine, acting as a loan shark by lending money to people at extremely high interest rates, and threatening them when they didn't pay on time. It could have been anyone.

Dad and David ran the clubs, and our family saw more of David at family dinners and holidays. We even took vacations together. David became like a son to Dad. Dad had the majority stake now, making even more money than before.

I graduated in June 1990, and Dad gifted me a new white Saab with a red ribbon on top. "I know how much you missed a car," he said, chuckling as he handed over the keys. A new phase of life beckoned.

15 Surrounded by Smut

After graduation, Dad insisted I get a job right away. Meanwhile, my college friends were backpacking around Europe or working at Club Med in Tahiti. It didn't occur to me that I had a choice; I just did what Dad instructed. Anne scored a job as a flight attendant for American Airlines and moved to New York. That was a perfect fit for her, and I wondered if I should do the same. Instead, I found a job posting for Playboy on the UCLA Career Center board, and a woman named Susan hired me immediately. I had previous legal secretary experience working for the strip club's law firm in high school. I was still 21 and now the legal coordinator for Playboy's Business Affairs department.

I moved to West Hollywood, ten minutes away from the Playboy building at 8560 Sunset Boulevard. I found a studio apartment with bars on the windows on Hollywood Boulevard that I could afford. I took Dad to see it and without even getting out of the car, he quipped, "No way is my daughter going to live there."

He insisted on subsidizing my rent and picked out my West Hollywood apartment with a secured gate in the front. Dad cased the entire building, bought dowels for all my sliding doors, and had an alarm installed. He made me so paranoid that every time I came home, I checked my entire apartment, including closets, under the bed, and behind the shower curtain. When I got to my car in the morning, I checked both underneath and the backseats, making sure there wasn't a creepy dude around before unlocking it.

He also gave me a Smith and Wesson.38 handgun. "Remember, Lip, if you take out the gun, be prepared to shoot or else someone could grab the gun away from you and shoot you instead. You wouldn't want that to happen, believe me," he said, resting his hand on my shoulder and looking at me with those piercing blue eyes.

He stored one of his cars in my parking garage and had a key to my apartment. I was used to Dad being in charge and didn't think anything of him having full access to my place.

I went grocery shopping to fill up my first ever refrigerator. At UCSB, I ate all my meals at the campus dining commons. So, as I didn't learn how to shop for my own groceries or cook for myself, I filled my fridge mostly with vodka, Jell-O, and popcorn. As a treat, I bought my cat, Bubby, fake crab meat at Trader Joe's, but if I got desperate, sometimes I ate that too, with a dollop of teriyaki sauce.

Mom and Dad had just moved to a swankier house in Westlake Village, this time in a tiny cul-de-sac with only two other neighbors who kept to themselves. They could hang outside on their front lawn or garage without people glaring or whispering.

During my first week at work, Playboy fired the department head for having an affair with his secretary ... spicy! I liked my job already. A nice woman named Lita, born in Jamaica and raised in Brooklyn, trained me before she transferred to the production department. Lita helped me ease into work life with champagne and strawberry pie lunches on the rooftop on Sunset Strip. I could even see some of Dad's old car lots I used to hang out at as a kid. The attorneys watched the movies that aired on the Playboy Channel, making sure there were no scenes with penetration. Most days, the office was full of seventies porn music and groaning sounds. I was surrounded by smut. I felt at home.

Soon after I started, I went to the mansion for our annual employees meeting, but didn't meet "Hef" I did check out the infamous grotto and played with the monkeys in their cage. Susan had been a games keeper at the mansion when she went to UCLA and told us stories about the animals there.

There was a scandal at work involving *What Gets Me Hot!* and *Those Young Girls* sensation Traci Lords, admitting she was only 16 years old when she made all but one of her porn films. She had gotten a fake birth certificate stating she was 20 years old, so basically, Playboy, along with all the other adult entertainment companies, was distributing child porn. Thanks to Traci, I was immediately put to work getting release forms filled out by the actors in our movies that aired on the Playboy Channel. I checked two types of identification to prove their legal ages. I also met with Playmates and had them fill out release forms. They were all really nice women, just like the strippers I met when I was a kid. Most of them had the body of an 11 year old, but with huge boobs, perfect hair, makeup. They looked like they might tip over.

When I worked at Playboy, a friend also got me a volunteer job at the Children's Hospital, where I sang and danced for babies and toddlers in hematology and oncology. My time with the children would kind of offset how I felt while working at Playboy encased in a great deal of misery among coworkers who wanted to be at a studio or network instead but needed the experience. I got so tired of explaining why I worked for "a company that exploits women."

I figured at Playboy I could at least tell coworkers what Dad did for a living without judgment. But several women said that strip clubs were disgusting and exploited women. "How is it different from what we produce here at Playboy?" I asked.

"What we do is an art form that's highly respected," they argued.

Centerfolds were always plastered in the mailroom, and in the fall of 1991, some female coworkers complained to human resources about it, but because centerfolds were our product, they stayed up. Later on, video producers at Playboy, some of them women, asked me for Dad's contact information. They ended up renting out the clubs to film Playboy videos like *Wet and Wild* and *Sexy Lingerie*. Even Rod Stewart shot some of his music videos at the clubs, using the dancers in his scenes.

16 May the Force Be with Me

In April of 1992, I had been instructed to go home from work, so I thought I would walk to the Beverly Center and catch a movie. I wasn't aware of what lay ahead. About halfway there, I noticed looting, cars on fire, and gunshots. In sheer terror, a man yelled at me to "go back home and lock my doors." Dad called and urged me to pack my car and cat and "get the hell out of there." I drove out to my parents' house where we spent the next few days watching the news. My hometown had turned into a war zone for six straight days. The LA riots came to a halt only after the California National Guard, the United States military, and several federal law enforcement agencies deployed more than 10,000 of their armed first responders. Sadly, sixty-three people were killed.

Two months later, I took a leave of absence from Playboy. I craved a change in scenery from the concrete jungle of West Hollywood, especially after living through the riots. I needed definitive space from fourteen years of strippers plus two years of centerfolds, porn movies blaring, penetration editing, and helicopters circling my apartment most nights. Family friends, Connie and Paul, lived in Jackson, Wyoming, and they invited me to stay with them. My Playboy boss, Susan, begrudgingly signed my leave of absence paperwork for three months. I drove with my cat, Bubby, and my mountain bike to Jackson. That summer, kitty and I lived in a tiny log cabin behind Connie and Paul's house. To punctuate the rangeland experience, I worked at a bead store in the town square.

The bead storeowner was a feisty German woman named Ingrid. She ordered her cosmetics from Neiman Marcus in Beverly Hills and was direct with people in that German way, not taking any bullshit from anybody. When I first started, she had just fired two employees for stealing beads. Beading and beaded jewelry were huge trends in the nineties, and her store was the happening place on the square.

Ingrid dated a local guy named Lane, half her age. He was tall and lanky, always in black clothes and black military boots, knocking his long, black, greasy hair around. He was obsessed with knives, but apparently not with deodorant. Every time he came into the shop, I had to breathe through my mouth, so I didn't pass out from the fumes. He always pushed knives on me, in many hidden forms, for protection.

Harrison Ford lived down the road from us in his big ranch, and I saw him driving by sometimes in his white Saab. *Han Solo drives a white Saab just like me!* Connie worked at the local private airport and knew all the celebrities that came through town. I peppered her with questions about Harrison. I don't think she understood my level of Force fandom, but she appeased me. Paul was hilarious and gave me Harrison's home number from Connie's home Rolodex. I called it once, panicked, and hung up.

Connie and Paul belonged to the Jackson Hole Land Trust, and a month after I moved there, a Jackson society woman named Emily Oliver invited us to a private party. Harrison was going, too! As soon as we arrived, I spotted Harrison. I tried to look natural, which I sucked at. Paul talked to Harrison about how well *Patriot Games* did at the box office, while Connie approached Harrison's wife, Melissa Mathison, and expressed that I wanted to meet him. Melissa was such a sweet woman and whisked me over to Harrison for the big intro. We shook hands, and I blubbered what a big fan I was. However, he didn't seem too taken with me, and soon there was nothing more to say, so I backed away toward the safety of Connie and Paul. Suddenly the lightbulb beamed in my head—I wanted to work at Lucasfilm!

After three months of hiking, biking, and beading, I returned to my zany life in West Hollywood and returned to work at Playboy. I'd given up my apartment, so I moved in with Dad's partner, David, in West Hollywood during the week and stayed at my parents' house on the weekend. My boss, Susan, was the only entity keeping me at Playboy. Lita lasted only ten months after I had started, before moving onto mainstream television production, everyone's dream who worked at Playboy. The Hollywood nightlife wore me out. I refused to wait outside with all the posers waiting to get picked to enter a club that was empty. Plus, I'd never lived outside Southern California except for Jackson. I wanted more independence and an apartment Dad didn't hold the keys or security status to. Explaining to people why I worked for a company that exploited women also exhausted me. I'd been around that my entire life, and those women made more money in a day than I made in a week! I wanted to be proud of where I worked.

After nearly three years, I quit Playboy and moved in with my parents. My friend, Debra, at Playboy helped connect me with a guy named David at Industrial Light + Magic (ILM), the storied visual effects division of Lucasfilm. I knew the mission statement: "From building galaxies far, far away, to resurrecting prehistoric creatures, and conjuring realms of wizards and superheroes, at ILM we turn incredible ideas into iconic moments." I flew up to the Bay Area, had a spirited lunch with David, chatting about our love for *Star Wars*. After a few months of flying up north for interviews, followed by lots of handwritten thank-you cards, I secured a position at ILM!

I moved to Sausalito, Marin County and started at ILM in July 1993. One of my first jobs was to clean the production office after the filming of *Jurassic Park*. Pure Heaven in technicolor! I passed George in the hallway, along with so many other stars like Geena Davis. At the time, everyone used ILM and Skywalker Sound for special effects.

Star Wars was everywhere—I was finally with my people. David and I became good friends and often had lunch together to chat about the latest work gossip. Lucasfilm didn't like hiring people who were *Star Wars* obsessed, so David warned me to dial down my enthusiasm. I also made the executive decision not to tell people how many times I'd seen *Star Wars* at the Jet Strip.

The Lucasfilm company holiday party approached. I heard amazing things about how extravagant it was, with open bars, catered food, and live entertainment. Playboy's infamous parties were held after work at a hotel bar on Sunset Boulevard, with Playmates and Hef's daughter, Christie, making an appearance. But this was Lucasfilm.

The Lucasfilm holiday party was on a Saturday night. I asked my sister to be my date, and we dressed up like we were going to prom. The evening did not disappoint. The venue was a five-story building in San Francisco's fashion district with endless food buffets, bars, entertainment, photographers, and dancing among celebrities there like Warwick Davis ("Willow") and Peter Mayhew ("Chewbacca"). I spotted George Lucas from across the room, grabbed Rachel's arm, and screamed, "There HE is!" over the loud music playing. She leaned in and finally saw him. I thought he must want to meet me, as his company hired me. After a few glasses of chard, Rachel and I walked over. I introduced myself.

"Hi George, I just wanted to say what an honor it is to meet you and thank you for hiring me! It's always been my dream to work for you." Surrounded by people, he stood there with a smirk on his face and his arms crossed. This meet and greet was not going well, and I wanted to get out of there, quickly. I shook his hand, but it was like a wet noodle. I said, "Happy holidays!" a little too loud and stumbled away, limping like Quasimodo from the *Hunchback of Notre Dame*. My sister burst out laughing and pointed out a chunk of sourdough bread lodged onto the right heel of my shoe. My heel must have stabbed it on my way to meet George. I still turn red thinking about it.

The following Monday at work, I announced that I went up to George and introduced myself, but it didn't go well. "Oh, that's a big no-no; he hates it when people approach him," a coworker scolded me. I sat nervously at my desk all day, waiting for George's assistant to call and demand that I pack up my things.

The following year at the holiday party, people surrounded George, taking photos with him, and chatting. This was bullshit! I went up to him again and asked for a photo, snatched the money shot, and didn't care this time. He was friendlier that year, perhaps because I didn't have bread stuck on my heel. We had matching red and black outfits on—it was the perfect photo for my 1994 holiday card: "Merry Christmas—love George and Woodsy!"

17 Address in Slumvato

After living in Sausalito for a year, Mom and Dad agreed to help me buy a condo, if I paid the mortgage. I hoped for a cool place in San Francisco or at least Southern Marin, but they picked the last freeway exit in Novato, thirty miles north of the Golden Gate Bridge. All my friends lived close to the bridge or in the city.

"You'll be safer up there, plus we're putting the money down on it. You can pick your own place when you can afford it," Dad retorted.

My condo was literally across the street from a cow pasture. Neighbors were all married with kids screaming through paper-thin walls. Not exactly how I'd imagined my first big move away from SoCal to be. Some work friends advised I'd never see a visitor all the way up there in what was known to the locals as "Slumvato."

On weekends, I hiked Muir Woods or the Dipsea Trail, camped in Point Reyes, or went wine tasting in Napa. I joined two volleyball teams and played twice a week. I went mountain biking in the woods and rollerbladed along the Marina in San Francisco. I spent lots of time with my new family at Lucasfilm, going to screenings, playing softball at Skywalker Ranch, and hanging out at Marin Brewing Company. I didn't miss Playboy, West Hollywood, or the red velvet ropes one bit.

I had even opened up to my coworkers about Dad owning strip clubs. We had an email group going around work for all the *Melrose Place* fans. The latest episode included one of the characters visiting a strip club, which happened to be Dad's Bare Elegance club. We were all discussing the latest drama, and I just decided to drop the bomb, "They filmed that at my dad's my strip club!" People walked by me in the hallways after, smiling coyly or asking for more detail. It felt dynamite to be out of the closet! I couldn't hide it anymore and couldn't keep my lies straight. I was 25 years old, and if fellow Californians couldn't handle what Dad's business was, fuck them.

A year after I moved to Marin, Anne switched bases from Miami to San Francisco and lived in an apartment with three flight attendants in Sausalito. After her lease ended, she asked to move in with me because I had a spare room. I felt guilty having more money than her, so I charged her a nominal rent. Plus, she had a new boyfriend, Craig, who was a winemaker, so she spent time a lot of time up in Napa.

One time, Anne called me at work. Every time we spoke it was filled with excitement, as if we hadn't spoken in months. "I'm in your bathroom cleaning your toilet, and I wanted to know what you wanted for dinner?" Anne harbored an obsession with *Cooking Light* magazine, using me as a guinea pig for her recipes.

"Don't ever let her go," Mom said, laughing when I told her about the call. What I couldn't do in the kitchen I made up to Anne helping her out with her phone or computer, as she was technology averse. I also took Anne with me to the Lucasfilm screenings, wrap parties, and holiday parties. She was an honorary Lucas employee. Anne even convinced me to go to therapy, to deal with my trust issues with men. I had put it off long enough. "Woods," she said, "I'd love for you to find someone to be with, you'd be so happy. You should try it!"

I still had only dabbled in boys, men, whatever they were, since my horrendous encounter with my childhood bully. Where was the bastard now, anyway? I prayed that he never hurt another girl or woman, that his assault on me had been an impulsive crime of opportunity. Today, I know this notion was insanely naïve.

18 Skeletons Aren't Dead

At the end of 1996, Dad learned the Orange County DA's office had reopened the investigation for Mac McKenna's murder. The investigators were making rounds interviewing former dancers and managers of Dad and David's strip clubs. The former employees called the other managers to give them a heads up. It was the same conversation the investigators had started with years ago: "Michael Woods killed Horace McKenna, and we want to tell us what you know about it."

The police investigators visited strip clubs in Los Angeles Dad didn't own, like the Kit Kat in Sunnyvale and King Henry VIII on Crenshaw, asking employees about the murder. Word of the investigation inundated the adult entertainment scene. The investigators flew to Seattle to interview an ex-manager named Terry, then to Colorado to interview an ex-strip club owner Dad knew casually. Each week, people tipped Dad off about whom the investigators had contacted.

Dad spoke to an attorney who said not to worry about it. After all, police harassed the clubs regularly, trying to nail them for prostitution, drugs, or gambling. Undercover vice also frequented the clubs, some asking for kickbacks to stay away. The investigation had spread to the East Coast when Dad found out that they paid a visit to an ex-dancer in Miami who had partied regularly with Mac at his penthouse in Inglewood. She told the investigators, "Yeah, Mike did it, I know he did. Who else would do it? He's a strange guy and I never liked him. You gotta get him." She was dying of cancer, and the investigators took these words as her honest-to-God dying declaration.

Dad knew he was probably under some type of surveillance, but he didn't care. He talked on the phone freely about it, making light of the investigation to his buddies. Mom and I shook our heads in disbelief. "Dad, do you think it's a good idea to talk so much about the case and business on the phone?" I asked him. But he couldn't help himself. He blabbed away on the phone like a teenager.

It seemed so ridiculous to us that they were chasing after Dad. He wasn't the murdering type. He was a family man, an ex-cop who never did drugs.

19 A Very Secure Room of One's Own

Anne broke up with the winemaker and declared that both of us needed to move closer to the city. A week later, after querying my therapist about it instead of my parents, I put my condo on the market, and we found a place in Mill Valley, twenty miles south on Highway 101. Our new pad was an end unit on a hill with pine trees and two decks, ten minutes north of the Golden Gate Bridge. I was 30 years old, and it was the first place I picked to live without my parents' approval.

"Woods, you're an adult, and you're the one living there. If your parents are giving you money, it should be yours to do with what you want, right? Why should your parents pick it?" Anne was right. Why had I felt like I never had a choice before?

I told Dad that I wanted to start making my own decisions, but he said, "You're lucky to have parents who love you as much as we do. I didn't have *anyone* taking care of me when I was your age." I felt ungrateful upon the weight of his words and the circumstances of his youth.

When Dad visited my new place, he assessed, "I never would have picked this condo, it's too dark and musty. Plus, anyone can climb up from the hill and jump over your decks to break in." He convinced me to install an alarm system that we usually set off by accident, pissing off the local cops who had to stop by each time. He also went to the local hardware store to buy dowels for my sliding glass doors. Plus, he installed sensor lights behind my condo in case someone tried to break in. Your garden variety coyote or raccoon loved to trigger them.

I loved our new place, and I loved being close to San Francisco, Muir Woods, and my friends. "Don't listen to your parents, Woods, this place is awesome!" Anne assured me. Anne spoiled me, doing most of the unpacking and organizing the kitchen. I set up our computer and TV, complete with a THX surround sound system I bought at a discount through work.

Our next-door neighbor, Wendy, was a therapist and single mother. She kept asking if we were a couple. After saying "no" for the tenth time, she nudged, "It's okay, you can tell me. I have lesbian clients too!" I guess it didn't help rumors much when Anne made me her official registered companion with American Airlines, meaning I flew employee status for *free*.

After we settled into our new condo, we took our first trip together and went trekking in Peru to Machu Picchu. It was my first time roughing it. Anne kept laughing at me with my hand wipes and sanitizer and my freaking out about the less-than-ideal toilet situations. I couldn't bring myself to pee in the bushes without her gentle persuasion!

After our long trek, we took a night bus to majestic Lake Titicaca on the border between Peru and Bolivia. We just liked saying that word so much, *Titicaca*, accentuating each syllable. On the bus there, we met these guys from Alabama, who offered us Rohypnol, aka roofies, swearing they helped you sleep.

Anne chirped, "Why not?"

I loosened up with Anne, not following all the rules or consulting my folks about everything. It was the best night's sleep I've ever had on a bus barreling down rickety roads. As such, we smuggled some pills back to the States.

When we returned home, I started a new gig at ILM. I'd been self-training to be a digital effects artist, and ILM hired me to work on the next trilogy of prequels to *Star Wars*, starting with *The Phantom Menace*, which flaunted a glittery cast, who would make my contribution come to life: Natalie Portman, Ewan McGregor, Liam Neeson, Jake Lloyd, Ahmed Best, Ian McDiarmid, Anthony Daniels, Kenny Baker, Pernilla August, and Frank Oz. Even though the company could only guarantee seven months of work, I didn't care. I had everything I wanted, including newfound freedom from my parents' control.

20 On the Edge

In the beginning of 2000, Dad was in the upstairs manager's office at the Bare Elegance with his partner, David, and the other managers, Johnny, Ricky, and Chet. They started talking about this ex-dancer they'd fired for doing drugs at work. She subsequently died of an overdose in her Hollywood Hills apartment, and was found alone, slumped over a table with the doors locked from the inside. LAPD investigated the case, but closed it, declaring it an "accidental overdose." Two weeks after the office discussion, the Orange County investigators began asking around if Dad was involved in the dancer's murder.

Dad talked to Ricky and Chet. "How the fuck do those guys know about her?"

"No idea, Mike, we didn't say anything."

A couple more conversations ensued in the office, which got back to the investigators. Dad decided the offices were bugged and hired someone to sweep the clubs, but they came up clean. "Sorry, Mike, there are no bugs in any of the offices."

"Then we got a rat on our hands, or someone talking too much. I think we're all talking too much around here," Dad huffed.

Then they came after Mom.

"*Who* came to the hospital?" Dad asked in disbelief. He was getting ready for work.

"Those two investigators going around asking people about you!" Mom slammed her purse and keys down on the kitchen table. She'd just got home from working the night shift.

"What did they want?" Dad's mind raced.

"I guess they came to the hospital last week when I was off and spoke to my supervisors. They pulled me into their office today after my shift, saying two police investigators came by and wanted to know about me. They said you killed your business partner and they were investigating the murder, looking at all leads. And now *everyone* at work knows about this!"

Mom had a habit of emphasizing "everyone" as if the world were a captive audience to our family's transgressions, the hills had eyes, and we were always under some kind of watch. It was tiring. I could sympathize. She craved a simple life … laced with some luxuries.

"That's it, I'm hiring an attorney!" Dad lost his cool.

"Are they going to raid the house again? I can't take much more of this, Michael!" The mere thought sent more blood rushing through Mom's veins.

"I don't know, Debbie, anything's possible." But this was one thing Dad couldn't make a phone call about or throw money at to disappear.

After the hospital visit to Mom's supervisors, Dad hired a criminal defense attorney. He also spoke with his private investigators, Jack and Frank, whom Dad had known for years. Jack and Frank told Dad to keep a low profile and not get arrested for anything, "not even a goddamned traffic ticket." He'd kept them on hand since Mac's murder.

Dad mentioned the investigation to Mom, Rachel, and me casually over the years, assuring us there was nothing to worry about. Plus, they never got anything on him in the past raids, so what could they find now? Yes, there was nudity involved in his business, but it was legit. Thinking about Dad's upbringing, I was still so proud of him and what he'd accomplished. Dad told us that eventually the investigators would run out of steam and we could relax.

Dad was my hero. I felt protected and safe around him, even just hearing his voice. He talked to me about strangers, sex, and drugs when I was 12. He said to never get into a stranger's car, or I'd be killed for sure. I needed to fight and scream as much as I could to avoid being kidnapped. He also told me to examine under my car and in the backseat before getting in and to lock the doors immediately. Finally, still without the knowledge of what happened to me as a child, he advised that if I were ever raped, I needed to "try and enjoy it" for the assault to be less detrimental. I decided not to share that enterprising tip with anyone.

PART FOUR

ORANGE IS THE NEW DAD

21 Into the Woods

The sun barely shone through the tall trees as I wandered through the lush, dripping coastal redwoods. The world smelled like fresh dirt, dry leaves, and wet ferns. At 10:00 a.m., the fog was still pumping in, as if from a machine. It was a Friday. Only a few people were on the trail. I sipped my soy latte and inhaled.

Steep Ravine Trail in Muir Woods was my favorite hike. It cleared my mind. In the shuffle of the dotcom bubble, my friends left for even more glamorous or higher-paying roles and though I never thought I would leave the Star Wars universe, my motivation left with all my muses. I quit my job as a technology manager at Lucasfilm.

Dad frowned upon my resignation without another job in place. Never in my wildest dreams or under any circumstances did I foresee managing my father's strip clubs as my next career stop.

That morning, as I often did, I drove from my home in Mill Valley, ten minutes north of the Golden Gate Bridge. With my sunroof open, listening to REM on the radio, I had planned a day involving a hike, a pedicure, a massage, and a lunch date.

With my eight-dollar latte in hand, I strutted down the trail, as my mind pivoted between reexamining and replanning my next steps in life. My friends were getting married, cooking, and breeding. I had three cars, two cats, and lived off protein bars and popcorn.

At 32 years old, I yearned for something more than corporate workdays boxed into cubicles. I had an interest in the nonprofit sector and doing something meaningful. Sadly, having only worked at Playboy and Lucasfilm, my expertise was in boobs and the Force. In the meantime, I was taking time out for myself and spending time with friends. The warm sun hit my face, making me smile.

I was covered in dirt and sweat as I climbed back up the steep trail. I hopped back in my car and continued north to Costco in Novato, passing by the Lucasfilm freeway exit. I became nostalgic and wondered if I'd made a mistake by quitting.

But then while driving, I made a mental list of all the guys I'd made out with at work whom I hoped to never see again. Suddenly, I felt better about my decision.

I parked and walked into Costco, flashing my membership card to the employee guarding the entrance. I was browsing the music aisle for some Nat King Cole to buy Dad for Christmas. He used to sing "Unforgettable" to me as a child when he put me to bed. I missed him. I tried calling both his car and cell phone to say hey. He didn't answer. That was unusual.

I came home from Costco, unloaded my car, and called Mom. There was no answer either. What the hell, man? At least one parent always answered. Two shots. I decided to conceive my costume for my friend's work Halloween party. I wondered what my sister, Rachel, was doing for Halloween and called her. No answer. I tried Dad again and it went straight to voicemail. *Where is everyone?* My heart began beating fast and my head tingled. I began expecting the worst, like a car accident or a heart attack. I distracted myself by putting together my Halloween outfit—a Playboy bunny.

Sometimes it's just better to go with what you know.

My phone rang about 4:00 p.m. *Finally*, Mom.

"Where the hell has everybody been?" I asked while foraging through my lingerie drawer for my red push-up bra.

"Laurel, your father's been arrested." I slammed my drawer shut as if locking this news away forever.

"*What?*" I screeched. "Are you joking? What for?" All I could think of was for speeding.

"For Mac's murder," she said robotically.

My mind traversed to Mac's hulk-like body pounded with twenty-six bullets and his last words to his driver being "Tell my mom I love her," according to the news. His murder had remained unsolved for the last eleven years.

"Can you believe those assholes?" Dad would often say about the investigation. "They're wasting their time and money. They got nothin' on me." He spent most mornings calling everyone he could, joking to an excessive degree about being a suspect. I'm sure his financial advisor *loved* getting those forty-five-minute phone calls. But to be frank, not even Mom, Rachel, and I ever took the investigation seriously. According to Dad, Mac had an enemy list a mile long. How could *my* perfect dad be involved?

"Why didn't you pick up your phone earlier?" I asked Mom. I felt hot and clammy.

"We were being held at gunpoint while the district attorney's office and sheriffs raided the house." This was now the second house raid by police I'd missed out on since Dad started working in the strip club industry. I was weirdly envious.

"Where is Dad now?" A painful nerve crept up my spine and my shoulders stiffened.

"They took him to Orange County Jail … where Mac's murder … took place, in Brea." Mom was out of breath.

"Should I come home?" I just wanted someone to tell me what to do. This time, Dad could not. I hung up and sat down on my sage green fleece sofa, wearing my pink Playboy shirt and bunny ears, staring at the hardwood floor.

I kept shaking my head with my bunny ears flopping as I got ready for my friend's Halloween party. Wayne, Mike, and some other Lucasfilm friends came over for beers before the party. We all stood in my living room as I told them about Dad's arrest. Saying it out loud made it real, and a huge wave of exhaustion suddenly enveloped me.

"Well," said Wayne, "you can't drive down to Los Angeles tonight since traffic's a bitch on Fridays, and there's nothing you can do for your dad yet. If you want, drive down in the morning, but unless you hear from your dad or his attorneys, there's little you can do."

"I know, you're right, I'm sure he'll get bail by the time I drive down there anyway." I was just so happy to have someone tell me what to do.

"Enjoy yourself at the party tonight and talk to your family in the morning," Wayne said as he hugged me and my push-up bra.

We drove to downtown Mill Valley for the Halloween party. Wayne's company had rented an old Victorian house, and we walked into cobwebs and strobe lights as the song "Monster Mash" played on the stereo. I saw this skinny guy coming down the stairs, wearing a loincloth. Orange makeup covered his body. I couldn't make out his costume, and he saw my inquisitive look.

"Hi, I'm Zack, I'm an orange Smurf!"

"Oh, wow, it must have taken a while to get all that makeup on."

"Yeah, my girlfriend helped me out. I just hope it comes off."

"I thought Smurfs were blue."

He went into this long story about the Smurfs, which he knew way too in depth, explaining the significance of the orange Smurfs. I smiled and listened. Then I started to cry.

"The police just arrested Laurel's dad," Wayne explained.

"Oh, I'm sorry," the Smurf said.

Oh God, I didn't want to be *that girl* at the party—that girl who cried over family drama. For the rest of the night, I pretended to have fun, avoiding talking to anyone in case I burst into tears again. I ended up dating the orange Smurf a few months down the road, until he ditched me for a tennis pro twenty years my senior.

The next morning, I packed my bag as if for a weekend trip. I figured the jail would release Dad and he'd be back home before I arrived. I pulled into Mom and Dad's driveway in the afternoon. Rachel was watching TV and crying. Mom was at Orange County Jail with Aunt Martha, Dad's only living sister, to visit

Dad. I took Dad's German shepherd, Trooper, for a run through their manicured neighborhood. "This is all a big mistake. Everything is going to be fine by Monday," I said aloud—to Trooper, to myself. Mom came home a couple of hours later.

"Did you see Dad?"

"No, he's not done being processed yet." She set her purse down on the kitchen counter.

"What does that mean?" I turned down the TV.

"Laurel, if I knew, I wouldn't have gone."

Mom sat down next to me on the sofa, giving me that look. That look that said she knew this would happen all along. She'd warned Dad for years to quit the strip club business. "You have more money than you know what to do with, Michael, don't be greedy," she'd often say to him. "Look at what happened to Mac."

Jack Scully, one of the private investigators Dad had hired when he realized he was being investigated, came to our house. He explained what was going on and what was about to happen. I took notes in my journal as Jack discussed jail and next steps. I didn't even have Dad's attorneys' information. I'd never felt more ill-equipped to face something.

Nothing could be discussed on the phone. Jack was a family friend who had known Dad for years. In the kitchen, he explained to us Dad's charges, the attorneys, and the process going forward. "Your dad's in great hands with his attorneys, Vicki and Richard. They only take cases they can win." I let out a deep breath. Mom stood there silent, a smirk on her face. "They're working with the Orange County D.A.'s office to get the discovery on Mike's case so they can understand the evidence behind these charges."

Mom asked Jack about visiting Dad in jail. "The jail is open for visitations Friday, Saturday and Sunday. Friday visits start at 1:00 p.m., Saturdays and Sundays at 7:00 a.m. Visits are limited to forty-five minutes. Remember, the jail records and listens to everything your father says. They want him to slip up."

I thanked Jack as he left the house. He reassured us it was going to be a long journey, but everything would turn out okay in the end. "The most important thing right now, is to not let your dad discuss anything, and I mean *anything*, about his case on the phone," Jack reiterated.

I remembered how Dad had mocked the investigation. I thought about how he discussed it with anyone who'd listen, even his financial advisor, on the phone. Dad even thought their house phone was tapped and still didn't care. "Yeah, I'm pretty sure a car followed me around yesterday as I hit the strip clubs," he'd say to me nonchalantly, again, *in the phone*.

"How do you know?" I'd ask.

"Because, Lip, I used to be a cop, remember? I know how to tail people."

22 America's Most Wanted

That Sunday night after private investigator, Jack Scully, left the house, Mom, Rachel, and I pretended to have a normal evening. We returned home from dinner with family friends and watched TV, simultaneously hoping and not hoping to find news segments on Dad. We found more than we hoped for. "America's Most Wanted" featured his mug shot. Dad would be so irate if he knew how bad his mugshot was!

The entire neighborhood had seen my parents' house being raided the day of Dad's arrest. Neighbors stood on the street watching and whispering, while helicopters, sheriffs, police, and investigators swarmed around. They had raided all of Dad's strip clubs, too. A constant barrage of friends called. No one knew what to say, and I didn't trust the phone lines, so I didn't offer much. I imagined a white van outside the house recording every conversation. It sent a chill up my spine.

Dad's first court hearing, his arraignment, was on Tuesday, October 31, 2000, Halloween day, four days after his arrest. I remembered the Halloween when Dad dressed up like Darth Vader. Now, he wore one of those dumpy orange jail jumpsuits like the ones sold at costume stores.

We left home at 5:00 a.m. and arrived at the court before 8:00 a.m. to meet the attorneys. I wondered if Dad would come home with us.

I ordered a small latte at the coffee cart outside. I certainly didn't need it, as I was already shaking from adrenaline. The barista handed me a large, so I informed him he'd given me the wrong size.

"It's my treat, because you said *please*!" he beamed. I was grateful for his kindness.

Vicki, one of Dad's attorneys, assured us the hearing would be short—it was to formally charge Dad, and then Dad could ask the judge for a bail hearing. Vicki also stressed that we could not talk with Dad in court. "No touching, no eye contact, no motioning." This very act of affection, not aggression, was classified as a misdemeanor—we could be arrested! My head swirled with all these new rules.

Nothing prepares you for seeing your parent shackled, in an orange jumpsuit, locked in a cage in a courtroom. The whole scene reminded me of those sad SPCA animal videos with Sarah McLachlan singing in tandem with a dog shaking uncontrollably in a shelter cage with those sad red eyes. Dad attempted a smile, but his puffy eyes, slouched shoulders, and hands cuffed behind his back told the true story. Dad had never shown weakness; he was the toughest person I knew. It scared me to see him rendered helpless and shredded my confidence for the day.

People I didn't know filled the courtroom—investigators, police, Mac's son, and a slew of reporters. Why was Dad's case such a big deal? These strangers were witnessing a private moment. I felt violated. *The Los Angeles Times* reporter approached us, but Vicki shooed him away.

"Absolutely no talking to the press," she pointed at us.

Vicki reminded us that it was a sensationalized case filled with murder, sex, drugs, strip clubs, and even tales about him being tied to the mafia. Soon, the case would, indeed, make it to numerous true-crime shows and movies milking the greed–power–sex–slaughter storyline.

The day of the arrest, David Amos, Dad's current strip club business partner, had asked Dad to lunch at Jerry's Deli in Woodland Hills. The D.A.'s office had arrested David for murder the night before and wiretapped him before meeting Dad. In the transcript of the wiretapped conversation, Dad and David talked about how to deal with the pending murder investigation.

"If I take the fall for you, what are you going to do? Are you going to look after my family?" David asked Dad.

"Yes, Dave," Dad replied. You could hear distant chatter and banging plates in the background.

At one point, Dad tells David he will use "the same old story" about why he gave him a stake in the clubs after Mac's death.

"I was scared to death … I didn't want to go by the clubs. So, I said, 'Here, Dave, you go. You run the clubs. I'll split it with you.' And that's the story I'm going to stick with," Dad said. David brought up Johnny Sheridan, the shooter who killed Mac, and one of their club managers, telling Dad he was worried about Johnny's loyalty, saying Johnny often complained he wasn't paid enough.

"Well, I hate to say this, but you're the one … you told me you would take care of Johnny," Dad pressed.

"I know," David responded. "I thought he forgot about it. I mean, you said you'd do it, and I forgot to give it to him … I mean he can't prove it's you."

"Yeah," Dad replied.

All at once, undercover cops had stood up from surrounding tables, shouting orders, and scattering around like roaches, arresting Dad there at the restaurant. Police rushed out to raid my parents' house and all three strip clubs. We found out from the attorneys that Johnny had confessed to the murder ten months prior, declaring that he'd "found God." He'd been arrested for the murder but was then released in exchange for cooperating with the investigators, gathering paperwork for a tax evasion case, and wearing a wiretap in the clubs.

Parts of the wiretap transcript were even printed in *The Los Angeles Times.* Thank God they left out the part where Dad gave David way too many details about his bowels. Nonetheless, it didn't look good for Dad. But for weeks, he refused to believe that David "rolled over on him," another new term I had recently learned.

Dad's arraignment lasted less than five minutes. We sat there, dressed up, with perfect posture. Sitting in a courtroom was like sitting in a church pew, with a priest at the helm instead of a judge. After a moment of silence, which seemed like an hour, the stodgy judge slammed his gavel down, with the words, "I'm denying the defendant bail at this time!" He set a court date of November 17, 2000, for a bail hearing. Dad looked over at us and nodded. I snuck in a wilted smile, my lips sticking to my teeth, before the court officer took Dad away, hobbling in his shackles and handcuffs. I could hear his chains jangling for several minutes after the door closed behind him. When we couldn't hear Dad's chains anymore, we arose from our pew and left.

Vicki met us outside with a steady stream of answers. "The charges are murder for capital gain, coupled with a tax evasion case, meaning the district attorney's office can seize all assets."

When she mentioned the word "seize," my heart stopped beating. I thought of what they could seize—everything?

"Well, they can take anything they suspect was purchased with illegal funds—the family's house, your and your sister's condos, your cars, your dad's boats, and all belongings," Vicki explained with boss-bitch authority. "Hard to say what they'll do. We're still not sure what evidence they have against your dad. But the sentence would be the death penalty because of the capital gain charge." *Death penalty*? Mom wobbled so I pulled her up by her arm.

"There's mention of another motive besides murder for capital gain because Mac made threats against the family. Specifically, he threatened to have the wife and daughters gang raped," she said as if she were talking about another family. I suddenly remembered hearing about the gang-rape threat from my parents in the eighties.

Vicki continued, warning us not to let Dad say anything about the case on the phone. All our phones and probably our houses could be wiretapped, and they probably had been for the last three years. I remembered the phone conversation the summer before, when I had called Dad from London on my way back from Africa with my friend, Erin.

"How was it?" Dad asked me.

"It was great! I slept with our African tour guide!" I started laughing.

"I wish you hadn't told me that, Laurel," Dad said disapprovingly. What other private, intimate moments had they overheard? I'd always told my parents everything. Well, and now the Orange County investigators knew everything, too.

"Don't worry, we'll get this all figured out," Vicki assured us. "I'm late for another court hearing in Santa Monica. I'll be in touch." Like a puff of smoke, the boss was gone.

We drove the long ride back home—a five-hour round-trip drive for a five-minute hearing. I couldn't have imagined then that these drives would become a daily occurrence. My body was stiff as if I'd been in a car accident. I couldn't move my neck. The thought of food made me nauseous. I was parched. All I wanted was water. Mom informed me that when your body is in shock, your kidneys shut down, dehydrating your organs.

At home, I paced the house, waiting for the phone to ring. That evening, Dad headlined almost every major channel for the five o'clock news. "Mike Woods, ex-cop turned strip club owner with possible mafia ties in Las Vegas," the newscaster began, "Woods, accused of murdering his strip club partner and thought he'd get away with it." He talked about Dad being involved in the porn industry and drugs. My dad, my hero. We changed channels, but the reporters were like parrots repeating the same phrases. What happened to "innocent until proven guilty"? They showed Dad's hideous mug shot and then panned to a family photo of the four of us in Hawaii at sunset one Christmas. How did they get their hands on that photo? A *Los Angeles Times* reporter came to the house and asked Mom for a comment. She slammed the door on him.

As a precaution, Anne's parents let Mom store her precious china set from her grandmother at their house. It was the one thing Mom didn't want to be seized. I drove them over cautiously as the dishes rattled in the backseat. Anne's dad, an FBI agent, waited for me at the door.

That night, I slept in the same bed with Mom. Every time a helicopter flew by, or we heard a siren down the street, we were certain the sheriffs were coming back for another house raid or to seize our assets. It would take years to get over that fear.

23 A Cold and Dazed Family

The day after Dad's arraignment, I didn't want to get out of bed. I found it hard to sleep at night. I had nightmares involving characters from all aspects of my life, from Star Wars figures to teachers and the child-monster rapist.

How would we survive if our assets were frozen? How would we pay what the attorneys said might be in the millions in lawyers' fees? How would they know what I bought with my own earnings versus what my parents bought me? Would they take my clothes? Would we get any notice? Mom could lose her home, her car, and most possessions in her house. Where would she go? Maybe she could live with Anne's parents.

Rachel had just bought a condo in Santa Monica and was moving in with her boyfriend from grad school. We warned her to get out of escrow if she could, but she went ahead with it anyway. Mom, Rachel, and I had eight animals between us. Would they seize them too? Would Dad have to downgrade to a public defender?

One night, after turning off the evening news, I crawled into bed, listening to the frogs croaking outside around the pool. I stared at the trazodone pills my doctor had recently prescribed me for depression and sleeplessness. They seemed to be calling to me, taunting me on these nights of feeling like my life was empty of meaning and filled with difficulty. I picked up the bottle and stared at it. Then I looked over at Mom lying in bed next to me, sound asleep, and I gently stroked her hair.

I worked to secure funds for the attorneys. Dad had spread his wealth around several banks. He kept cash and paperwork in safety deposit boxes. I visited the local banks, giving the tellers my elevator pitch. "Hi, my Dad's been arrested for murder, and I'm wondering if he has a bank account or safe deposit box here?" I then slid my driver's license and power of attorney papers underneath the glass for them to look at. The typical response was silence and an open mouth, followed by a mad dash to the nearest manager.

On the third day of this, I was in the same outfit I'd worn the last couple of days, Old Navy khakis and tee shirt. I was waiting in line at Bank of America, but my mind was elsewhere. I was remembering my friend, Heidi. Her son, Sean, was disabled, and every day of his too-short life was a struggle. He has since passed away. "The one thing about going through a catastrophic event," she'd say, "is that you don't give a damn about anything else. Nothing else matters." As I stood there at the bank with my dirty clothes, ratted hair, and unbrushed teeth, I finally knew what she meant. All I cared about was getting Dad out of this mess.

A day after I'd done the rounds at the banks, a judge granted the D.A.'s office warrants for searching Dad's safety deposit box at Bank of America. All they found was an empty box accompanied by a Post-it Note with a smiley face stuck to the bottom. By this point, I knew I was being followed 24/7 and decided I needed some levity. After Dad's trial, all the paperwork they seized was returned to us, including the smiley-face Post-it Note.

It was the following Thursday, and Dad had been in jail one week. I thought about the last time I'd seen Dad before his arrest. I'd flown to Los Angeles for a quick visit, and I was pissed. Dad had picked me up at the airport an hour late. I let Dad have it. "You knew what time my flight arrived. Why are you so late?" He laughed his signature hyena laugh, gave me a hug, and told me how excited he was to see me. I acted like a petulant child on the ride home. Now, I wish I could go back in time and tell him it was okay, all that mattered was that he took time out of his day to pick me up. What I wouldn't have given to get that car ride back.

Back at home, I set the alarm for 1:45 a.m. Friday. The drive to jail took two and a half hours. Jack said to arrive by 4:30 a.m. to ensure a visit. It would be our first. I went to bed at 11:00 p.m., lying there in anticipation of the alarm going off. When it exploded, Mom, Rachel, and I jumped out of bed, threw on jeans and tee shirts, and hopped into Dad's black Lexus. I felt jet lagged. David Gray played on the radio; his album, *White Ladder*, had just been released. That album still haunts me. As I drove Mom and Rachel down to Orange County, I looked around at the other cars on the freeway. Where were they going this early in the morning?

We parked in the parking structure across from the jail, grabbed our things, and walked in. The visitor center was a big, cold building with fluorescent lighting and rows of plastic molded chairs with fixed armrests, so you couldn't lie down. There was one vending machine with soft drinks and water. The trashcan spilled over with soda cans and fast-food wrappers. The women's bathroom was stainless steel and smelled like shit, with no toilet paper. There was piss on the seats and no soap in the soap dispenser. The processing booth was in the right rear corner, encased in bulletproof glass with Orange County Sheriffs chatting away inside. We saw people being released from jail, mostly for DUIs. They were shaking their heads, sobering up, clutching their belongings in a brown paper sack, looking for a ride home. It was a constant rotating door of those being released and those being booked. It was kind of a hotel lobby of guests checking in and out, except without the grand floral arrangement. I found the whole thing fascinating. What was the nice-looking boy being arrested for? That sweet old man? Teenage girl cowering in the corner?

People gathered in line in front of the booth, so we got in line with them. I stayed in line while Mom walked over to a sheriff and asked what the process was.

"You see that ticket number dispenser? You get a number, and we process the visits based on those numbers. Today visiting starts at 1:00 p.m. Come back by noon."

It was like taking a pink ticket number at the local deli. What were we supposed to do for the next eight and a half hours? Mom came back in line, gave Rachel and me the scoop, and we got our number. The people in line with us were women—wives, girlfriends, mothers, sisters, and daughters. They were covered in tattoos and piercings. The three of us stood there, clinging to each other. We must have looked like lost Stepford wives. Mom wanted to spray everyone down with sanitizer and used a tissue when touching any door handle.

The other visitors knew each other and chatted away. No one spoke to us.

After getting our "deli ticket," we guarded it with our lives, as if it came from Willy Wonka himself. We hopped back into Dad's car, drove to South Coast Plaza Mall, parked in front of Old Navy, and slept in the car until the mall opened. This became our Friday ritual, and over time, I acquired an entire wardrobe from Old Navy, and instead of size eight, I was now a size two, thanks to my "Dad's-in-jail-for-murder" weight-loss program. We shopped, got coffee, and stared at our watches.

I found myself staring at a woman one day. She was about my age. She was wearing yoga pants and had a coffee in her hand. I had a flashback to my hike in Muir Woods, the day I got the call. It seemed like a lifetime ago.

We arrived back at jail in time to wait in another processing line, when the sheriffs checked out what we were wearing to make sure it was appropriate and did a background check with our driver's licenses. We sat down and waited for our names to be called. There was no "How are you today?" There were no smiles and no eye contact.

"Woods?" we heard at last.

We got up and followed the officer leading the rest of the crowd, through the metal detector and up the stairs. The walls were white-painted brick. We walked deeper into the jail, and the interior was as cold as a meat locker. We arrived in the visiting room—six small booths, each with a phone and an orange-clad inmate on the other side of the glass. We walked by each one afraid to look up until we saw Dad. My mouth tasted salty as I clenched my jaw, forcing a smile. It was so hard looking at him, that occasionally I had to turn my head away and recompose myself. Rachel was full-blown bawling, while Mom stood there, motionless. I'd never seen Dad scared before, with that caged-animal look. An inch of glass separated us, but it seemed like a brick wall. There were cameras everywhere, and the phones recorded every conversation. I wanted so badly to hug him, but he was trapped behind the glass. We could only smile to offer any reassurance.

Dad was pale and covered in goose bumps. He'd always had a huge presence—powerful, larger than life, and fearless. Now, he tried to keep up his joking facade, but I saw fear in his glassy eyes as he bit the skin off his lips. This was a scene right out of a movie. There was no way this could be real.

We let Mom sit down in the one chair to use the phone, while we crouched on each side of her so we could all hear the earpiece.

"How are you doing Michael?" She pressed her hand onto the glass.

"Eh, I've been better." Dad placed his forehead in his hand.

"What are they feeding you?"

"Mostly meatloaf, cold hamburgers, and fries," Dad shrugged.

"How are you sleeping?"

"Oh man, it's freezing in here, and I have a blanket that's no better than a flimsy airline blanket. I need a court order to get an additional blanket. My attorneys are working on it."

He started talking about the case, so I pulled the phone away from Mom. "Dad, don't say anything. Your attorneys told us to tell you to keep your mouth shut."

"But I have to have someone to talk to about this," he said, leaning forward in his metal chair.

"Dad, *please*, you could jeopardize your case!" My voice rose sharply as Mom put her hand on my arm.

Rachel continued sniffling.

Our visit lasted forty-five minutes. We tried to fit everything in, sometimes mouthing words so the guards couldn't hear. Dad told us over and over how much he loved us. When the guard motioned that visiting was over, it was too soon. And just like that, the phone line went dead. Mom got up and Dad turned to look at me, pointing to Mom. "Take care of her. I'm worried," he mouthed.

We were cold and dazed. The guards herded all of us back to the main visiting area, and we exited the building. The other women chatted about how great their visits were. The sun was bright and bold and warmed my chilled skin. I had escaped. We were silent on the walk back to Dad's Lexus. It was an odd feeling, leaving Dad behind. I looked at the large brick jail building. Dad was probably only about 100 feet from us right now. I imagined Superman busting into the side of the building and pulling Dad out with one arm.

I drove us home, and Mom made us lunch even though we weren't hungry. I was running on fumes, my exhaustion and adrenaline constantly battling it out. Last week, I'd hiked Muir Woods with my latte. Now I'd just experienced my first jail visit. Mac's murder had been nothing but a faint murmur in the background of our ongoing lives. Now it consumed us. I had questions for Dad. How much did he know? Who were Mac's enemies? Why didn't he go to the police about the gang-rape threat?

Whenever I'd watched the local news, and they'd talk about some poor schmuck arrested and awaiting trial, I'd assumed that schmuck was guilty. Otherwise, why would they take the time to arrest him? They'd show interviews of the family supporting the defendant and I'd think, *shit, this family is wasting their time.* Now that "poor schmuck" was *my* father, while Mom, Rachel, and I were the supporting family members.

24 Olivia Newton-John Will Save Us

The attorneys said Dad would be released in two weeks. Two more weeks of this hell. I couldn't eat. None of us could. We were up at all hours of the night watching TV, making tea, talking to Huey, our pet parrot, or staring at the ceiling fan while lying awake in bed. I drove six hours north to my place in Mill Valley to get away from it all. But as soon as I got home, I felt helpless again. I wanted to turn around and go back to Mom's, but I knew there was nothing I could really do. Mom and Rachel worked, but I had no job to keep me preoccupied. I longed for my days back at Lucasfilm. This was no longer the dreamy break between career changes I had imagined. Thankfully, I had an amazing support group of friends. As word about Dad spread about my inner circle, and within my Lucasfilm community, people called to see how I was doing, told me they loved me, and told me not to hesitate to call anytime.

Vicki, Dad's attorney, told us that we needed as many people as possible at Dad's bail hearing. Also, we needed to collect letters from family and friends addressed to the judge, about what a great family and community man Dad was. We needed to maintain Dad's image as a devoted husband and father, instead of a strip club owner/murderer. I called everyone—my close friends, Dad's boating and car friends, family friends, my old piano teacher—and asked them to write letters.

I sat down to write my letter and thought about what an amazing father I had. He gave me my first cat, Coco, took us camping and trick-or-treating, taught me how to ride a bike and drive a car, and cried at both my high school and college graduations. I needed the judge to see Dad through my eyes. I took a breath and began. My letter of support began with how instrumental Dad was in shaping me into the strong, independent woman I am today. I wrote about Dad's abusive childhood, growing up on the streets in Hoboken, neglected by his mother and abused by her boyfriends. I explained that my father never went past seventh grade but later received his GED when he went into the Army. And I showed how important it was to my dad for his kids to have a better education—a better life.

He encouraged my accomplishments in school—National Honor Society, French Club President, and maintaining a 4.0 GPA in high school, UC Santa Barbara, UC Berkeley, and at Université de la Sorbonne in Paris. Dad encouraged me to do as much as I could with my life.

As I wrote these things down, tears streamed down my face. My letter of support covered everything needed to portray my father as the man I saw him to be—loving, devoted, empowering, caring, and innocent. The judge had to grant Dad bail. I corralled friends to come to the bail hearing. "This is it," I told myself. "He will get out, and then we can sort out this whole mess."

The night before Dad's bail hearing, I had a dream. I didn't usually remember my dreams, but this one was vivid.

Dad and I were eating dinner at the theme restaurant at LAX Airport. Dad took us there for dinner often. The restaurant looked like a building popped out of the "Jetsons" in the middle of the terminals. In my dream, he told me that he was arrested but the guards released him for a few hours. The restaurant was packed with people. Music blasted; we couldn't hear to talk. We sat across from each other at a table, drinking glowing neon green cocktails from martini glasses. Dad wore a mustard-colored turtleneck dickey—one of those faux-turtlenecks men wore underneath sport coats in the 1970s. It was an ugly shirt. But I looked no better—I had my long brown hair in a side ponytail and was wearing a grey sweatshirt dress with pink polka dots and a large white belt, and a pink bandana around my head, just like Olivia Newton-John in her video "Let's Get Physical." By the way, this was an actual outfit I did wear in high school in the eighties!

In the dream, Dad told me how the guards were treating him in jail. Suddenly, helicopters surrounded the restaurant and the searchlights shone into the restaurant's floor-to-ceiling windows. "Oh well, I guess my visiting time is up," Dad said. We hid underneath our table, as policemen rappelled down ropes from the helicopters, smashing through the windows while glass shattered everywhere. People screamed, but Dad laughed. The policemen came over to Dad and picked him up off the ground and handcuffed him. "Mr. Woods, you need to come with us now," they said, taking Dad away. The dream seemed so real.

The next day, I packed my car and began the monotonous drive back down to LA. Most of the time, I was in a trance. I had to get to bed early for the dreaded drive. At 4:30 a.m. Mom, Rachel, and I began getting ready for Dad's bail hearing. We were nervous, but we were certain that he'd get out. We left the house before sunrise and drove without saying a word.

At the courthouse, I walked down the hall. It was full of friends who had turned out for Dad's bail hearing. I hugged each of them, tearing up, not wanting to let go. In the courtroom, I found my friends, Erika and Richard, Susan, my old boss from Playboy, my friend Jill, Dad's managers, family friends, Stanley and Patti, among others, and of course, Anne. There must have been thirty-five people there to support Dad. On the other side of the courtroom, Mac's son, Orange County investigators, the district attorney, and reporters sat and glared at us. I'd never met Mac's son before. Dad told me he didn't have a close relationship with his dad and was raised by his grandparents. Once again, Dad's attorneys warned us not to expect much.

The D.A. began describing Dad as a killer, a mobster, and a pimp driven by greed. He ended his rant by calling him a psychopath. I saw Dad shake his head. The D.A. said Dad was a flight risk with ties to hidden funds in Europe. *Europe?* I couldn't even find funds at the local banks. The D.A. ended by pleading with the judge to deny bail. I snickered and rolled my eyes.

Next up were Dad's attorneys, Vicki and Richard. They described my father as the family man I wrote about in my letter to the judge—father, husband, businessman, and community member. They described our family, and I sat up straight as the judge studied us. The attorneys assured the judge Dad was not a flight risk—he had a business and a loving family to attend to. As the grand finale, Vicki asked us to stand up in support of Dad. We were surrounded by people I knew and loved, who had taken time out of their busy workday to be here with us. Vicki held in her hands copies of the letters we wrote.

The judge sat there in silence for a moment. What did he need to think about? "I'm denying the defendant bail."

My chin dropped to my chest. The prosecution smiled. I hated them. I could hear the disappointment on our side of the courtroom. Dad's jaw dropped so much I thought he was going to start drooling. Even now, when we discuss his case, he has no recollection of his bail hearing.

The attorneys met with us after the hearing and talked about the next steps. "There will be a pre-trial to determine if there is enough evidence to go to trial."

"When?" I drilled.

"We'll be in touch," Dad's attorneys replied, each leaving with their small wheeling black suitcases full of case paperwork.

I stumbled down the courthouse hallways. I was cold and had that sinking feeling of jet lag again. My friends hugged me and took off for work.

"Oh Woodsy, I'm so sorry," Anne said.

I watched them leave to return to their normal lives and jobs. We drove home. I sat in front of the television watching "Alias" while Mom fussed in the kitchen. I watched this strong female character conquering evil as my realization set in—this was not some horrible mistake that would disappear anytime soon. We needed to prepare. I thought back to the day of Dad's arrest—my hike, my coffee, my leisurely lunch, and shopping. How relaxed I was, planning out my trip with Anne and my next career move. I wondered when I would have a moment like that again.

25 Time for Dirty Santa's Little Helper

People said the holidays were hard and I never understood why until Dad went to jail. I lived for the holidays—eating honey-baked hams, guzzling spiked eggnog, laughing with family, lying on the couch watching *Star Wars*—the perfect excuse to be a sloth. But this year was different. It would be our first Thanksgiving without Dad carving our turkey.

I got my nails done at Kathryn's salon. I tried to smile, but the sniffles gave me away. Kathryn came over, gave me a hug, asked how Dad was, and I broke down sobbing. "Oh, you poor thing, I'm sorry this is happening to you," she said, rubbing my back. Kathryn had been cutting my hair since I was 10 years old. She was like family to me.

We went to Ron and Sandy Shaw's house for turkey dinner. Dad had known Ron for years, from the car and boat business. Ron owned his own upholstery business, and Dad used him for his boats, cars, and furniture upholstering. Sandy was a schoolteacher. They had two kids who were also hardworking. It was rare for Dad to have friends outside the club business, and I think Mom wished they knew more people like Ron and Sandy. After David had wiretapped Dad, it was hard for him to trust people. The Shaws were an exception. Ron was the Energizer bunny and hopped around, talking about twenty subjects at once and pouring us wine. Sandy was the opposite—calm and patient.

The Shaws insisted on serving us, keeping us out of the kitchen. Mom didn't know what to do with herself. We didn't say grace before the meal, but I saw Mom say a quiet prayer of thanks. We talked about Dad's case, and Ron was very positive. He cracked jokes and made us laugh. I didn't want to leave the mirth of their home. We sat around the dining room table as we sipped red wine and slouched in our chairs. Pumpkin-scented candles lit up the mantel. Then the moment was gone. Dad called to wish us a happy Thanksgiving. Dad's attorney had filed a court order to allow Dad to make collect calls with his calling card at the jail, so he'd been calling us often. When it was my turn, I took the phone into a bedroom for some privacy. As soon as he said, "Happy Thanksgiving, Lip!" tears streamed down my face. Dad's nickname for me was always "The Lip." Apparently, when I was little, I pushed out my lower lip, pouting, when I didn't get my way. I swear I've changed.

I told him how wonderful the Shaws were and what a great meal we'd had. "Huh, I don't even want to know what you ate. We had cold meatloaf for dinner. I pretended it was your mother's turkey." I didn't talk much after that. I felt so guilty telling him about our lives on the "outside," and I wished I could protect him. I came out to the main dining room and passed the phone around so people could say hi and cheer Dad up. Ron was great at getting him to laugh. "Don't worry, Mike, I know it's hard now, but everything's gonna be okay."

The next day, I drove home to Mill Valley for a two-week break from the madness. I couldn't wait to leave Los Angeles and all it now meant. My friends tried to distract me by calling me and taking me to lunch. But every time I turned on the TV, there was more news about the case. And Dad called my cell phone several times a day, talking for an hour at a time. It was impossible to escape.

Mom and Rachel worked, so they had an excuse for not answering. I had none. At first, I answered his calls because I felt bad for him. Sometimes I'd leave my friends alone at a restaurant table for an hour, while I talked and cried on the sidewalk. I'd tell Dad I was at lunch, but he never took the hint. When I'd get back to my seat, my friend would pay for lunch. I called these "sympathy lunches," and friends joked that I cried to get out of paying.

"How did you know my scheme?" I'd challenge.

"Brilliant, Woods, brilliant," my friend, Erin, said to me. Sometimes a smile would even surface on my ghostly face.

Before Dad's arrest, I never cried; my therapist even said that I needed to cry more. Now, I cried when I woke up, when I saw friends, when I talked on the phone with Dad, and when I went to bed. One Friday night, I had dinner plans with my friend Sheila. "You need to get out, Lew (one of my nicknames). It's no good staying at home, crying. Come out to dinner with the girls!" So, I did my makeup and hair—and was fine. I had to be at Sheila's house in San Francisco in half an hour. Just as I was about to leave, an emotional tidal wave flooded me, and I was sobbing on my kitchen floor. My cats stared at my pathetic state.

I called Sheila back. "I'm sorry, I can't come. I can't stop crying, and I don't want to be around people and pretend everything's okay." Sheila asked if I was sure, and I kept sobbing. "I'll call you tomorrow, I'm so sorry."

Two days later, I packed my bags and drove the six hours down to Los Angeles. It was Christmas time now, and I hated the holidays. I'd be spending my first Christmas in jail. When I arrived, Mom had put up a tree and decorated the house. I decided to get into the spirit and went out to look for a Santa's little helper costume for when we'd visit Dad. I found a costume rental shop in the Yellow Pages. The guy running the shop looked out of place for Thousand Oaks. He looked more like a Vegas pimp. He was wearing big gold chains and chunky gold rings. He gave me two costume options—one was the normal costume and the other one was the "Dirty Santa's Little Helper" costume, complete with G-string. I went into the dressing room, covering the mirror, which I assumed had a camera in it, and tried on the normal costume.

Mom and I did our usual drive to jail. We got up at 2:30 a.m. and made the two-and-a-half-hour drive. I wore my non-dirty Santa's Little Helper costume.

"Don't be so certain they'll let you in with that costume on," Mom said.

"Why not? It's regulation. It's like a dress. And give me a break, it's Christmas!" Mom rolled her eyes.

"Well, you know how the guards are," she said. "It depends on who's there and what their mood is."

Once, a guard had accused me of sending in Bobby, a friend of Dad's, to get my visiting appointment. When I came back to the jail for the evening visit, after signing in at 4:30 a.m., like always, my name wasn't on Dad's list of visitors, but Bobby's was. The guard said that he wouldn't let me in because I had someone else wait in line for me. I asked him to pull up the surveillance video of the morning showing me waiting in line. He huffed about before letting me in. "Don't try and pull that again."

I entered the visitor center looking like a Rockette. Everyone stared. I signed in with a smile so they wouldn't turn me away for the outfit. The guards giggled. "Nice costume!" "Merry Christmas!" I said in return as Mom and I sat on the cold chairs. Some child visitors approached me, wanting to sit on my lap for a picture and to tell me their Christmas wish list. I held back tears as I obliged. How would I have handled this as a young child? The kids were sweet with a sense of innocence I was now longing for.

We'd planned to smuggle presents in for Dad. I'd bought Dad two Hawaiian shirts. The sizing had been tough because he'd lost thirty pounds. As I went through security, the alarm went off. I'd used foil wrapping paper, which had set off the metal detector. I held my breath as I attempted to joke about it, "Well I guess you caught me!" I said, smiling at him. Finally, the guard chuckled and waved me through.

Mom and I walked down the cold cement hallway to see Dad. I pulled myself together and launched a Rockette kick in the air. He looked pale and cold, but he smiled. Mom and I shared the chair and sat in front of the glass. Dad asked where Rachel was, and we said she and her boyfriend went to a spa in Palm Springs. We took turns talking on the phone and opened the presents for him we brought, saying we'd hold them until his release.

"Next year, I won't be in here," he assured us.

When our forty-five-minute visit ended, we waved goodbye, and a guard escorted Dad to his cell.

On the ride home, we reminisced about how Dad had dressed up as Santa Claus each year on Christmas Eve. He owned a Santa suit and wore 1970s aviator glasses with it. He'd knock on the door after our family meal and come in yelling "Ho ho ho!" to the crowd, dragging a sack of presents behind him. Mom acted as his helper, reaching into the sack to hand him gifts. Dad would read the name off and ask if that person was naughty or nice, then he'd chuck the gift at them. Sometimes you had to duck, he'd throw them so fast.

New Year's Eve was as uneventful as Christmas. Well, almost. We ordered a sushi platter for the four of us—Mom, Rachel, her boyfriend, Seth, and me. We lounged on the sofa in front of the TV, trying to relax and enjoy the evening. Rachel and Seth got into a big fight—she accused him of taking up too much space on the sofa. The tiff spiraled into a loud and vulgar screaming match, and Rachel drove an hour home to Santa Monica, leaving Seth behind without a ride.

It wasn't unlike the last year's New Year's Eve, before Dad's arrest. The family, including Seth, went to Maui for Christmas and New Year's. It was the Millennium—2000—and my parents planned our trip a year in advance. We landed in Maui, and Rachel came down with the flu. Seth, Rachel, and I were sharing a room, and within a day, Seth and I were also sick. We were in Maui for seven days, and I spent four days in a hotel bed. After dinner on New Year's Eve, we walked down to the beach by Black Rock Point by the Maui Sheraton. You could see fireworks going off from sailboats, and the ocean glistened in the moonlight. We sat down in the sand, and Mom and Dad served us champagne for a toast.

Dad raised his glass in a toast when Rachel and Seth started fighting. Dad tried to calm them down, but Seth stood up, crying, and ran away.

"What did you say to him?" Dad asked Rachel.

"I just broke up with him," she said.

"Did you have to do it on New Year's Eve, in front of everyone?" Dad put his champagne glass down in the sand and took off after Seth, and Rachel went back to the room. It was Mom and I on the beach.

Mom raised her glass. "Well, cheers to another fucking family vacation."

26 Making It Rain

It took not even two months of Dad and David being locked up before the clubs' cash receipts began dwindling away. The clubs were a cash-heavy business, and skimming was common among the employees. After discussions with Dad's private investigators and the club accountant, I decided to take on managing daily operations of the strip clubs to have a better eye on cash flow and the employees. We limited Dad's involvement in the day-to-day operations of his clubs, due to his inability to avoid saying things that might further incriminate him.

During this time, a friend reminded me that working for strip clubs doesn't attract Harvard business grads. Boy, was that an understatement. The adult entertainment business drew more, shall we say, street-savvy employees, with resumes including prior arrests for gambling, carrying concealed weapons, assault, and burglary. The dancers were pretty clean. The real problem was the bouncers, managers, and bartenders.

Dad was hypervigilant regarding the finances of the clubs and whom he hired to work at the clubs. Before Dad's arrest, one of his longtime managers, Ricky, stopped making cash deposits for one month. At the end of the month, Dad's accountant told him $190,000 in cash was missing. Ricky eventually admitted to stealing the money. His dishonesty infuriated Dad, but Dad forgave him and kept Ricky on as manager so that he could eventually pay back the club with a payment plan.

That never happened.

When I informed the general managers that I would be coming on as operations manager, I visited each club and met with the managers. Each time I walked into the dark interior of these clubs, it took my eyes several moments to adjust from the Los Angeles brightness and sun. Everyone stared at me.

The managers dressed in nice suits with flashy ties, expensive watches, and shoes. They walked around observing the patrons and employees while taking mental notes. They got their cars detailed in the parking lot while at work. They hung out at the bar, or upstairs in the manager's office, bullshitting and watching the security monitors while the cook served them food and beverages. Bouncers also kept a close eye on the stage and lap-dance action, asserting themselves if a patron touched a dancer or attempted to follow a dancer to her car.

The morning I did my first rounds at the clubs, my adrenaline was pumping, and I suddenly realized how angry I was that I had to step in. I already had my plate full of attorneys, jail visits, taking care of Mom, communicating daily with our extended family about what was going on, and getting some sleep.

"You're the only one I can trust," Dad told me at jail the day before.

I had high expectations of creating better workflow processes, as I carried my notepad and pen around. I started at Bare Elegance, following the managers upstairs to meet in the back office, which they swept for bugs each week. After the LAPD, sheriffs, and the Orange County District Attorney's Office had raided the clubs, we assumed everything was being recorded. The managers immediately conveyed their concerns to me, catching me off guard. These were big, thuggish guys whom I had known most of my life. Now with their employers arrested and a possible tax evasion case, they were like scared little kids. The managers with prior arrests were especially anxious.

Cliff, one of the main managers, spoke for the group. "You know, Laurel, it's very stressful around here now with your dad and David in jail," he said with his East Coast accent.

"Why are you guys stressed?" I was already irritated.

"Well, you know," he nervously chucked as he leaned over putting his hands together, "people are coming around asking questions, like the cops. The guys here don't want any more trouble, and customers are afraid to come in."

"So, Cliff, what do you suggest we do?" I let out a deep sigh and sat back in my chair.

"Well, uh, honestly, we'd like a raise. And I know Ricky wants a company car because his car is falling apart." *You've got to be kidding me*, I thought. The vultures were already coming out.

"Well, okay. I'll have to talk to my Dad and David about it before I can do anything."

"Yeah, that would be great, Laurel. I mean, we really do feel sorry for your dad and David, but you know, uh, we have to take care of ourselves in this mess too. I can't even sleep at night."

I stormed into jail the following weekend to discuss it with Dad in person. I thought he'd be fuming when I told him.

"Nah, I don't care. Give them raises. I mean if they leave, I'm fucked. At least I know what they're capable of. I can't hire new managers now with everything going on."

"And what about the company car for Ricky?"

"Sure, let him get one."

"Are you serious? After all he's already taken from you?" I leaned forward, shaking my head.

"Lip, what am I gonna do? I can't do anything in here! Plus, I need them on my side, so they can testify at the trial." I couldn't believe what a pushover Dad had been with these guys.

The following week, I hired tax attorneys to sort out a formal process with the employees. The attorneys implemented at-will employment contracts with salary information on paper. Cliff called me irate the next day.

"Hey Laurel, so what are these agreements we all received from your attorney?"

I told him I wanted to start documenting everything.

"Uh, Laurel, we can't have on paper what our salaries are. That's just, uh, really bad for us. And what is this clause in our agreement about at-will employment? It says we can be terminated at any time. I mean Laurel, the guys are going apeshit over here about that."

"Cliff, you guys have *no* employment agreements now, so it's essentially the same thing, just on paper. No one's getting fired." My patience was draining from the bottom of my flip-flops. I paced on the phone in Mom's backyard watching the waterfall spill into the pool to calm me down. What type of business did Dad run? I was so disgusted by the greed surrounding me each day. To make matters worse, every morning I woke up to the same stupid song "Like A Rhinestone Cowboy" playing over and over in my head.

After five days of smoothing over the mess I'd created, I met with the clubs' accountant, Mark, at his office in Santa Monica. He did my taxes too, but we had only ever spoken on the phone. I couldn't believe how normal he looked after what I had experienced in the clubs. Mark was your average, conservative accountant with a dry sense of humor, and I had found an ally. I told him about the employment agreements I tried to implement.

"Yeah, I can't imagine that going over well with anyone there," he laughed.

I could see small planes coming in for a landing at Santa Monica Airport from his office window. It reminded me of the first time I went to the Jet Strip.

"Mark, they acted like such babies, I could not believe it. They're not even the ones in jail!" It was so nice to have someone to talk to. We discussed everything—employment, deposits, and payroll, and coming up with a formal process for handling the money and depositing it into the bank as quickly as possible. We agreed that he would handle the deposits, not the managers, and Mark agreed to visit the clubs more often, which was a relief. Besides reducing employee theft, Dad and David needed money for their attorneys' fees. Dad's defense attorneys alone cost $450 an hour.

I hired Dad's private investigators to escort me to the clubs—to protect me and to instill fear in the managers. Sometimes the meetings were formal and scheduled.

Other times, I dropped in unannounced. Pauly, a friend of a friend who came highly recommended, was looking for a job in Los Angeles. I'd met him a couple of times, and convinced Dad to hire Pauly as a manager at the Odd Ball. Pauly ended up being the worst offender out of the bunch. We showed up at his club, waiting for him for an hour in his office. He always had an excuse. He was stuck at the Mercedes dealership, there had been an accident at the off-ramp, he'd been locked out of his house ... Once the first club figured out my unannounced visits, the clubs called each other with a heads-up. I couldn't believe what I was dealing with—a bunch of entitled, gossipy thugs. More so, this is what Dad dealt with each day. And they made so much money!

Dad had a longtime friend named Bobby. They met in the 1970s in the car business. Bobby spent half his time detailing cars in the San Fernando Valley and the other half moonlighting as a baccarat dealer in Vegas. He was a hard worker and a straight shooter. When I was a kid, we visited Bobby's home in Vegas. Rachel and I thought that he had the coolest house, filled with kitschy Disney memorabilia and blue shag carpeting. Bobby worked for Dad in the eighties as a club manager, but after a disagreement, he moved back to Vegas full-time. Bobby heard about Dad's arrest on the news and called Mom to see how we were doing. He drove 300 miles to Los Angeles right away and visited Dad in jail, offering his services. "Anything you need, Mike," Bobby told Dad.

After several jail visits, Dad decided to hire Bobby as the new manager of club operations for all three clubs. After four months, I had some relief and could focus on Dad's trial. Dad's attorneys had banned him from discussing anything case- or business-related on the pay phones, but he needed reminders. Dad's attorney even used the expression "Loose lips sink ships." It fell on deaf ears. I told Bobby not to discuss anything work-related in jail, and that I'd fill him in later in person. I conducted meetings face to face to avoid wiretaps, bugged phones, and big mouths.

His first day on the job, Bobby came to my parents' house, and we discussed the clubs in the backyard. Mom had made us iced tea and we sat down by the waterfall, both wearing shorts and flip-flops.

A week into Bobby's reign, I received a phone call from one of the managers.

"Hey Laurel, how are you and the family holding up?" Cliff asked.

"Oh same, thanks." I twirled a pen through my fingers. I knew something was coming.

"How's your dad doing? People ask about him all the time."

"He's trying to stay positive, but you know, it's hard." Huey kept saying "hello" in the background.

"Laurel, we have a problem with Bobby." I froze.

"Oh really?" I looked up at Mom cleaning the kitchen.

"Yeah, I mean we know he means well and all, and is friends with your dad but he's not getting along with some of the employees."

"How so?" I collapsed into a shabby chic chair in the sunroom.

"He keeps telling the crew and dancers what to do." My shoulders shot up into my neck.

"Yeah, that's why we hired him." I was about to lose it.

I talked to Bobby, the attorneys, my trusted accountant, and the private investigators. I thought I'd left the club drama behind, but I was continuously pulled back in. It was nonstop. I wanted to cry. The stash of trazodone pills sounded like a good idea again.

Bobby lasted three months before the club crew threatened to quit and gave me an ultimatum—them or him. After several discussions with the managers, I decided to fire Bobby. I felt terrible about it, but he was gracious. "If it ain't working out kid, it ain't working out." He said his goodbyes and moved back home to Vegas, landing a baccarat dealer gig at Mandalay Bay Resort. I let the clubs run as well as they could, accepting the drama, gossip, and daily chaos. I gave up. The clubs operated like a circus—that's how they liked it—and I learned to accept a few truths: First of all, everyone was a thief because it was a cash-only business. I could not trust anybody. Strippers were super fucking flaky, so you had to have a schedule airtight with plan B. Strippers' boyfriends were very problematic for the girls who had daddy issues—they were controlling and picked fights with the patrons. Then there was the issue of touch because undercover vice was in and out all the time.

27 Women Talking

With the continued chaos around Dad's arrest, I decided to relocate to Los Angeles for the next year. Going up north had been my way of trying to escape and have normalcy in my life, but I just felt out of the loop too much.

After the New Year, I packed my car with my two cats, clothes, and favorite CDs, and headed south on Interstate 5. A friend rented my place out while I was gone, with the agreement that I could stay there when I visited the Bay Area. I drove by several prisons along the way. I'd never paid attention to them before. Now I thought, *Dad could end up as permanent residence in one of these*. I made my usual stop at the Chevron & Taco Bell combo somewhere outside of Bakersfield. I told myself I deserved it.

After Dad's arrest, I lost thirty pounds as a result of stress and pneumonia. I was gaunt, but I didn't see it. I bought boys clothes at Target because nothing in my closet fit me after I moved to LA, and size zero in women's clothes was too … sizeable at this time. I went out to lunch with my friend, Erin, from Lucasfilm. The last time I'd seen her, we were in Namibia together before Dad's arrest.

"Woods, you're too thin, you need to eat something," she insisted, tucking my stringy hair behind my ears.

"I do eat, I swear. I think it's all the adrenaline from Dad's arrest. I feel like I'm amped up on drugs or something all the time."

Erin frowned. "I watched you eat, and you barely touched your meal."

"It's not on purpose, but sometimes the thought of food isn't appetizing." I examined my plate like a scientific experiment. She was right.

One weekend, I went alone to visit Dad in jail. As usual, he gave me a head-to-toe once-over.

"Wow, Laurel, you're too skinny, what's happened to you?"

I clenched my teeth. "Now I'm too skinny? All those years of you commenting on my weight, ass, and hips telling me how big I am, and now I'm too thin? Which is it?"

He opened his mouth, but no wise words tumbled out.

I stared at him until he looked down. "I'm sorry, I always think you look great," he said at last.

"Well maybe if you didn't comment on my appearance, I wouldn't be insecure about my body. I don't drive to jail five hours roundtrip to be criticized."

Of course, at this point, I was snappy. Mom and Rachel kept telling me to "go easy" on Dad, but the pressure had gotten to me—so much so that I was now making rash decisions without thinking about what consequences might be. Thus, in a daze, I moved back in with Mom!

I had moved out of my parents' house when I was eighteen and lived on my own ever since. My parents had a 6,000-square-foot house. I shouldn't have been in the way, but I was. I stayed up later than Mom and watched TV too loudly. I bought my own groceries but when I attempted to put them away, I was told I disrupted the way she organized her kitchen. I always seemed to shower when she planned to—the water heater couldn't take two showers at once. I never parked in the right spot, even though the driveway could accommodate six cars.

I grew to enjoy the times when Mom was at work or running errands. Mom had lost control of her life, so she dug in harder to control the things she could. She didn't deserve this life, and I felt sorry for her. I stayed in my wing of my parents' house as much as I could. I coordinated attorneys—at one point, we had eighteen—and I went to court hearings during the week and jail each weekend.

Every day waking up to this nightmare was like the first day, and I felt like I was drowning all over again. Then I came home to my parents' house and tried my hardest with Mom. If I loaded and ran the dishwasher, she'd unload, reload it, and rewash the dishes. If I did laundry, she'd come downstairs in a fury telling me I didn't know how to use her machines, stop the machines, and then redo everything. It reminded me of the petty fights I got into with roommates in college.

If Mom came home from work and wanted to watch something on television, she'd make me go into her bedroom to watch television instead, even if I was mid-show. She also demanded that I take my feet off the sofa. I was 32 years old and my mom was treating me like a 13-year-old. It didn't occur to me to get my own place amid the crime and chaos juggling act—this was all temporary, I told myself.

My parents had a koi pond in front of the house. Two years ago, the koi began getting open sores and dying. Dad spent hours in the pond trying to figure out the dying koi mystery. Finally, Dad hired a koi expert to examine the fish. The koi dude tested the water and found out a parasite was killing off the fish. Those koi were $200 a pop, and Mom didn't know what to do with them, so she wrapped them in Saran plastic wrap and put them in the freezer. They were still there in the freezer after two years, and each time I opened the door to retrieve ice, the dead koi stared at me. I discussed disposing of them, but Mom wasn't ready to let them go.

One day, I was on the phone with an attorney, and Mom got a call on the other line. I told her friend Mom would call her back and continued my conversation. When Mom threw a fit, I made the appeal that we needed to see a therapist. I had stopped therapy a year prior and now deeply regretted it.

Mom and Rachel were separately seeing this French therapist fittingly named Claire, so I called their shrink and made an appointment.

"Hello, how are you today?" she responded when I called. Her accent was amazing.

I explained way too much and cried to this stranger on the phone. We could both tell—I was losing it.

"Sounds like we need to address matters immediately," she finally cut in. "Can you make it in Thursday?"

"Yes," I said, sniffling.

"Don't worry, we'll work this out together." Lovely French Claire was calm and reassuring, and I breathed a sigh of relief.

On Thursday, we went to Claire's office and sat down in chairs facing her. I had never been in therapy with someone else before, and I wasn't sure how it worked. Claire asked us why we'd come to see her.

"Laurel is the one who insisted we come see you, so ask Laurel," Mom spat before clamming up. I repeated to Claire and Mom what I'd said on the phone. The laundry, the dishwasher, phone calls, TV ... I thought it would be easy. I thought Claire would correct my mom's behavior, and I could get shit done for Dad's case. Instead, Claire explained that I was imposing on my mom's physical space, and I needed to be more aware of her feelings.

"But I don't even want to be here, I have my own place and my own life." I folded my arms. I explained I didn't want to cohabitate with my Mom, but I had agreed to come down and help the family, which included taking care of Mom.

"Yes, but I didn't ask for your help," Mom snapped.

My face stung from the inside out, "So are you saying you don't want my help?"

Mom just shrugged her shoulders, looking down at the beige carpet in silence.

"Well, that's all the time we have for today," Claire let out a sigh. "Let's pick this up next time, shall we?" she said, nodding.

I stormed out to my car and took off. We both got home around the same time and Mom ignored me for the remainder of the day. I went upstairs and cried into my pillow.

That weekend, I went to jail alone and visited Dad. I was an emotional wreck. I didn't even have my mom on my side.

"Laurel, I know what you're doing for me and I appreciate it." Dad tried to cheer me up. "You know your mother just isn't capable." The guard walked behind Dad and gave me a cross look.

I twisted my hair around my fingers. "I know but she's shut down and I don't know what to do. Whenever I try to talk to her, I get the silent treatment," I said tearfully.

"Now you know how I've felt all these years. She's so stubborn." Dad chuckled. "Just know that I love you, Lip, and I wish I could be there to help out. You have no idea how hard it is being cooped up in here. I feel so helpless, and I worry about your mom." Dad's eyes welled with tears. I hated making him cry.

Mom had agreed to go to therapy three times, and we had our third appointment with Claire scheduled for Tuesday. I asked Mom to be ready to make compromises or I'd move back to Mill Valley. She shrugged her shoulders, tilting her head at me. We drove to Claire's office in silence. *This all could be avoided if Mom would just talk to me and be normal*, I thought. Instead, we were paying a professional to work out our "roommate" issues.

Claire crafted a plan that benefited Mom. Because it was her house and I was a guest, I needed to ask permission to use the washer and dryer, and if Mom wanted to watch television, she could boot me off the sofa. I had to follow her house rules of no feet on the sofa, no loading or running the dishwasher, and no going through the mail and picking out recycling. The only thing I didn't need permission for was using the phone. Because I used the landline for business reasons, although not often because, after all, our phones were tapped, I had the right to ask someone to call back if I was on the phone.

I walked out of Claire's feeling like the high school principal had chastised me in her office. I became even more isolated. Mom had shut down. In turn, Rachel threw herself into her job and relationship with Seth. I couldn't connect with the only people who were sharing the same experience I was going through. I wished Dad were here. He'd let me eat Fruit Loops with my feet on the couch, just like old times.

28 The Clearing

Dad's attorneys prepared for his trial and began jury selection. The attorneys hired a jury consultant, a human behavior expert with a PhD in psychology. She guaranteed us prospective jurors would be questioned about their backgrounds and potential biases before being chosen to sit on Dad's jury. We watched as the expert curated questions, which included what the potential jurors did for a living, if they felt that they could be impartial for the defendant, and if they had any hardships preventing them from sitting on a jury. One woman said she had acid reflux and couldn't sit that long in a jury box. Another potential juror, a doctor, said he couldn't leave his private practice because he worked alone. "Do you take vacation?" The judge asked him. "Of course, I do," the doctor responded. "So, you do have coverage when you're out of the office?" the judge retorted. The specialist didn't pick the doctor anyway—Republican.

We watched the group answer the attorneys' questions, as they listed excuse after excuse. It seemed as if they had researched answers that would dismiss them from their civic duty. It was hard to find someone compassionate toward a strip club owner and ex-cop. People hated one or the other, or both. Those who had seen Dad in the news and had concluded he did it were out. Dad's future lay in the hands of these people, and the jury selection process worried me. Dad's sentencing still had the potential of the death penalty. My heart beat faster and my chest tightened as the days progressed.

In the end, the selected jurors included a woman my age, a retired woman, a young, single guy who seemed normal, and some conservative Orange County people the D.A.'s office picked. The prosecution selected a Black male juror they were happy with because Mac was Black. I tried to make eye contact and connect with the group, but they looked away. After an eight-hour day, the attorneys set a court date with the judge and D.A., and we went home.

We secured funds for Dad's trial by selling his beloved six cars and three boats. Luckily, the police hadn't seized any family assets. The D.A.'s office was too busy now with the murder to worry about tax evasion. But we were encouraged to sell as much as possible now. If the court exonerated Dad, the attorneys warned us that the Orange County D.A.'s Office would throw the tax evasion charge at him. As we rummaged through the garage, I remembered Dad trusting me to drive his beloved right-drive convertible Bentley to high school. Emptying Dad's garage made it feel like he'd died.

I spent more time up in Mill Valley and started dating the orange Smurf from the Halloween party. But I couldn't focus on the relationship. All I could think about was what Dad knew, and whether he was involved in the murder. Why did the District Attorney's Office have it out for Dad? Mac had acquired a lot of enemies over the years, yet Dad was the only suspect. What about the evidence—David's wiretap tape, Johnny's ten months of wiretap tapes, Dad's motive? At this point, I knew that Mac's threat to gang rape us was real. And I knew how protective Dad was of us. What else did they have? What really happened?

During the pre-trial, Vicki informed us that Dad admitted to knowing about the murder.

"*What?* When did he say this?" I couldn't believe it. I thought Dad told me everything.

"He told us last week during a visit, that David told him sometime after the murder. We're still trying to figure out exactly when your father knew about it. Once we get all the information, we're hoping to ask the judge for a lesser sentence of accessory after the fact, which is still a felony, but only a sixteen-month prison sentence."

Mom hardly showed any emotion in the weeks after the jury selection. She cleaned the house even more often, laundered clean clothes, and reorganized cupboards.

The investigators and attorneys kept reassuring us that we had nothing to worry about. There was no solid evidence to convict Dad beyond a reasonable doubt. They had to be right. Dad would never be involved in something that could hurt the family. I couldn't wait for the trial to start. The attorneys' confidence rubbed off on me. I was almost excited as I reserved an Embassy Suites room near the courthouse for the six projected weeks the trial would take.

Smurf insisted I go to psychoanalysis to deal with Dad's situation. He said he was in love with me and this was for our future. I made three appointments, at $600 not covered by insurance, with a doctor referred by his psychiatrist. He dumped me a week later for a 55-year-old tennis pro with droopy elbow skin. My new shrink told me I was stable, considering the circumstances, but said my ex-boyfriend had issues.

"I have a regular therapist," I said, "I just have been taking a break this past year."

"It might be good for you to go back to him when you're ready. Don't beat yourself up about it now. You have a lot on your plate." He walked me to the door, shook my hand, and said with his thick-rimmed glasses and curly gray hair, “Good luck, and take care of you too.”

I ran into the shrink a couple of times at the local supermarket. He always came up and asked how I was doing with that sunken face someone exhibits just for you when they know you’re going through a traumatic situation.

29 Destruction

The trial began on August 22, 2001. The attorneys took Rachel and me out to breakfast, to prep us as character witnesses for the trial. We met at their hotel, which was much nicer than ours. Rachel and I were both dressed as if we were going to church on Easter Sunday, with heels, hosiery, and modest dresses in pastel colors.

"I don't think they'll ask much if anything. They want your dad. It would be stupid for them to attack the girls on the stand," Vicky said as she took notes. Rachel and I politely drank our coffees and sat up straight. We decided I would take the stand first because Rachel was more nervous. I was nervous for her too; she cried a lot during the court hearings and jail visits this last year.

Dad's attorneys called me as their first witness, and Mom squeezed my hand hard. I sprang up and walked onto the stand, raising my hand to the court reporter swearing to "tell the truth, the whole truth, so help me God." I sat down, straightened out my dress, smiled at the jury, and nodded at Dad. *I got this*, I thought. Until, in no time, I didn't have *this*, when the prosecutor began by asking me how I landed the job at Playboy. I thought that was an odd question to ask, wondering what my career choices had to do with the trial. I think he hoped it was through Dad so he could show the whole family was a perverted bunch. He was caught off guard when I said I got the job through the UCLA career center. He continued asking me a litany of questions regarding Mac's son. Why hadn't I contacted Mac's son after his dad died? Did I feel sorry for him? What would I say to him now? Was I sorry his father died? Did I go to Mac's funeral? He berated me with other questions about the clubs, my relationship with Dad, and my relationship with employees at the club. Rachel received the same treatment, and I worried she'd have a meltdown on the stand. She cried but didn't have an outburst, luckily.

The Orange County District Attorney meant business with this trial. At first, the D.A. had told Dad's attorneys that it wasn't a "big case" for them. Clearly, this was not true. It was the first of many dirty tricks the D.A.'s office played. As the *coup d'état*, the D.A. had suppressed the defense's main witness. Only the week before the trial began did we find out that Johnny, Dad's manager and the admitted shooter, wouldn't be testifying. Dad's attorneys could no longer impeach him on the witness stand with his conflicting comments on his wiretaps. Johnny had secretly cut a deal with the D.A.'s office for a ten-year prison sentence and no trial, dependent on him not testifying at Dad's trial. Johnny pleaded the Fifth Amendment, refusing to testify, and blindsiding Dad's attorneys and their defense plan.

By day two of the trial, the dirt on Dad piled up a mile high. They even accused him of faking his motorcycle accident to retire early from the CHP. The Orange County investigators had interviewed hundreds of people Dad knew from all aspects of life—Mom's old hospital coworkers, Dad's estranged brother, Uncle Chuck, club patrons, and Mac's friends. They all said the same thing about Dad—he was arrogant, flamboyant, greedy, and frightened of Mac.

The prosecution presented the B-movies Dad and David made together years after Mac's murder, in 1994 and 1997, as evidence to the jury. David had become friendly with Arnold Schwarzenegger and Sylvester Stallone from riding Harley Davidsons together around Hollywood. Dad and David both wanted a foray in the movie business, so David did grunt work securing a project, and together they made their first unwatchable movie, *The Takeover*, a wannabe *Pulp Fiction*. Dad executive produced and David co-starred in it, alongside other actors like Billy Drago, the villain in *The Untouchables*, and John Savage, well-known for *The Deer Hunter* and *Do the Right Thing*. Official movie synopsis: "Both Danny Stein and Tony Valachi are drug lords in a struggle to gain control of the same territory. Jonathan and Mickey are ex-cons who come in wearing white hats and attempt to settle the dispute." The dispute was over control for nude clubs across Los Angeles, ending with the murder of the clubs' owner. Jose Menendez's company, Live Entertainment, distributed the movie. Jose Menendez died five months after Mac, when his sons murdered him and his wife, Kitty, at their home in Beverly Hills, a national news story in and of itself. Three years later, Dad and David produced another flop called *Flipping*, also about gangsters and the violent struggle for Los Angeles strip clubs. The prosecutors wanted to show the jury that Dad and David were so cocky about getting away with the murder they even made movies about it!

The more dirt the prosecutors uncovered at the trial about Dad, the more my family looked like a joke. As each day passed, and more information came out, the belief I once held in my dad, the image of him as a good father and husband, started to erode. Why would he make those movies if he knew about the murder? Why did Dad brag so much about his money and flashy possessions to *everyone*, as my mom would underscore? Why didn't Dad hire an attorney the moment he heard the investigation reopened, instead of three years later?

The "evidence" the prosecution ratcheted up was so outlandish, people would laugh in the courtroom. David and Dave Smith, the other ex-boxer Brit Dad hired as his muscle man and chauffeur, had both spent time with my family. Dave took the witness stand stating that Dad had offered him money to kill Mac years before his murder. He told the jury his nickname was "Secret Squirrel" and that he was a spy. People snickered. He said he knew about Dad's involvement in other murders.

David Amos was the star witness of the State's prosecution team. He testified against Dad and professed they were both involved in Mac's murder, having given Johnny the money to kill him. I thought about our vacations with David and living with him in West Hollywood and how much fun we had. When I was 15, Dad used to make me challenge David at backgammon until I beat him. Now I was sitting in court for Dad's murder trial, watching David's deadpan expression, as he pointed to Dad. "He planned the whole thing," he testified. He also confirmed that Mac did indeed threaten to gang rape Mom, Rachel, and me. David was convincing. It didn't hurt that he had an English accent.

Throughout the nightmarish trial, love and support surrounded us. Family members from Wyoming, Texas, and New Mexico came out for the trial. Aunt Deanie and Uncle Derrick and their kids, plus Connie and Paul, helped out at home and went to court hearings with us. I clung to childhood memories like Dad teaching me to drive a Subaru Brat truck in my school parking lot. It felt like all I had left.

On September 7, 2001, after a week of waiting at the hotel with family and friends, the jury foreman, a woman who reminded me of myself or someone I'd be friends with, read Dad's verdict in court. *Guilty*. Dad's head dropped.

Mom, Rachel, and I screamed out loud. We sobbed so loudly in the courtroom that the judge hushed us, saying we'd need to leave if we couldn't be quiet. Dad turned to us and mouthed "Don't cry."

Reporters and onlookers filled the courtroom, as flashes went off in all directions and people cheered. Mom, Rachel, Aunt Deanie, Uncle Derrick, Connie, Paul, and I all exited the courtroom as soon as they dragged Dad away in his navy business suit and shackles. I kept my head down until we got into the safety and peacefulness of Mom's car. My thirty-third birthday was two days later on September 9, 2001, and I spent it in jail crying behind glass. I was the first person to visit Dad since his verdict. I didn't know what to say to him—there was no more talk of hope and I couldn't fake it anymore.

Two days later, two airplanes crashed into the World Trade Center. We woke up early when a family friend called telling us to put the news on. We sat glued to the television. I didn't get out of my pajamas or brush my teeth all day. I called Anne and my friend, Kelly, because I knew they were in Boston working a flight. Luckily, they were safe but grounded for five days like the rest of the country. They were in shock because they knew coworkers who died on American Airlines flight eleven. Watching people as they jumped to their deaths out of the towers gave me the gift of perspective on Dad's conviction—he was alive, safe, had food and a roof over his head.

When President Bush lifted the flying ban, our family friends packed and went home. I discussed the case and verdict ad nauseam on the phone with Dad when he called collect. He still wasn't supposed to talk about it as the appellate process started right away, but I was tired of commanding him to keep his mouth shut.

I put his stories and the evidence together and still wondered if he could be involved. David and Dad discussed the murder on David's wiretaps at Jerry's Deli. Dad's admittance to knowing about the murder after the fact startled me. Why had he not said something before? And why was he trying to protect David in the beginning?

30 Trauma Pasta

The trial was over. I moved back to Mill Valley, taking Huey and my cats with me. I felt emotionally spent. I fluctuated between numbness and sobbing outbursts. I couldn't fathom working full-time, and Dad still had court hearings I needed to be available for. I was emotionally incapable of doing much of anything, except getting out of bed.

Anne suggested going back to school. She knew how much I loved school and she said I'd be both busy yet flexible. Man, she always had my back! After sending off several applications, I received a letter from Mills College in Oakland, accepting me into their business school program with a scholarship for the following fall. Even through the haze, I knew I needed a purpose—a new thing to strive for. Hell, if I could run three strip clubs, I could ace business school. But I wasn't free. We didn't know what the appeals process entailed. Would it take a month? A year?

Each time we visited, Dad broke down what went wrong with the trial and where his attorneys failed. At one point, he even accused me of not getting him better attorneys.

"You know Laurel, I told you I wasn't happy with Vicki and Richard, and you guys didn't do anything about it," he said, leaning forward, shaking his finger at me behind the jail glass while the guards looked at us.

"But Dad, you hand-picked them yourself."

"I wouldn't have been convicted if I had stronger attorneys," he insisted.

"Dad, you admitted to knowing about the murder after the fact. You *are* guilty of something." There, I said it. It took almost everything I had.

"The only thing I'm guilty of, Laurel, is trusting the wrong people."

I just shook my head. What else was there to say? When I thought we might have closure, Dad became laser-focused on his appeal, pressuring us to find him the best appellate attorney and demanding that we gather boxes of evidence that the attorney would need. You know what I needed? A fucking break from everything. Would this never end?

It took all my inner strength to focus on business school and studying. I was so happy to be doing something for myself. I quickly made friends with my peers and enjoyed my professors. As the oldest student in the group, I shared my work experiences at Playboy and Lucasfilm as the others listened in awe. When the professors weren't around, we talked about managing strip clubs. It was nice to have structure and a new circle of friends. I also got back into therapy and was feeling more grounded. Most importantly, I had a legit excuse for not answering Dad's relentless phone calls.

Dad's sentencing hearing was in February 2002, sixteen months after his arrest. The same judge he had during the trial took pity on him because of his age, and because David and Johnny, his "alleged cohorts," would be released from prison in ten years. We consulted a parole attorney, who calculated that Dad would be eligible for parole in seventeen years, going by time spent in jail, the year of the crime, and future good behavior. The judge said to the court, "Who would you want knocking on your door, the guy who made the call or the actual killer? I speak for myself when I say that I wouldn't want the killer knocking on my door." In the beginning of this mess, the prosecution was threatening to seek the death penalty. Thankfully, life without parole was given to Dad with the jury's verdict. Twenty-five to life with the possibility of parole seemed like a pretty sweet deal, considering he started with possible execution. Mom, Rachel, and I were happy he was alive and had a chance to get out.

Dad didn't share our relief. "SEVENTEEN YEARS? ARE YOU FUCKING KIDDING ME?" he screamed. Everyone permitted him to have his moment of fury.

In April 2002, Mac's son, Michael "Big Mike" McKenna, filed a wrongful death suit for $10 million collectively against Mom, Dad, Rachel, David Amos, and me. They eventually settled out of court, Dad and David paying him a combined $800,000. Big Mike died four years later of cardiac arrest.

Uncle Derrick died of liver failure right before Dad's sentencing. It was one thing too many. I organized a two-week trip to Italy for Rachel, Mom, and me. We desperately needed to escape our lives. We invited Aunt Deanie to come along at Uncle Derrick's funeral, and surprisingly she said yes, with a helpful nudge from her kids. So, the four of us spent two weeks on a bus tour around Italy. The attorneys told us they would only contact us in an emergency. They likely picked up the fact that I had felt and/or looked suicidal during this whole ordeal more than once. Dad couldn't call us abroad, so he'd call Aunt Martha at home collect, and she would conference-call him in on our cellphones. With the time difference though, we didn't speak often.

Italy was magical. We forgot about jail, guards, reporters, and the media, and we plunged ourselves into beautiful architecture, art, wine, and pasta. We were still emaciated from the stress, so we ate whatever we wanted. We tossed coins into the

Fontana di Trevi, spent two days exploring the Vatican, cruised the Amalfi Coast, walked around Pompeii, and took a boat tour around the island of Capri. We had a break from Dad. We laughed together. I no longer felt guilty about having a nice life. I didn't need to drop everything each time Dad called in a frenzy. We were in another country and he was doing just fine. No matter how much he fought it, the trial was *over*. Why couldn't Dad focus on us for a change, and our happiness?

After we returned home, we started the next chapter of our lives. We put Mom and Dad's house up for sale and moved Mom into a condo in a gated community less than a mile away from my parents' old house. We were afraid that she might have her place raided again or be harassed by someone from the clubs or the trial and wanted her in a safe place. In her entire life, it was her first time living alone.

After Mom finished unpacking her new place, she booked a trip to visit her mom's sister, my great Aunt Dottie, and cousins at their trailer park outside Orlando, Florida. It was the first time she'd organized her own trip. She called me from her rental car. "Hey, babe! I just wanted to let you know I landed, and I'm in my rental car that I rented all on my own!" I smiled. I'd never heard her sound so free.

Business school was going swimmingly. I had a routine, friends, and a public relations internship that turned into a job at Design Within Reach, a high-end furnishings company. Meanwhile, the club business still tanked as Rachel and I became the legal owners of the three strip clubs. We sold Bare Elegance and the Odd Ball Cabaret to a guy named Mike, who quickly turned the businesses around and made money again. Dad and David kept the Jet Strip, and each month I cut David a check for his share of the profits, which his dad collected. David's brother called Mom to apologize for what his brother had done to our family, asking if we needed anything. But Mom wanted no ties to David. The year prior, Dad reiterated how David was like a son to him. Dad instructed us to "take care of David" after their arrests. How things had changed.

PART FIVE

TALES FROM THE SLAMMER

31 Prison for Dummies

Dad knew from talking to other inmates that he'd be taken, snatched from his cell without notice, so he asked one of his jail buddies to call us collect when it happened. Prison guards took him in the middle of the night. Dad had been having panic attacks regularly, but this move sent him over the edge, going to an unknown environment. They transported him shackled in a white sheriff's van to Wasco State Prison, the reception center for new California inmates. They picked up other prisoners along the way, kind of like a prison fieldtrip. The prison was northwest of Bakersfield, surrounded by farmland, and a five-hour drive from Mill Valley each way. At least for Mom, it was only three hours.

At Wasco, they threw Dad in solitary confinement, or "the hole," as the inmates called it, and observed him before placing him in the general population. Because Dad was an ex-cop, he was placed in protective custody in the prison system. Instead of the mainline yard, he was in a separate yard with other ex-law enforcement, informants, and sex offenders. These were the people inmates wanted to hurt or kill in the mainline yard, especially the pedophiles. The prison administrators still allowed us to visit Dad during the observation period. However, he was still required to sit behind the glass partition using the grimy black phone.

After three months, Dad's evaluation period ended, and his counselor approved him for general visiting.

Rachel and I were the first to visit. Before we left, we looked on the California Detention Center website, soon to be our new prison bible, to make sure to wear regulation clothing. We also called the prison to check to see if Dad's yard was on lockdown. This would happen whenever there was a prison fight, a missing utensil, or a tuberculosis outbreak. Sometimes the prison guards didn't update the hotline, and we'd show up thinking it was open when his yard was on lockdown. Not cool.

We could bring in thirty dollars, a valid ID, a car key, unopened pack of tissues, and six photos, all in a clear plastic pouch. The dress code included no denim, no khakis, no blue, orange, or green colors, and nothing tight or sheer. Wearing a bra was mandatory, but you couldn't wear one with wires. Some of the women who visited were quite large with melon-sized breasts. I don't know how they found wireless bras to fit them. Dresses and skirts had to be no more than three inches above the knee. The list goes on and on.

The visiting room resembled a school cafeteria with vending machines and round, low tables so you couldn't pass contraband underneath. It also included an eerie children's play area. Armed guards with bulletproof vests surrounded the room. Visitors routinely hid contraband in baby strollers and diapers, so those were searched meticulously. Even after all our jail visits, prison was a shock. But we were looking forward to seeing Dad without glass between us. Rachel and I sat at the table the guard assigned us to and kept the chair that was facing front open so Dad could sit there, because inmates needed to be visible from the guard booth. Dad came out of a side door with a group of other prisoners. He looked around searching, so we stood up and walked toward him. He had a different uniform on now—double denim instead of his orange jumpsuit.

We hugged Dad and cried for so long that the guards had to tell us to stop fawning over each other. On the wall was a visiting rule list the guard pointed to, which stated that visitors and inmates were allowed "one hug in the beginning" and "one hug at the end." As the other inmates and families laughed, conversed, and shared stories, the three of us sat there in silence, holding hands with Dad and crying. With all the tears shed, I'm really surprised I still had eyeballs.

"How could they find me guilty? *How?*" he kept repeating.

We walked Dad over to the vending machines and bought him grapes, a cheesecake, a super burrito, and Yoplait yogurt. It was the best food he'd had since his arrest, now almost two years ago.

Dad had just lost his first appeal at the state level, but his attorney told us it was to be expected. "He'll have a better chance at higher level courts," he assured us.

Nonetheless, Dad had his things packed, thinking he might be released, "Lip, I gotta have hope. It's all I got!" he said.

Five months later, when we got the hang of Wasco, the CDC transferred Dad to the maximum-security Calipatria State Prison, outside of Palm Springs near the Salton Sea. I'd spend a fortune on prison visits with flights, hotels, and car rentals. From the Bay Area, I took a one-hour flight into Ontario airport, spent the night at a Motel 6, and drove three hours in a rental car the next morning to prison, returning home the same way that night. Dad hated Calipatria. From Mom's place, it was a four-hour drive each way. It was forty-five minutes north of the Mexican border.

A year later, after the prison accepted his transfer request, Dad relocated to Corcoran State Prison. He was close to Wasco and Harris Ranch, where you could smell the foul stench of cows being slaughtered. My Corcoran commute was a four-and-a-half-hour drive each way, with usually a four-hour visit. You could visit from 8 a.m. to 3 p.m. pending free tables, but no way was I staying the whole time. Luckily, the drive was only three hours for Mom.

The prison excursions wiped me out for the weekend, and all I could focus on when I returned home was wine and laundry. Sometimes Anne would surprise me at my door with flowers and fixings for dinner. Just seeing her smiling face and the way she said "*Hiiiiii*" calmed me down, like a yoga class. We'd hang out, drink wine on the deck, and reminisce about high school and our fun times living together. I wished so badly my life could go back in time to those days.

Dad hated Corcoran too, his third prison in less than two years. But who really likes being in any prison? Unless maybe you're lucky enough to get Martha Stewart's deal. Corcoran ended up being Dad's home for the next nine years, where he shared a roof with famed music producer and murderer, Phil Spector, and cult leader and depraved daddy of the murdering Manson family, Charles Manson.

32 Seeking Sanity

Dad had now been in prison now for four years. But it wasn't over. We were all working on his appellate case. I started back in therapy, filling my therapist in on the last couple of years of my life, apologizing for not coming in sooner. I was really apologizing to myself.

"Well, Laurel," my shrink said, "Don't be hard on yourself. You're here now, and perhaps you weren't ready to come in before. Therapy only works when you're ready to focus on yourself and it sounds like you've had your hands full."

I skipped out of his office as I left. I was so happy to be back and take time out for myself. The feeling was foreign to me.

Mom was coping with living alone better than I'd expected. She still worked as a nurse but now had the freedom to work day shifts. She wanted to travel more, so Rachel and I organized annual trips for us and took her to places like Costa Rica, New Zealand, and Africa, places she never dreamed she'd visit. "Your father would hate it here," she said on our trip to Tanzania. Dad viewed every place outside Los Angeles as a third-world country. But Mom was discovering her inner travel bug. She wanted to explore everything. I look now at a picture of her jumping over a waterfall in Costa Rica with a yellow helmet on after white-water rafting. The look of pure joy on her face is something I'd never seen before on her, and it still makes me smile. Mom and Aunt Deanie even traveled together, doing a week-long white water-rafting trip down the Colorado River. She glowed as she spoke about the adventure, camping in tents, and meeting fellow travelers. She was 56 going on 16.

After two years, I graduated from Mills College with an MBA. I felt such an insane amount of accomplishment, my cheeks hurt from grinning so much. I got my game back and I was ready to conquer the world again. Plus, I finally got Glen Campbell's "Rhinestone Cowboy" out of my head.

Mom came to my graduation ceremony, and I threw a joint graduation/Mom's birthday party that night in San Francisco with all my favorite people. Anne took care of Mom's birthday cake and we all sang to her as Anne lit the candles.

I explored different industries and found a job at Pottery Barn corporate, as an inventory forecaster. The number crunching in Excel spreadsheets prompted a daily headache. But something about it being straightforward and not the same as stripper stress made it more satisfying. I still thought about Lucasfilm and if I had left such a rare, rewarding company impulsively. At the same time, freeing Michael Woods had become my full-time job for so long. I may have been forced out anyway.

I tried to reestablish my friendships back up north, but most of my friends were married now. I felt like crazy Aunt Laurel, driving around the Bay Area visiting my friends with kids. I succeeded in entertaining everyone but myself.

Anne met her fiancé in first class on a flight she was working from JFK to SFO, and in 2000, she moved in with him south of San Francisco, in Saratoga. I was secretly devastated at losing my life partner in crime, but I was truly happy for her. It was all she ever wanted. In the beginning, I was so lonely but eventually got used to living alone again. And now I had to make my own meals and clean my condo! Damn you, Anne! The other flight attendants I hung out with were engaged now as well. We'd meet at a bar in the Marina and they'd boast about their engagement rings, dresses, and honeymoon plans. There was always this awkward moment of silence, chirping crickets, before they finally turned to me.

"Uhm, so Laurel, are you dating anyone?" Jeez, I was just happy to not be suicidal, let alone worry about being single.

"No, I'm just focused on getting my life back together." I felt inferior to them. I glanced at the sailboats whipping past Alcatraz in the distance, waiting for the topic to change.

Then the lecturing began. "Well, you know you *must* be doing something wrong, because you should be going on dates and getting out there." My jaw clenched and my neck stiffened. I began breathing heavily through my nose. Their comments made me feel inadequate, and I wanted to scream at them. Didn't I get any points for surviving the last few years?

"You know, you really need to get on Match.com or something. We're not getting any younger. That biological clock is ticking." I tilted my head and sipped my chardonnay.

One of the women present was engaged to a man who, on several occasions, screamed at her saying he never loved her, and kicked her out of the house. She had slept in her car outside on the curb overnight several times. Yet I was the one being scrutinized. Thanks to therapy, I stopped surrounding myself with those types of people.

I did date a guy named Forest briefly, who lived in Atlanta and was visiting a friend from Pottery Barn. After the three of us spent the day together touring San Francisco, I invited them over to my place where Forest and I sealed the deal in my hot tub. We were instantly smitten with each other and began dating long distance.

My Pottery Barn friend warned me that Forest, while fun, was cheap and selfish. In the end, she was right. He dumped me after three months and went back to his ex, a week after we spent Christmas in Hawaii together, which I'd paid for. It was my first Christmas away from the family, so on top of nursing a wounded heart, I was dealing with a heavy guilt trip. Plus, because he'd been two-timing me, it reinforced my lack of trust with men. I could hear Mom's words playing over and over in my head, "Men are pigs." I cried; I cried so hard, feeling even more sorry for myself than usual. Was something wrong with me?

"Everyone should live in New York, Woods, for at least six months," Anne huffed as we hiked 9000 feet up Half Dome in Yosemite for our birthdays, hungover from the night before.

"Really? Think I could handle it?" I'd been filling Anne in on my drab life in Marin, where I spent most weekends talking to my pets. I also hated working at Pottery Barn, except for the discounts. I had heaps of linens, candles, and cookware.

Nicely decorated table for one, please.

"I just don't feel like I fit in anymore. Everyone's moved on. It's like trying to go back to high school. I think I've outgrown the Bay Area." We stopped for a break on the trail. We waited for people to pass us so we could go pee in the bushes. Anne gave me some hand sanitizer afterward and asked if I needed a tissue or a piece of gum. I wished Anne and I were still living together. She was the only one who got me and all my "isms".

"Woods, you totally got this, and the great thing is, if you don't like New York, you can always move back!" She was right. Although I had lived in my Mill Valley condo for eight years, the thought of moving my shit terrified me.

"The fact that you've been in one place so long is exactly why you should move, Woods, shake things up! I loved New York when I lived there. All the Broadway shows, the restaurants, tons of people. You've got to get out of Marin. It's like a retirement community." The mere thought of a change of scenery terrified and exhilarated me. My head tingled and I beamed ear to ear. With Dad's incarceration, I didn't think I had a choice to leave California. But Anne was right, even if it was only for a year. Suddenly, I imagined myself living in New York, riding the subway, dressing up, and going to fancy restaurants. The most popular restaurant in proximity currently was the Cheesecake Factory, where people wore fleece and hiking boots.

I contacted Quinn, one of my Pottery Barn bosses who'd transferred to West Elm corporate in Brooklyn. Both brands were now under the Williams Sonoma parent company. I flew out the next week and interviewed with Quinn and her team.

"So, what do you think?" Quinn asked.

West Elm seemed way more laid back than the uptight, preppy Pottery Barn crowd, plus West Elm had no dress code. "I think I'm in," I said to Quinn. If I overthought it, I'd never make a move.

"Okay, I'll contact HR and have the paperwork sent out within the week." And just like that, I landed a job in New York.

My parents were less than thrilled. "What are you going to do about visiting Dad?" Mom drilled.

"I'll still fly out; I just won't see him as often. Am I supposed to put my life on hold?" I clenched my teeth until my jaw hurt.

"Well, don't you think it's a little selfish of you to move when your sister and I are staying here to be close to him? That puts the burden on us to visit him more." How could Mom be so full of contradictions? She was having the time of her life working, traveling, and making new friends.

"No, I don't. And it doesn't mean you have to go to prison more. I've done enough for him, and I want to move on with the rest of my life now. We all need to. If the tables were turned, I doubt Dad would visit me as much as I visit him."

My call with Dad came next. "New York is dangerous. You can't move there. You're too nice," he said. I had him on speakerphone as I folded my laundry. I already knew how he'd react and shook my head. I had become accustomed to his constant disapproval and let out a heavy sigh as I defended my decision. "Dad, nice people live in New York too."

"Yeah, well, you can't move there with three animals. What are you going to do with them?"

"I'm taking them with me. Why wouldn't I?"

"Well, you'll have to sell your car."

My back stiffened and my cheeks burned. The prison recording came on telling us our conversation was ending in sixty seconds. *Thank God.* "Why? I can leave it here and store it with someone or ship it if I want to."

"Oh, you can't ship it, that's too expensive and no one has a car in New York."

"Well, Dad, I'll just have to figure these things out then," I said as I emptied out the dishwasher. And just as he began to rebut, the line went dead. I turned off my ringer and unplugged my answering machine. I filled my glass of chardonnay to the rim and lit up a cigarette on my deck. I inhaled the hot smoke into my lungs and stared into the pine trees.

The only person happy for me in my family was my sister. "I'm glad you're moving! I think it's exciting!" Rachel screeched. "I wish I had the guts to move to New York, that's my dream city," Rachel hugged me. She was now a successful architect and loved the old buildings and cobblestone streets in New York.

I kicked myself for letting Dad's comments get under my skin. He was in jail for murder! Why did his opinion still matter to me? But at least I wasn't heeding his advice anymore. In New York, I'd be free. I'd be a new and improved me.

33 She Really Doesn’t Sleep

Transferring high schools and moving to New York City were two of the biggest decisions I’d made on my own. They were also the best decisions of my life. Although with New York, it took a while to realize it. I’d found an apartment in a prewar walkup on the Upper West Side at 69th Street, half a block from Central Park. Anne helped me move. We took the animals with us in first class on American Airlines. Flying with three animals, especially a parrot, was an absolute riot. Huey laughed his ass off going through security, and my male cat, Tenzin, almost escaped from his carrier. The first-class flight attendant threw a fit, saying he was allergic to animals. Luckily, the purser also had a parrot and took pity on me, and the flight attendant was relegated to coach, not me.

The cats had a smooth flight, and Huey only squawked when I used the lavatory, his separation anxiety kicking in. The other passengers glared at me, as if I had a screaming child, but fuck them with their warm nuts and champagne. Huey laughed again as we landed, and, luckily, we made it without any puking, pissing, or shitting snafus.

We hopped in a yellow cab and arrived at my new New York City apartment. My hand trembled as I used my keys to open the three locks on my door for the first time. It was really happening. I was so happy that Anne was there for a little longer. I was on the top floor of the four-story walkup, and had the quintessential New York apartment with hardwood floors, vaulted ceilings, a marble mantel, and a fire escape. I felt like I was on vacation. Anne spent the weekend with me, taking me around to some of her old haunts. We went to the ballet with her Aunt Martha at Lincoln Center and got all dressed up. I was drunk with excitement. I did the touristy thing and took a picture of myself jumping up into the brightness of Times Square. I felt so carefree and safe with her. I wished we were moving in together. For a moment, I forgot about everything going on with my family and enjoyed our moment. Her levity and laughter were contagious. At the end of the weekend, Anne left for home to start planning her wedding. I didn't want her to leave and held onto our hug for an awkwardly long time. She chuckled. I tried to.

When it got dark, I went up to my rooftop with a glass of wine and inhaled the brisk air. The water towers rose impressively from the skyline. The taxis honked their horns. At 37 years old, I was on my own for the first time.

It took me two years before feeling settled in New York. I took everything in like an eager student. Discovering New York was like learning a new language. There were people everywhere—in grocery stores, on sidewalks, in parks, alleyways, and theaters, all packed in like sardines. I loved the sounds and smells and grit. The sensory overload of pizza, curry, urine, exhaust, trash, cupcakes, and coffee. I was less fond of the rats and cockroaches running in front of me as I scurried down the sidewalk to the subway. My cats played with the cockroaches I'd find in my apartment. At least I didn't need to buy them cat toys.

I fed the rats my power bars in the subway as I waited for the next train. I'd grown up without using public transit. The subway seemed like a miracle. I reveled in the fact that I could get from point A to point B without having to drive. In the subway, I'd get in trouble staring at people for too long. But it was like a free circus, complete with outfits, hairdos, and habits. The homeless could clear out an entire subway car with their putrid smells.

In February 2006, just after moving in, I experienced my first blizzard. I put on my powder blue puffy coat Mom had bought me with snow boots, and I resembled a walking sleeping bag as I ventured into Central Park. Everyone was out, sledding or cross-country skiing. The taxis slid down the streets in slush. I strolled past the Dakota Building, Strawberry Fields, Bethesda Fountain, and Tavern on the Green. All places I'd heard of and now I lived down the block from. It felt right. Dad had just lost his second appeal, and I was glad I didn't have to be the one visiting him. My ears were ringing thinking about it.

I was so happy with my decision to move and thanked Anne every time we spoke. She felt responsible for me now, but I assured her that I was happy. And I was—for the first time in a long time. "I knew you'd do well in New York. It suits your vivacious personality," she told me. As a housewarming gift, Anne had given me Carrie Fisher's pillowcase, from the fluffy airline pillow provided to her in first class. Anne just happened to be working on a flight to London where she spotted my favorite princess. Anne was not a *Star Wars* fan, but she appreciated my galactic fandom. I couldn't believe it as I opened up the package—Princess Leia's pillowcase.

My job at West Elm sucked just as much as it did at Pottery Barn, with even more spreadsheets and meetings. But everything's a lesson, and my lesson was to never work in retail again. I quit and landed a job at MTV in Times Square, managing the design department for MTV and VH1 digital. I relished being back in a creative digital environment again, and with a great team of people. I loved working in Times Square. It was central to everywhere, and I enjoyed discovering the local places to eat and drink. In the beginning, I'd politely wait as tourists snapped away, taking photos, but after a few months, I hardened, and photo bombed everyone in the way of my morning commute across Broadway.

I rewatched "Seinfeld" and "Sex in The City" and felt a new kinship with them. At Thanksgiving, Mom and Rachel visited. We watched the Macy's Parade downstairs on my street, taking turns standing on my kitchen ladder as the colorful balloons floated by, the crowd cheering. Then we had our Thanksgiving meal at my apartment. Mom said grace and instead of praying for Dad, I prayed for myself and my new life ahead of me. Mom reminisced about seeing the parade with her family as a kid, and I watched her ease into accepting my move, as she explored New York with me.

At the end of their trip, I drove us out to Wyckoff, New Jersey, and visited the cemetery where most of Mom's family was buried. We walked around the cemetery in the bright wintry sun and chilled air. We separated and read all the tombstones, until Mom stumbled upon her family's. I saw Mom's breath as she stood there in silence, staring down at the wet grass outlining ten tombstones, including aunts, uncles, grandparents, and finally, her mother. She placed her hand on her mother's tombstone, and I saw unspoken pain in her face. I was almost the same age as her mom when she'd died.

Dad even lightened up about my move over time. He called, telling me stories about riding the subway and eating Nathan's hot dogs in Times Square, back when it wasn't a safe area, filled with XXX video stores and peep shows. With both work and the time difference, I only spoke to him a few times a week. He still called my landline, leaving me collect-call messages, saying he loved me.

34 Daddy's Dialing Again

I'd found myself a great Upper East Side therapist and worked on boundaries, especially with my family. Dad had recently called me to tell me that he wanted to have phone calls discussing his advice on how to run my life, saying I was lucky to have someone who loved me as much as he did. My therapist reminded me that love didn't mean controlling someone or giving unsolicited advice.

She helped me see things I never saw before, like the guilt trips and the controlling. She also taught me that I didn't need to share everything with my family. I'd always been so open with them. Through therapy, I realized that I didn't need to tell them everything, all the time. I cringed at how much of myself I'd already given up to them. I felt empowered keeping things to myself. It was like discovering a superpower I didn't know I had, and I had to practice using it daily.

I had a great circle of friends; we went out bar hopping, and I'd occasionally bring home a stranger for the night. It felt good to let loose and not think about consequences. Even though I'd been surrounded by the sex industry for most of my life, I still had very few sexual experiences under my belt. I knew deep down inside I was still scared of relationships with men, but one-night stands were an easy way out. Besides men, I also took advantage of the theater, ballet at Lincoln Center, ice-skating in Central Park, and the Oyster Bar in Grand Central Station.

During a work conference in Boston the previous year, I'd met a handsome Brit named Henry, along with some of his colleagues. We went out that night in Boston and I promised to show them around New York City when they came into town from the UK—and I delivered.

One night, I took Henry and his mates out in Times Square to my favorite spot, Bar Centrale, an art deco lounge for pre- and post-theater crowds, including Broadway stars. Henry and I sat next to each other in the booth, and I could feel his knee rubbing up against mine. A pulse of electricity zapped my body. We talked about work and New York, ignoring the rest of his mates. At the end of the night, as we said our goodbyes, our attraction was apparent to everyone. But

… he was married with two small children, so I just admired him from afar. My therapist urged me to stop going for unavailable men. She thought perhaps I was afraid of being controlled, like I had been with Dad, or how Mom was. Maybe she was right—and I couldn't stop.

I found myself visiting Dad more living in New York than I did living in Mill Valley. We'd chat about the weather before he'd change the topic to himself for the duration of the visit. It got to the point where I didn't even bother saying anything about myself after a while. He'd just lost his third appeal, this time at the federal level.

Dad badmouthed his appellate attorney, as expected. "He doesn't listen to me," he complained, leaning toward me and resting his elbows on his knees.

"Dad, I'm sure he knows what he's doing," I replied.

"I mean, Lip, every day I wake up and think they're going to let me out, realizing this was a mistake," he said pointing at the guards.

"Dad, you have to stop being so hopeful, and focus on your release date instead."

"If I didn't have hope, Lip, I'd kill myself in here. I must think I'm gonna get out, or else I'd be even more depressed than I already am!" he said, raising his hands in the air. And then I just let him go on with his usual ranting, not sharing anything about myself. It was nice having some privacy in my life.

A week later, Dad called me in the morning before I left for work. I actually had a contact named "PRISON" on my phone now.

"You know, I called you on your home line last night, and you didn't answer. Don't you think you were out late for a work night?"

I began explaining where I was and then stopped myself. "Dad, I'm 41 years old. If I want to do cocaine in the gutter all night, it's my choice," I snapped.

"You're lucky you have someone that loves you as much as I do. My parents never gave a rat's ass what I was up to when I was growing up, just remember *that*," then the line went dead.

Mom followed up with a similar phone call, pretending she and Dad hadn't already spoken about my "late" night. I had installed a landline solely to receive Dad's endless collect calls. But the prison phone system, a monopoly overcharging inmates' families phone calls, now allowed collect calls to cell phones. I swiftly canceled my landline and it felt so good. My parents didn't like that.

Dad called my cell phone, and it rang throughout the day. At first, with the switch to cell phone calls, I answered his calls at night, no matter whom I was with or where I was. If I was out at a social event and it was snowing or raining, I'd run outside just so I could hear his voice.

"Every time you answer the phone, you're at a bar. Don't you think you're going out too much?" he said. Was he fucking kidding me? Then I stopped answering his calls altogether, picking up maybe once a week. My therapist suggested it as a means to empower myself.

I called Anne to calm down, and she informed me she was getting married.

"*Oh my God, I'm so happy for you, baby!*" I screamed into the phone.

"I know, right? Who knew this day would ever happen," she laughed as I heard her pop open a bottle of wine. She wanted to remind me that once she got married, my American Airlines companion pass for flying free standby would default to her husband.

"Dammit!" I screamed louder.

"Yeah, Woodsy, I knew that's all you'd really care about," she said giggling. I milked those passes as much as I could, flying out to Los Angeles every three months. I usually flew first class. One time, I made out with a fellow first-class passenger after too many glasses of champagne. Those were the days. Once I landed, I'd ditch the puffy coat and drive to prison with the sunroof open and the radio blasting. I missed driving.

It had always been Anne's dream to travel to Africa, so, before her wedding, I took her to Africa, along with Mom and Rachel. I wanted to thank her for all those passes she gave me. Africa was Anne's dream. It was her goal to travel to all seven continents.

In 2008, we went to Africa. They filmed a lot of *Star Wars* along with *The English Patient* in Tunisia. We went wine tasting one night in Botswana, and Anne threw up on someone's front lawn. Mom didn't like that, surmising that *everyone* was watching. We saw penguins in South Africa. Shantytowns, real poverty. We were on swanky tours. In Botswana, in robes, we were drinking brandy. Hippos were coming through the camp, and we were warned to stay away from them. One night, we just went looking for them and found guards with machine guns! We were forbidden from going hippo hunting at night again, as we were supposed to be appeased like all the other tourists by 5:00 a.m. sightings of lions, tigers, and wildebeests.

Every night, the Amarula drinks hit us. I have a picture of Anne dressed in all khaki saluting her dream of traveling the seven continents come true. We were loud and constantly shushed for "scaring the animals away." My enthusiasm for adventure travel grew.

35 Huey's Last Squawk

In March 2009, Huey began losing weight, so I took him to the vet, who discovered a mass in his rectum. She said we'd keep an eye on it, but his health declined rapidly. I'd have to put him down. I brought him to the clinic and held him as I slobbered tears all over him. Finally, I got up and gave him one last kiss. He had been in my life for thirty years. Outside of my family, the bird was my longest relationship. My family never thought that squawking Huey would ever die. As I put him back in the cage, I walked upstairs and could still hear him screaming "goodbye" to me. I cried harder.

That night, Dad called collect and I told him about Huey's death. I felt responsible. After Dad recounted the story of how he got Huey from Big Wally, he mustered an unselfish offering, "You gave that bird a damn good life."

Huey's body was still warm when I received my first jury summons. I was excited and told all my friends, "I got a jury summons!" I was excited to be on the other side of jury selection, after sitting through Dad's jury selection process where people came up with any pathetic excuse to get out of it. I was thrilled and sure I'd be selected. "They'll never pick you because of your dad," most said. Why not? I wasn't defendant sensitive. Hell, I thought O.J. was guilty. But the night before I reported for jury duty, I had nightmares about Dad's trial.

The morning I arrived for duty, I had butterflies in my stomach. I sat in a room waiting for the jury coordinator to call my name, wondering if anyone else had a family member in prison for murder. I was shocked to overhear people discussing how they could get out of jury duty. I wanted to beat the shit out of those ignorant fools. It was a privilege to sit in judgment of someone's life. The court official came back out to read yet another list of names, as I held my breath.

"Woods, Laurel," she announced.

I grabbed my purse and book and walked to the courtroom. I hadn't been in a courtroom since Dad's sentencing. My palms were beginning to sweat, my hair stuck to the back of my neck and my mouth went dry.

Inside the small, plain courtroom, the judge stood with the defense attorney, prosecutor, and defendant. The judge was friendly and welcomed us, thanked us, and acknowledged that we had left work or school to be there. He introduced the attorneys for both sides and the defendant as well, stating that the charges against the defendant needed proving in the trial, reminding us that he remained innocent until the verdict. The court reporter typed away at her desk in front of the room as the judge gave us instructions. "I'm bringing you up to the jury box in three groups," he told us. I was in the second group. The two wooden jury boxes each had three rows of tiered seating. I felt like I was in a choir.

The judge laid out the case, a drug deal, and our roles as potential jurors. The judge and attorneys asked group one questions and dismissed potential jurors. My group was next. The judge went around to each of us, asked us our occupation, group affiliations, and highest education. Next, he asked about prior arrests, or if we knew anyone in the NYPD or D.A.'s office. Finally, the judge asked if anyone knew someone who spent or was spending time in prison or jail. My heart stopped. Some dude raised his hand. "When I was in college, a guy in my dorm was arrested for a DUI and spent two nights in jail." *What a moron.*

"Do you think this will affect your ability to give this defendant a fair trial?"

"No, I'm good."

"Thank you," the judge responded.

"Anyone else?"

I raised my hand. "My father is serving a life sentence in prison." Every head in the room turned around and suddenly, I could hear myself breathe.

"What is his … conviction?" The judge fumbled his words.

I paused. "Murder." People were craning their heads now, as if they were stretching in a yoga class.

"Where is he serving his sentence?"

"In California," I offered. I tapped my heels on the floor.

"Do you feel that your father's conviction will prevent you from being able to give this defendant a fair trial?"

"No, I do not." I sat on my hands.

"Thank you," the judge said, nodding to me.

Next, the attorneys each asked detailed questions. The defense attorney singled me out right away. "Were you involved at all in your dad's trial?"

"Yes." I had sudden flashbacks of being cross-examined by the bulldog prosecutor during Dad's trial. He tore apart every phrase of my testimony, trying to put words into my mouth. I learned quickly never to offer more than what was required of me.

"Can you elaborate?" she asked.

"I sat through my father's jury selection and his trial."

"Every day?"

“Yes.” I was shaking.

“Did you have to testify?”

“Yes.” With everyone staring, I had stage fright. I couldn’t get out more than one syllable at a time.

“And you still feel that you can give my client a fair trial, given your dad’s conviction?”

“Yes, I do.”

“Thank you.” She seemed disinterested in my answers as if she made up her mind to dismiss me.

After both attorneys finished, the judge read the names for dismissal. I wanted the attorneys to select me more than anything. I wanted to give the defendant the fair chance Dad didn’t get. “Laurel Woods,” the judge said as the group stared at me with drooping faces. I gathered my things, stood up, and walked out of the courtroom. Everyone else was trying to get out, and I was trying to stay in. I felt rejected and exhausted. I knew it then—they’d never pick me.

I donated Huey’s birdseed and toys to his vet clinic. His vet told me that they had a baby parrot named Rocky, who was looking for a home. “Just think about it,” she said. “You already have the cage.”

I ran it by my therapist. “Why don’t you take that energy and focus it on a relationship with an actual person instead,” she suggested. I hated it when she was right.

36 Christmas with Phil Spector

The alarm went off at 4:45 a.m. on December 25, 2009. My flight from JFK to LAX had landed nine hours earlier. I had that first-day-of-school feeling. Mom fed the cat while Rachel packed a cooler of refreshments for the day. At 5:30 a.m., we took off in Mom's Lexus.

The trip to the maximum-security Corcoran Prison took three-and-a-half hours. As usual, we called the prison hotline to ensure that the inmates weren't on lockdown. We also checked Dad's schedule. He had gotten a job as a porter, delivering meals to inmates who couldn't leave their cells, mostly disabled inmates. Sometimes they'd schedule Dad to work during visiting hours and the guards wouldn't release him to see us. It was draining getting physically and mentally prepared for prison. Maybe more so now that my regular life was thousands of miles away.

We drove by Magic Mountain. I remembered the Free Fall ride from my high school trip, dropping fifty stories in half a second and leaving my stomach back at the top. That's how it felt driving to prison. We made a pit stop at the county line in Bakersfield for one last restroom break because prison restrooms had no toilet paper or soap. I'd seen Himalayan outhouses that were cleaner. Halfway to the visitor center door, I realized my bra had the contraband underwire and had to rip the wires out right there in the parking lot. I noticed another woman changing clothes in her car, and we nodded at each other and smiled.

It took three hours to get processed because it was Christmas. We entered the crowded visitor building and signed in. The guard gave us each a form to fill out the inmate's information—*Michael Woods, CDC number T-47887, Daughter*. Other information included my address, driver's license number, and the list of jewelry I was wearing. An hour and a half later, the processing guard called us up to the front counter. He looked at our forms, our IDs, and our outfits. We were wearing matching red and white striped shirts, and Mom had on her festive Christmas jewelry with red and green blinking lights.

The guards relaxed behind the counter, chatting away and flipping through magazines. A visitor commented to me about how slow the guards were. "If they could just do their jobs instead of standing around, we'd get processed faster," she whispered. There were three male guards and one female guard. By now, we knew which guards were naughty and which ones were nice. The female guard, usually in the "nice" bucket, was in a foul mood today. I blamed it on the crowd.

We continued to sit and stare, watching people cough, blow their noses, and apply lipstick. Was I being held up in Purgatory, waiting to go to hell for taunting those poor nuns in school? After three hours of waiting, we heard the guard call our names to go through security. After clearance, we passed through the electric gates and followed the yellow path to Dad's facility as the tower guard watched us with his rifle. We had to stay within the yellow path lines and walk slowly or else we could be mistaken for a runaway inmate and shot.

The inmates working the visiting room took family photos behind a painted mural on the wall. We bought dockets for a photo, but they ran out of film when it was our turn. The guards maintained the camera, but it was a low priority for them. We bought Dad some fruit from the vending machines, because the inmates couldn't get fruit at *chow*, as Dad called it. Prisoners had been known to ferment the fruit into alcohol. Some even fermented packs of BBQ sauce into wine. Inmates were like Eagle Scouts. I decided that if I were ever trapped on an island, I'd want an inmate with me or, well ... Brad Pitt.

Dad came out dressed in his best double denim and his hair combed. This was my tenth anniversary of spending Christmas in prison since Dad's murder conviction. I was 41 years old.

I already knew what we would talk about during our visit. Dad rehashed the same stories over and over, breaking down his trial and bad-mouthing his attorneys. "I told you I wasn't happy with them," he pointed at me, as if this were the first time I was hearing this. Then he began rambling on about the evidence, what his attorneys missed, and how they didn't listen to him.

Mom calmed him down about the trial. "Michael, can you please discuss something else?" she said, putting her hand on his knee. So, he moved onto his next subject, his cellmate.

"The guy never showers, and he sits on my bunk in the cell when he's brushing his teeth. I keep telling him to get off my bunk, but he doesn't listen."

"Dad," Rachel said, "have you tried talking with him about it?"

"That guy is so stupid; I can't even have a conversation with him. And I know he's lying about why he's in here. Some of the other inmates say he's a pedophile."

Then he went on a rampage about the sex offenders. "I can't stand those 'chesters' [prison slang for child molesters]. They find religion when they get in here, carrying around their Bible preaching at everyone. As if that's going to save them, we all know they like little boys."

"Michael, please lower your voice," Mom said.

Then Dad started pointing out the sex offenders in the room. "There's another one over there who just got here."

"Dad, put your finger down and stop talking so loud, they can hear you," I said. "Would you want one of them pointing at you talking behind your back?"

"I'm different," he said.

"No, you're not, you're in here just like the rest of these inmates," I responded. Having some distance now from him lowered my tolerance for his rants.

"No, Laurel, you're wrong."

I glanced at Mom hunched over, staring at the floor, squeezing hot sauce packets between her fingers. Even with her holiday cheer on, Mom sat slumped in her seat. In some ways, Mom was freer and happier than she'd ever been. She finally had a close circle of friends, loved adventure travel, and joined a book club. But she still missed Dad. She still loved him. She didn't sleep in her bedroom, but instead, fell asleep in front of the TV on the sofa. The TV kept her company now, and she had it on all day long as comforting background noise.

Call me crazy, but I looked forward to one thing at prison—burritos in the vending machines. Forget about finding any worthwhile Mexican food on the East Coast. I got *The Bomb*, a meat and cheese burrito with red flames on the wrapper. I waited in line with other inmates to microwave my Christmas meal. I could still hear Dad blabbing from across the room. I came back over to our table, doused *The Bomb* with extra hot sauce, and dug right in.

As I came up for air from *The Bomb*, I realized that Phil Spector was sitting across the room. I didn't recognize him at first without his big, puffy, afro-like wig. He looked more like Benjamin Franklin now, balding and old. I smiled at him, and he winked back.

"Inmate restroom break," a female guard broadcasted. Phil stood up and strolled by me. I smiled again. Dad said he had given Phil nail clippers when he first arrived, but they didn't speak much.

Rachel was opening the New York cheesecake we bought for Dad from the machines. Dad looked over at Mom and squeezed her knee. Mom perked up. "Michael, why don't you ask your daughter how she's doing?" He switched gears and asked me about my car. I'd been trying to pinpoint the cause of a slight vibration for months now. "Did you try cleaning the engine mounts?" he offered.

"Yeah, I did that already and tightened up the exhaust."

"You should sell that car," he said. Just when we thought we'd gotten him to ask us how we were doing, he jumped right back into his ranting.

"Inmate visiting over in fifteen minutes!" the guard announced on the intercom.

I let out a deep breath. I could not wait to get the fuck out of there. Dad walked us to the door, squeezed me hard, and said, "Take care of yourself, Lip. I love you."

I clenched my teeth so my lips wouldn't tremble and gave him a big kiss. I waved goodbye to him through the windows as the guards herded the prisoners back to their cells. I knew the rest of Dad's day would be spent locked up in his shitty, smelly cell, reading a book or watching his TV with his headphones on. An organic hot meal and presents waited for Mom, Rachel, and me when we got home.

Mom sped away as we left the prison, and a cop pulled her over for speeding. Poor Mom. She wanted to get away from that place as fast as she could; we all did. The cop gave Mom a ticket, letting her know he wrote down a reduced speed of sixty miles per hour on the ticket instead of her actual speed—seventy-five miles per hour in a forty-five zone. The cop wished us a "Merry Christmas," and Mom pulled away. The drive back home was quiet. After nine years, we were still adjusting to Christmas with sex offenders, drug lords, murderers, and Phil Spector.

I flew back to New York after Christmas, and I was in my own world again. I had my own space, and people were cross-country skiing in Central Park. I felt as if I'd injected myself into a snow globe.

On Monday, my boss caught up to me in the hallway, asking how my holidays were. I smiled and said, "Fine, thanks. And you?"

37 I Didn't Stalk Carrie Fisher!

In 2010, MTV launched a new franchise called MTV Geek. The producers asked me if I wanted my own blog covering all things *Star Wars*, and I got up and hugged them in my cubicle. I scored a press pass to *Star Wars* Celebration that year and reconnected with Lucasfilm coworkers. I interviewed Warwick Davis, took a selfie with Mark Hamill, and sat next to Anthony Daniels at breakfast. I was sweating profusely, but I was over the moon. The Lucasfilm public relations department granted me access to all the great panels featuring George Lucas, Mark Hamill, and Carrie Fisher.

The only thorn lacerating this star-studded celebration was that I had to try my best to stay away from Carrie Fisher due to a previous "stalking" incident. I'd been front row for her show on Broadway, "Wishful Drinking," and "sometimes" when you sit in the front row you get noticed. Well, that seventh time, she noticed me. The last time I saw her show, she pointed right at me and called me a "stalker." I couldn't help myself; I loved how she turned tragedy into humor with her parents' divorce, her bipolar disorder, and drug addiction. And how did she recognize me anyway with all that electroshock therapy she said she endured?

I was so happy to be around my people again. Mom and Rachel came with me too, and we got pictures taken with R2D2 and Chewbacca.

Anne just had a baby boy named Connor, so I bought him a *Star Wars* onesie that said, "Who's Your Daddy?" on it. I wanted her son to get to know *Star Wars*, before getting swept away by some other franchise. It felt so weird that my best friend was somebody's mother, but I was happy for her. It was all she ever wanted, and luckily, it didn't change her. We spoke just as often about all my inappropriate behaviors in New York, the most recent being sex with my neighbor whose girlfriend was out of town.

Dad's pot got stirred again when David and Johnny were released from prison that same year. Because of their cooperation and plea deals, they only served ten years. Dad still had about seven or eight more to go. "I better not see those fucking assholes on the street," Dad said.

As David was now free, he offered to buy Dad out of his share of the Jet Strip, through their attorneys of course. Dad countered his offer with another $50,000, and David accepted it. I think Dad was sad to let the Jet Strip go. It had been a part of his identity for thirty-three years. I thought it was kind of sad too, like saying goodbye to an old friend—one that I had since the age of 9. But Ricky, still the manager, said that the business wasn't doing well, and Mom said it didn't seem healthy for Dad to have ties to David anymore.

"I hope that asshole rots in hell," Dad said. Nope, not bitter at all.

Over the years, whenever I had my doubts, I'd bury them. But it wasn't always easy. It was about this time when I started questioning Dad's innocence again. I mean, at this point, he'd been in prison ten years and was still playing the victim card. I kept waiting for a turn in him, for him to see things differently, stop the blaming and finger-pointing, have more compassion for us for a change. If I had been wrongly accused of murder and my friends had to visit me in jail, I'd be thanking them and begging their forgiveness for getting involved in such an outlandish situation.

I asked Mom about it. "Oh Laurel, your Dad didn't do it, that I'm sure of. He could never fake how terrified he was after Mac's murder. There's no way your father could put on an act like that."

True. But was he terrified because he thought someone might come after him, or terrified he'd get caught? I thought back to how he admitted to covering up the murder, after telling us he knew nothing all these years, and how his attorneys said they were still trying to pinpoint exactly when he knew, and how that didn't make sense.

38 Framing the Framed

I had recently returned from seeing T-47887. Even though it had only been a few months in between, he looked so old. Dad now walked with a cane and wore a neon yellow vest alerting other inmates that he was handicapped. The withering, the weathering of Michael Woods was simply surreal.

During the visit, Dad made a comment about how Mom, Rachel, and I always wore the same outfits, saying we needed to step it up! He then complained that Mom looked frumpy and needed to wear lipstick. Wow, did he have any idea how hard it was getting cleared by those guards? I could feel my empathy for my father evaporating like dry ice.

He called me the next day to see how my flight home was, then switched topics to his day. Someone had stolen his shower shoes, so he had to wear used tennis shoes a size too small that another inmate lent him. Instead of listening, my mind wandered off thinking about how much we'd all aged these last ten years—our grays multiplied, we lost hair and gained wrinkles. Dad's hair, once dyed brown, was now nothing but a few silver strands in a comb-over. I could see the scar from his scalp reduction, where he had slivers of his bald head removed to move his hairline up. Mom said he might start looking like Mickey Mouse if his ears moved up too high. Dad looked more like my grandpa than my father. Our family unit was dissolved. We had dwindled to four individuals related by blood and circumstances.

I was successfully dodging Dad's attempts to micromanage my life. I slept over at Anne's parents' house when I craved positive parental attention because they doted on me, listening to and remembering my stories. They poured me wine without judgment. I'd forgotten what it meant to be a part of a loving family, to feel like a daughter instead of a personal assistant.

Dad was newly obsessed with getting released early after reading about some inmates being pardoned. "Hey Lip, I need you to call my attorney's office and get some evidence delivered to my new appellate attorney," he instructed one day.

"Uhm, why can't you do that? You have access to a phone, and I don't even know your appellate attorney." I had him on speaker phone as I folded laundry in my bedroom.

"Yeah, but every time I call, he's not there, and I waste a pay phone call just leaving a message. I need you to talk to him in person and report back to me." I could hear the guards on the speaker in the background.

I rolled my eyes. But a small part of me couldn't let go, as I still hoped for him to say, "Hi Lip, I just want to tell you how much I love you, and how much I appreciate all you've done for me. How's your day going?"

Another day, he insisted that I could get him a connection to Governor Jerry Brown to get him pardoned. "I know you're well-connected in the entertainment industry. You have to know someone who knows someone who works for the governor. I mean, you worked at Lucasfilm, and George Lucas knows Steven Spielberg, and I know Spielberg knows the governor."

"Yeah Dad, it's not that simple." I was getting coffee with my friend, Kristine, in Central Park. Her eyes widened and she shook her head listening to my discussion with him.

"But Laurel, you don't know until you ask. I mean, this is my life here. I need to exhaust all my options; you know what I mean?"

After he hung up, I filled Kristine in on Dad's latest prison break scheme. Kristine said she actually did know someone who worked for Jerry Brown. However, she was certain her friend wouldn't be comfortable asking the California governor to pardon a previous strip club owner-turned-convicted murderer.

I was having a moment where I was so sick, so sick of everything. I was exhausted all the time. I dreaded Dad's phone calls and his demands. I was losing steam daily. Dad knew I was angry with him, but he dismissed my feelings, brushing me off as "bitter Lip."

Whenever I shared how depressed I was, he brought it back to him, "Oh *you're* depressed? My cellmate just sold my TV without me knowing about it!" He also went into great detail about his cellmate's bowel movements. "I mean the punk doesn't even have the courtesy to flush as he's taking a dump!"

I stopped expressing any feelings.

I kept waiting for this change in him. Why didn't he ever admit that it was his fault for getting himself arrested? He still kept rehashing the trial, still blaming his attorneys, his investigators and the jury consultant. He went into super victim mode about how David and Johnny framed him. Yet Dad seemed to continually gloss over the fact that he admitted to accessory after the fact, and as a proud ex-CHP officer, why wouldn't he have reported it?

In February 2011, a producer from KCRW, an independent radio station in Santa Monica, asked to interview me about my experience growing up with Dad and his conviction. They were producing a prison-themed episode for their show,

"Unfictional," and heard about my story via a friend who also worked there. My therapist had suggested I start blogging, and I even had a couple of articles published. It was just fun to do some creative writing and storytelling as an outlet, trying to make chicken salad out of nasty chicken shit.

The producer set up a recording session for me in New York City at a studio in the Flatiron District. My heart pounded with nervous energy. Would I say something that I would regret, that would tarnish the family or implicate Dad further?

"What are they interviewing you about, Lip?" Dad called one night after I got home from work and was feeding the cats.

"They are doing an episode about prison-related stories and want to hear my story," I said full of enthusiasm.

"Well, be sure to tell them that I was framed, and I didn't know anything about what was going on." Then the prison recording interrupted us, to let me know once again I was speaking to a California inmate.

"Dad, this isn't your story, it's *mine*," I sighed.

"Well, I know you can say whatever you want, Lip. So just be sure to get the point across that Johnny and David said they were going to pin it on me, and that I didn't do it." I sat silent, waiting for the fifteen-minute mark.

Two weeks later, my segment aired on KCRW and NPR. My blog statistics were sky high with hits. I also had several attempted atrocious, degrading comments on my blog. It was the first time I realized some people still had so much hatred for my father.

The following week, Dad called. I looked at the phone twice before picking it up. "Hey Pops, how's it going?" I decided to empty my dishwasher and had him on speaker.

"Hi Lip, hey, whatever happened to that radio show you were on?"

"It was fine. How are you doing?" I just wanted to change the subject.

"I need you to send me a copy of the transcript."

"There isn't a copy of the transcript," I replied, robotically. For a second, I actually thought about transcribing the interview for him. I'd done plenty of transcribing at Playboy. Then it hit me, why waste my time?

"Well, how can I hear what you said? Mom, Rachel and Aunt Martha all said they heard it."

"Oh really? No one said a word to me about listening to it." I had only told Dad about it.

"Well, they're just really worried what you were going to say about the family." I knew they were spying on my blog. Dad even slipped and admitted to me that Aunt Martha had printed out all my blog posts and sent them to him.

"I can play the show on my stereo and place the phone against it, if you really want?" I figured he would say no.

"Sure, that would be great!"

I wiped my hands off on a dish towel and turned on my stereo, plugged in my auxiliary cable into my laptop, and pressed play on my segment. "Machine Gun" by The Commodores began playing in the background as I began speaking about Mom being a nurse and Dad being a cop. I continued talking about Dad transitioning into strip clubs with Mac, Mac's murder and Dad's arrest, and how it had turned our family upside down. I let Dad listen to the segment for a few more minutes before coming back on the phone.

"What did you think, Pops?" I slapped my laptop lid down to shut off the show.

"Lip, you got it all wrong. I wasn't a *cop* … I was a California Highway Patrol Officer." The rest of his words were like white noise, as I pulled out the auxiliary cable and turned off the stereo.

"Yeah Dad, who cares? It's the same thing." Then we got cut off and I didn't pick up when he called back. I sat back down on my sofa as the room spun around. This crack in his armor I'd been waiting for, the one where he finally acknowledges what he'd put us through, was never going to happen, was it?

After Dad's critique of my radio segment, I sat in my work cubicle, staring out the window at the St. James Theatre, recollecting the times Dad thought he was above the law. I remembered the time he gave me a ride to LAX after a weekend visit when I lived in the Bay Area. We took a right turn on La Cienega and Dad plowed his black Lexus into this poor Latino guy on his bike in the crosswalk. The guy and his bike literally fell onto the car's hood with a loud thud. We pulled over, as Dad told me to stay in the car. It was a pretty quick transaction as I saw Dad give the guy, with blood running down his arm and a blank look on his sweaty face, a piece of paper and some money. Dad hopped back into the car and sped off.

"What did you just do?" I asked.

"I gave the guy a piece of paper with the name 'John Smith' and a phony number and handed him a $50 bill. I want to get away before he gets my license plate number."

"DAD! You can't do that! What if that guy's really hurt?" I looked into the side mirror to see how the guy was doing, as he sat on the curb with his head down, his front tire bent from the crash.

"Oh Lip, he'll be fine. And believe me, if I gave him my real information, he'd try to sue me."

I remembered the time Dad thought Rachel wouldn't get into college because she had mediocre grades in high school. He told her to put on her application that she was part Cherokee Indian, "If you're a minority, especially Native American, you'll have a better chance getting accepted." Luckily, Mom put her foot down on that one. Or the time in high school when we went to dinner at the Spaghetti Factory in Los Angeles. We checked in at the hostess podium and we were told it was a two-hour wait. Ten minutes later, when the hostess was on her third sweep through the lobby calling "Beverly party of four," Dad had me go up and tell her I was the Beverly party. It was so embarrassing, and the hostess totally knew what was going on, but she didn't say anything. Dad gave her a $20 when we sat down at Beverly-party-of-four's table, as other patrons still waiting to be seated glared at us. Mom still cringes when I bring that night up. Dad laughs, saying, "I remember when you used to be able to get away with that shit."

Then I let my mind wander to all the times he used his CHP badge to get VIP parking at restaurants and events, or how he always escaped getting a speeding ticket. I wandered around New York City the next few days in a deep haze as all these events churned around in my head, balancing them like spinning plates on a highwire, cross-referencing them with Dad's continual "I was framed" mantra.

One night, I was on the subway coming home from work. I exited at Bleeker Street and walked toward my building, looking up as the snowflakes landed on my glasses and the taxis honked away on Bowery Street. I hadn't spoken to anyone regarding my new epiphany as it swam to the surface the past week. I thought I was going absolutely mad as I recalled the last ten years of Dad claiming his innocence. I called Anne, but her phone went to voicemail, meaning she was probably flying. So, I called my friend, Erin, from Lucasfilm. Erin had been a great comfort to me in the early days of Dad's arrest, and still checked on me to see how I was doing.

"Hey, it's Woods," I said as she picked up. I poured myself a super-sized glass of red wine, anticipating a lengthy conversation.

"Woooooodsyyy, how are you, man? I was just thinking about you, what's up?"

I took a big gulp of wine and began telling Erin about the radio show, and the other instances of Dad's "shortcomings" I recalled.

"Uh-huh, uh-huh," Erin kept replying as I babbled away. It felt so good to get this all off my chest, it was like a free therapy session.

"Where are you with all this now, Woods?" I leaned back into my sofa and got lightheaded, as I let out a deep breath. I could hear a taxi fight going on outside my window.

"Erin, I think my dad's guilty, I mean like not just accessory after the fact. I totally think he had Mac killed." Even though my apartment was warm, my teeth began to chatter.

"Honey, we *ALL* think he did it." My eyes widened as I inhaled too quickly, choking on my own saliva. I coughed into the phone before coming back up for air.

"Why didn't anyone say anything to me?" I was angry, ashamed, and most of all, I felt like the biggest loser for not realizing this. How could I have been so snowed?

"Well, Woodsy, I asked you about it in the beginning and you were adamant that your dad was innocent. I didn't want to say anything to burst your bubble. None of us did, we love you and supported you as best we could." I could hear Erin's dogs barking in the background as she inhaled her burning cigarette.

"So even when I had all you guys write letters for Dad's bail hearing and his appeals, you guys thought he was guilty then?" I could feel a migraine piercing the back of my head, like a dagger.

"Yep. We did it for *YOU*, not for him." I thought of all the lunches, dinners, and drinks I had with my Bay Area friends, all talking about what a big mistake it was about Dad, crying like a little girl, and how friends just listened and comforted me. It didn't even occur to me that my friends would think Dad was guilty of murder. All the walls appeared to be moving in closer in my apartment.

I poured myself another glass of wine.

"Erin, I feel so bad putting you guys all through this when you didn't even believe my dad was innocent." The guilt ran strong in my veins. Years of practice.

"Woodsy, we all love you so much and want the best for you. It's not our place to tell you your dad's guilty. It's like when you don't like your friend's boyfriend, you can't just say you hate the guy, unless you want to sever a friendship. You needed to see it for yourself."

God, she was right. We hung up and I sat on my sofa with the cats, pouring the last drops of wine into my glass. All the times I felt guilty for having my freedom, a tasty meal, a good night's sleep, a private bathroom, a vacation. Unbelievable. I was done being a doormat.

A few days later, I talked to Mom. I wasn't going to, but I couldn't help myself. I told her I thought Dad was guilty. "Oh no, Laurel, you're wrong. There's no way he could fake how scared he was after Mac was killed. Remember how much he worried about you and Rachel and your safety at school?"

Okay, so that was a dead end, I told myself.

Then I called Rachel. "You know we never talk about whether you think Dad's guilty. Don't you wonder?" I then told her about my revelation.

"You know what, Laurel? I don't care either way, I really don't." I could hear her honking at another driver on her phone.

How could neither of them see what I saw? It didn't make any sense.

39 Still the Man of the House

In April 2011, a panel of judges at the California Supreme Court in Pasadena heard Dad's appeal. My family had waited for this moment since Dad's conviction on September 7, 2001. I was in New York in my cubicle at MTV, staring at my computer screen, while Mom and Rachel were sitting at the Richard H. Chambers U.S. Court of Appeals in Pasadena to support Dad. This appeal counted the most, at the Ninth Circuit level. Dad's attorney had been explaining to us how at the higher-level court, the better chance Dad had of winning an appeal and getting his case overturned. I wished I could protect them from reporters, from fear, and the unknown. I couldn't call them for updates during the hearing because they couldn't use their phones.

I sat there 3,000 miles away, biting my cuticles. With my newfound belief in Dad's guilt, I was completely depleted of any sympathy for him—no tears, no guilt, nada. I couldn't comprehend how eleven years had passed. Those old feelings and emotions buried by work, New York City living, and travel, suddenly resurfaced. I couldn't breathe, my hands tingled, my right lip crease and cheek went numb, my jaw locked, my back hurt, and my head felt like a worm was creeping around inside. I'd recently become convinced, based on my online research, that I had multiple sclerosis, and my doctor prescribed an MRI. My results came back normal. "Never underestimate the physical power that stress can have over you," my doctor insisted.

My symptoms stayed with me throughout the year-long preparation for this appeal. I got used to them because I had no choice. Dad's attorneys had continued to appeal his case since 2001. It broke my heart to watch Dad keeping his hopes up. But as I considered the possibility of his release, I felt terrified.

I thought about Dad picking every place I lived till I was 30 years old, picking the cars I drove, influencing my finances. Didn't all dads do this? Now I knew better. I'd stopped filling Dad in on my life and kept my sharing superficial. Our discussions omitted any work drama, late nights out, or how I invested my 401K.

"You know," he said, "I know you're there when I call sometimes and you're not picking up."

A volcano erupted inside. Then the words spilled out. "Yeah, that's right! You criticized me for not being home enough when you called my landline. And now you're criticizing me for being out too much when you call. Do you realize how many times I've interrupted my life, my conversations with friends, dinners, events just so I can pick up your call, and pay for it, and all you can do is criticize me?"

"I'm still the man of this household!" he yelled at me.

"No, Dad, you're the man of the big house." Then we got cut off.

I started sending him postcards instead. Dad seldom wrote back. He said it was depressing, and he had nothing to write about. I'd get cards at the holidays that Mom bought for Dad to send us, or a prison art piece of a flower, Snoopy, or Boba Fett.

At 42 years old, most of my friends were on their first divorce, second marriage, or third kid. I had two parents trying to impose a curfew on me from 3,000 miles away. I relished in the normalcy of my New York City life. I slept without crying myself to sleep, saw a nutritionist, joined a gym, and developed a healthy sense of humor about the whole calamity.

My therapist could not comprehend the stories I would tell her. "You know," she would say, "I can't believe you're not crazy, on drugs, or suicidal given your circumstances. Your resilience to this situation amazes me, and I'm proud of you." It felt good to hear someone acknowledge that what I was going through was not normal. My sense of humor was my savior. I enjoyed dropping the prison bomb on my new friends and coworkers—the look of shock was invaluable. "It just rolls off your tongue, doesn't it, Laurel?"

The thought of Dad winning his appeal made me want to pop Valium. Dad hoped for his release so he could sue the shit out of everybody. The other two options were a lesser prison sentence or a retrial. Thinking of a retrial and the media attention sucked the life out of me. I couldn't bear the thought of going through that again. I couldn't think about what his release would do to my newfound freedom, either. I was never hopeful about Dad's appeals and was vocal about it, even before my realization.

All Dad talked about was who he would sue, what cars he would buy, and how he and Mom were going to relocate to Florida or Nevada to save on taxes. Mom had no intention of leaving Southern California, but Dad didn't ask her. If Dad won his appeal, I knew I would be summoned, Daddy-ordered, to quit my job at MTV, move back to California, and help him with his new trial. There would be jail visits, hiring attorneys, gathering the evidence from his previous attorneys, sitting through his jury selection and trial, and testifying again. My therapist insisted I didn't need to do any of this, but the way I saw it, I didn't have a choice. The family needed to be supportive because it sent a positive message to the judge. All I knew was that I had a life I didn't want bulldozed again.

Three weeks after Dad's appeal, I flew to Los Angeles to visit him for his sixty-ninth birthday. The day before we left for prison, Mom, Rachel, and I received an email from Dad's attorney that the California Court of Appeals denied his appeal. I felt relieved as I laid back in my chair at work and exhaled. I could keep my life. And I didn't feel sorry at all for Dad this time. I didn't shed one tear. I felt bad for him, but not sorry, or sad.

Mom wanted to tell Dad in person. When we arrived at Corcoran State Prison, Mom, Rachel, Aunt Deanie, and I sat around the table at the visitor center. I began the conversation, detailing how I ran into Carrie Fisher on Easter at a restaurant in the West Village. She recognized me, as usual now, and ducked underneath her table to hide from me. Dad told me I'd better be careful. "But I was there first!" I whined, trying to keep the conversation light.

We all listened to my cheerful Dad ramble on again about the list of things he would do when he won his appeal. I couldn't take it anymore. After an hour, he got up to throw something away. I looked at Mom, "You have to tell him now," I whispered, squeezing her hand. She nodded back. He came back and sat down, put his hand on my knee and smiled.

"Michael, you lost the appeal," Mom said, devoid of emotion as we all put our heads down.

"What?" He stared at her.

I held his hands as he shook. In those dark, smothering moments, it felt like telling someone they had six weeks to live. It was the first time I'd ever seen Dad rendered speechless. Mom repeated herself a few more times before the news set in. All the color faded from Dad's face. His mouth hung open, and his eyes were glassy—I thought he was about to have a stroke. My need to flee was unbearable.

I flew home to New York City and partied with Henry the Brit and his UK coworkers. They asked about Dad, but I was so sick of talking about it. All I wanted to do was drink until I saw the bottom of the bottle and talk about nonsense.

While Dad now waited for his parole hearing, which would happen in about six years, I could take a breather from all those phone calls dictating what I needed to do for his case. I could continue my life knowing that I wouldn't be moving back to Los Angeles for another retrial. Dad's parole date of 2017 seemed like light-years away.

40 Big Girl Feelings

In November 2011, Henry the Brit's company invited me to their thirtieth anniversary party in London. We danced and watched live music and I mingled, as Henry took me around to meet the rest of his coworkers. Some shot us inquisitive looks. Later, we took cabs around town, bar hopping, and ended up back at the hotel pretty "pissed," as they say, in the lobby. Henry was sitting, smashed up against me, going through all my photos on my iPhone. At 3 a.m., we decided to call it a night and hopped in the elevator. Henry got out on my floor to walk me to my room. I opened my door and Henry slammed me against the wall in a scene of hot desire. The next thing I knew, my clothes laid in a pile on the floor.

The next day, I woke up to a dry mouth and pounding headache. Henry and I had hooked up. He was sharing a room with a coworker on a different floor and had to sneak back in. I laid in bed, looking at my pictures from the night before. God, he was sexy! I couldn't believe what had happened and kept playing the night back in my head. I was so excited, and a little sore. He really did like me … maybe? But he was married. I'd never hear from him again. I rolled over and spooned my pillow. Then my phone started beeping like crazy. It was Henry texting me how much fun he'd had the night before.

"You up? Last night was mental," he texted.

"Yeah, I'm awake, I have the worst headache. Did anything special happen last night?" I hoped he wouldn't pretend nothing happened.

He sent a few smiley face emojis, then texted, "I had an amazing time with you."

I beamed as I sprang up and got dressed. I picked up my underwear from underneath the bed and packed my suitcase. I was beyond tired and ecstatic at the same time. I ran into some of his coworkers in the lobby as I was checking out. They seemed to examine my body for hints at something scandalous. Was Henry a talker? He had already left for work.

I flew back to New York City, and Henry and I struck up a long-distance relationship. I didn't know what to expect. My head was like a big whirlwind and

I could barely focus at work. I was so happy, and I wanted to tell everybody, but I couldn't tell anyone. I told Anne about it who said, "Just try to have fun. That's all it's ever going to be."

I tried that, but my emotions took on a life of their own, growing stronger by the day. I'd never felt this way before. I tried having no expectations and simply enjoying the attention. Over the next few months, we emailed and talked on the phone every day for hours at a time. He even sent me letters and postcards. It was weird the first time I saw his handwriting. It seemed very personal.

"How long have you thought of me romantically?" I asked.

"Since the day we met," he confessed.

"Why now? Why did you make a move after all this time?" I wondered.

"I wanted to be happy," he said.

We shared childhood stories, talked about work, friends, and little details about our daily activities. Henry was different from the nice, shy guy I'd pegged him for. He had a sense of humor, opinions, and dreams. We both loved Pac-Man, Legos, *Star Wars*, and Citroëns. It was refreshing to have a man in my life who listened and remembered things I said. I started to think I could get used to this. My emotions shifted between elation and sadness. I had never let myself go like this before, and I knew the longer I stayed in this, the more I'd get hurt. Henry was like a drug that I couldn't say no to. My head tingled whenever I looked at a photo of him.

In April 2012, Anne surprised me with a visit. She picked up a last-minute trip to New York and had a layover until the following day. I hadn't seen her since she was pregnant, and she showed me pictures of her son, Connor. "Dude, I can't believe you have a kid, and I have a married boyfriend."

"I know, it's crazy, I don't get any sleep, man," she said as she yawned.

I loved her honesty about it all. We stayed in, drank wine, took selfies, and drunk-dialed a bunch of friends from our Marin days together. Then she fell asleep on my sofa. I covered her in a blanket and watched her, snoring in peace. I loved that woman so much. After her catnap, she woke up, put her black boots and coat on. We gave each other a super tight hug and kiss goodbye. I watched her cross the street, staggering, before she slipped and fell on some black ice. We were both totally laughing at 2:00 a.m. on my street. Someone yelled "QUIET" from the windows and then we shushed ourselves, still giggling. I watched her hail a cab and waved. I wondered when I would see her again.

Henry came to Manhattan a month later with coworkers for a work conference. We hadn't seen each other since *that* night. It was great to put his face to all those romantic letters and emails he had been sending me. It made everything more real once I saw him in person. I went out for drinks with him and his mates. I sat next to him, and he grabbed my knee. I was dying to kiss him. We couldn't stop touching each other under the table. He snuck away and came to my apartment.

He examined every inch, looking at my photos on the wall, my refrigerator door full of pictures, notes, and magnets, and played with my cats.

"It's nice to see where you live," he held my face in his hands. I cried when I kissed him goodbye.

A few months later, I went to London to visit some of Henry's officemates who I had become close friends with. Henry had told me we were going to a music festival and made me a mix CD of the bands performing before I arrived. I played it over and over, mostly the Lana Del Rey songs. Henry and I snuck out around town as much as possible. We all went together to the House Festival in Chiswick House and Gardens that his company paid for. Henry kissed me when he thought no one was looking and held my hand. At some point, he didn't even care as people took pictures of us, arm in arm. We drank champagne, ate raw oysters, and danced to Lana Del Rey, Basement Jaxx, and Keane. We all went back on the bus to our hotel and Henry snuck in to my room for a few hours. The day I left, I had decided I was going to tell him I was in love with him. My palms were sweaty, and my lips kept sticking to my dry teeth. He drove me to the train station, gave me a goodbye kiss, and walked away. I ran up to him and told him I loved him, grabbed my suitcase, and ran away as fast as possible. My heart hammered. He chased after me, clenched my arm, and kissed me. "I'm in love with you too," he whispered in my ear. And that's when everything changed.

Back in New York City, I started crying. A lot. We spent the rest of the summer on the phone. I wanted to be together for real. He told me he couldn't change his "situation at the moment," but he wanted us to continue. I told him I didn't want to end up another statistic. He tried to reassure me that our story was unique.

Anne wasn't pleased with me. "Woods, what the hell are you doing? It'll never go anywhere. He's got his cake and is eating too!"

I never planned on falling in love with Henry. I thought I could control my feelings. Even though I thought I had been in love before, this was truly the first time. My feelings for Henry whirled around my head every moment of every day. I had a hard time focusing at work. We texted each other all day long talking about our jobs, what we had for breakfast, and what exciting plans I had that night—plans that were now never as exciting without him in them. Every time he told me what he was up to, he always used "I" statements. I didn't even know his wife's name. It was as if he were single.

I started opening up to friends about Henry and me, and I was surprised to hear how many people had been in similar situations. One of my friends admitted to me that she was dating her fourth married man! They mostly had the same story—they never left their spouses. Henry and I were different; we had something special.

I told Mom about him. She really didn't say anything, except "Hmmm." I think I wanted her to know more because I was finally in a long-term relationship with a man, and happy. I wasn't sure if she would inform Dad or not. I really didn't care either way.

That fall, Henry proposed that he come out to New York City and spend a week with me to see how we would be together as a "real couple"—out in public, doing everyday things, as opposed to hotel rooms and the back of dark bars. A test. Our week together was magical. He took his ring off and we were like any other couple living together—making tea for each other in the morning, riding the subway, holding hands on the sidewalk, playing Ms. Pac-Man video game at my favorite bar, Barcade, in Williamsburg. I organized happy hour for him to meet some of my friends and they adored him.

"I've never met your friends outside of work," I said, strolling in Central Park one day.

"If I had you, I wouldn't need any other friends in my life," he responded.

"Oh yes you would, I'd make you." I stopped walking and looked at him. "You can't rely solely on one person to make you happy. You should do things for yourself as well." I felt like I was guiding someone along in life who had been living in a remote cabin.

I usually hated couples displaying PDA, but now I didn't care. I couldn't take my hands off Henry wherever we went. I wanted everyone to know how happy we were. I kept touching him to make sure he was real.

Henry carried home a fifty-pound box of cat litter for me, and we did laundry together. He told me he loved me at unexpected, mundane moments. We laughed about silly things. "Everything is easy with you," he said. "I'm so happy here, right now. My marriage is just about raising our kids now."

The next day, I walked him to his taxi, he gave me a long kiss goodbye before hopping into the taxi, jetting off for JFK.

He called me from London the next day with a painfully dry message: "I'm just not ready to make any changes right now. I need to work on myself and figure out what I really want."

I couldn't believe the words coming out of his mouth. I was still sore from the sex marathon. We had the perfect week as a "real couple," dammit! Why hadn't he been working on himself since last year when we first hooked up? I told him not to contact me. I screamed in my apartment so loud that my cats ran and hid underneath my bed. I was so sick of crying. Discussions that went nowhere. Most importantly, I felt like the biggest fool, and had no one to blame but myself.

Luckily, I had a few distractions to keep me occupied. Dad had been requesting a transfer to another prison. Instead of getting his prison of choice, they sent him even further away, to Tehachapi, near the Mojave Desert. He hated it and called every day to complain about it. I didn't believe how bad it was until I went out and visited him. The prison looked like an abandoned high school after a nuclear bomb had gone off. Dad said the guards were mean but if I worked there, I would probably be mean too. We had our normal visit, the one where he talks, and I stare. He asked me if I was dating anyone and I said "no." Yep, Mom told him. I almost liked doing something I knew he didn't approve of.

When I returned home, Mom called to tell me that she had breast cancer. It was stage one—they caught it early—but we were all worried, except for Mom. "Well Laurel, there's nothing I can do but just deal with it." She had toughened up since Dad's arrest, and she finally had a great group of her own friends.

In October 2012, on Henry's birthday, I quit MTV after seven years and started a new job at Gilt, a high-end fashion retail site. Henry sent me several emails begging me to respond, saying he couldn't live without me—you know, the usual. I didn't have time to dwell on Henry right now. I was nervous starting my new job. I swore I would never go back to retail, but Gilt seemed like a great opportunity.

Plus, Mom's diagnosis was my priority. The thought of losing her terrified me. I made her tell me exactly what the doctors said to her. She often put off doctor appointments. I harassed her incessantly and she got angry with me about it. Mom found out from her doctor that her cancer only required a lumpectomy and radiation. That news lifted my spirits. She didn't need chemotherapy. I called it "cancer lite" and it made her laugh. I just wished Mom didn't have to go through this alone. My boss at Gilt told me I could fly out and see her anytime I wanted. Between Henry, Dad, Mom's cancer, and a new job, I felt overloaded by life. I tried to hold it together for Mom.

41 Worst Week in History

I always thought Dad's murder conviction was the worst thing that could ever happen to me. That was until I got the call.

After Mom's surgery, the doctor said that her cancer had spread more to her lymph nodes than originally expected. She would now require chemotherapy, as well as radiation. I couldn't imagine Mom without hair. She had been through so much. The chemo scared her, and it horrified me. Dad would often "forget" to ask about how Mom was doing when he called her.

She went through her first chemotherapy treatment alone, although I called her every day to check in. She felt ill, miserable, lonely, and depressed. I've had several friends with breast cancer—some made it, and others didn't. I told Mom I had to fly out for her next treatment and stay with her.

I got the time off work and made arrangements to fly out on February 11, 2013, for Mom's chemo treatment the next day at City of Hope Hospital. Mom called me when I was at JFK Airport to tell me they rescheduled her chemotherapy for the following week, due to her low white blood cell count. I boarded the plane anyway. I told her we could take a road trip to Santa Barbara.

I landed at LAX and was in the rental car line when my friend, Craig, texted me.

"Where are you???"

"Hi!! I'm at LAX! I'm out here to take Mom to chemo but it just got rescheduled!"

"Can you call me?" he wrote. His sense of urgency began to worry me.

"Yeah, I'll call you when I'm driving out to Mom's house, settle down you little girl," I giggled in line.

"Ok, please call me as soon as you can." Why was he being so formal, I wondered.

"Ok, you asshole, I will!"

I'd known Craig since college. He was a winemaker, and we were roommates briefly when I lived in Novato.

I rented a bright green Jeep Cherokee to brighten up Mom's day, and settled into my car, adjusting the seat and radio. I thought about where Mom and I would stay in Santa Barbara, and how pretty our drive would be along the Pacific Coast. I put my earbuds in and called Craig as I turned the ignition on. I rolled down the windows, letting the warm air in and admiring the signature Los Angeles palm trees as I left the airport.

"Hey what's up, dude?" I said to Craig as I drove onto the 405 freeway.

"Are you sitting down right now?" he asked.

"Of course, I'm sitting, I'm driving, you idiot. What's up?" I was getting annoyed with these questions.

"Anne's brain dead on life support in a hospital in Saratoga." Then silence.

"What are you talking about?" My jaw hung open. I could feel my mouth water.

"She collapsed from an aneurism this morning and was taken to the hospital, but she was already brain dead on arrival." He and Anne dated for three years after meeting through me in Marin and remained good friends ever since.

"Wait, what?" My lips trembled, my mouth tasted salty, and tears rolled down my face. The car's brake lights in front of me blurred.

"Her brother, John, just called me from Hawaii to tell me. I'm so sorry, Woods."

"Where are her parents? Who else knows?" Maybe if I prolonged the conversation with frivolous questions, this wouldn't be happening. Stall the reality setting in. I was trying to calm my panic. Anne was a fighter. This wasn't over. It couldn't be.

"Her parents just flew up there, and John's on his way."

"Okay, thank you for telling me. I know it must have been hard—and I'm—so sorry." I was sobbing.

"I'm sorry, Woods." There was a deep sigh, then he hung up.

I cried the entire drive out to my mom's house. My friend Jill, Anne's coworker, called from the hospital. She happened to be working the American Airlines flight Anne's parents were on and drove them to the hospital.

"How is she?" I prayed for a miracle.

"She's on life support and has a tube coming out of her mouth, but she looks beautiful."

"I'm going to drive up in the morning, please give my love to the family."

I cried the whole drive north to Saratoga, making phone calls to close friends of Anne's and mine from high school and Marin, and her flight attendant friends. When I got to Anne's hospital room, I couldn't enter. I felt cold, and my neck was stiff. I finally walked in and saw Anne lying in her hospital bed, connected to monitors and other machines beeping. There was a breathing device, like a plastic accordion moving up and down, pumping air through a tube taped into her mouth, and she had a neck brace on. She was in a coma. I gave Anne's parents a hug and then walked over to Anne.

"Hey, it's Woods," I whispered into her ear, and stroked her hair.

I spent three days in the hospital with her family, her 3-year-old son, and her friends. The doctors ran dozens of tests, but they all said the same thing—there was nothing we could do. I was in her room when the doctor finally called her time of death.

I wanted to jump on Anne, shake her, and scream, "Wake up!" Instead, I said goodbye to her, torturing myself by holding onto her warm hand, looking at her face through my blurred vision.

Anne's family scheduled her funeral for a week later, so I drove back down to Los Angeles, visited Dad in prison, and took Mom to her chemo treatment. A miserable series of activities. However, Mom was in a chipper mood, with her Starbucks latte and shiny bald head. I fell asleep on the hospital floor while the IV dripped into her arm, and she draped her hospital blanket over me.

Anne's funeral didn't feel real. When the pallbearers carried her casket past me, my knees suddenly buckled, so Jill held me up. There was a reception afterward, and I caught up with Anne's friends from work and high school. I flew American Airlines home to New York City and cried the entire flight, wondering if the crew knew her.

I went back to work and immediately came down with pneumonia. My boss sent me home, but I felt guilty for being gone for so long, and after a week, I returned to the office. After coughing on my boss at lunch, I was sent home for another two weeks. I lay in bed with my cats, thinking about what mattered to me. I realized something. I was done with New York. I was ready to move back to California. I missed my close friends, driving, sunshine, and the easygoing California lifestyle. I missed Anne.

42 Is the Afterlife Calling Me?

The summer after Anne died, I went back to the UK to see friends. Life was short, I told myself, so I caved and texted Henry the Brit. He picked me up at the train station and took me to a pub. It was awkward. We chatted about the weather, work, and what I'd been up to. Then I asked him straight out, "Are you separated yet?"

He gawked at me, surprised, "I thought you were dating someone at your work now?" He leaned back in his chair.

"Why would you think that? All I think about is you, asshole!" I said as I punched him in the arm.

Then he pulled up my Instagram account on his iPhone, showing me a picture of me with my art director at work. "Well then who's *this* guy I keep seeing you post about?" Wow, I'd never seen him act jealous before, and it was kind of flattering.

I scanned the picture and laughed. "You mean Scotty? That guy is like a brother to me. We've known each other for years. Plus, he's married!" He tilted his head and raised his eyebrows at me. I felt tears running down my cheeks.

We sat in the back corner of the pub, making out and having a frank conversation. "I thought you'd given up on me," he said, "so I have been trying to move on." He gave me all the presents he had been saving to give me in case he saw me again, including a vintage pack of Pac-Man trading cards he bought off eBay. We stayed at the pub for five hours, occasionally glancing back at the front entrance when someone walked in.

The next morning, Henry met me in a cozy park, and we sat on a bench holding hands as people walked their dogs. He declared that he was going to make the changes necessary for us to be together. He didn't want to lose me! I couldn't believe what I was hearing, and I totally believed him.

Back in New York City, I spoke with him on the phone. "How did it go?" I was aching and dying to know how soon we could start our life together.

"I told my wife I want a divorce; it wasn't easy, and my life is tense right now, and it's all depressing, but it's done." He sounded exhausted. I was beaming, but somehow for the first time, it all hit me—how it would affect his family. I felt numb. But I pushed it aside. Henry and I were going to be a couple. We were going to start our new life together in England.

I researched apartments online for us to live in. He wanted us to get married at the Neon Museum in Vegas. It was all happening. We spoke on the phone again a few days later. After two long years, I was eager to start making concrete plans.

"How's it going?" I asked.

"Oh fine, my kids kept me running around all weekend, and work is mental."

I pushed again. "No, Henry, I mean how's it going with you moving out and starting divorce proceedings?"

"Oh, well, that's kinda on hold at the moment."

I plopped down in my chair with a cat on my lap. "What do you mean?"

"Well, I've already committed to taking care of the kids for the rest of the summer, and we have a family vacation planned in the fall."

"Uhm, okay," I choked out.

I got off the phone and screamed. I was furious. Mostly at myself. Our two-year relationship had become a true-life game of pong. My friends told me he was an asshole.

"He has kids. It's a lot harder," I still defended him.

My therapist was displeased, I could tell. Somehow, at least partly, I knew this was about Dad. She agreed. "You put men on a pedestal. You find the one thing you truly admire about them and ignore the rest. With your dad, you make excuses about him being a strip club owner. That was a highly toxic environment for two little girls. And with Henry, you make excuses for him being married. He's not treating you with the respect you deserve."

She was right. Some of his coworkers, plus a client of theirs, came out for work. I took them out bar hopping in the West Village, and we ended up at the Spotted Pig. Probably out of spite, I went back to the hotel with their client, Ian, and spent the night with him. A short tangle in the sheets didn't make me feel any better.

After Anne died, I knew I wanted to move back to California. But it wasn't until I was able to see Henry for who he was that I made it happen. Everything I loved about New York in the beginning I hated in the end—crowds, people, yelling, cost of living, snow, walking, subways, and tourists in Times Square. I lost interest in going out, and I had become obsessed with dying. I started researching the afterlife.

In December 2013, I gave my notice at work and packed up my Upper West Side apartment. When I left LA in 1993, I couldn't wait to get out of there; now I couldn't wait to go back. My therapist cautioned against it, but I saw it as a great way to practice setting boundaries. My last night, I became nostalgic, thinking about everything I experienced while living in New York City—working at MTV, Carrie Fisher, even Dad losing his appeal, one-night stands, Huey dying, Anne, and Henry. I hadn't expected any of it. It had been glorious; it had been terrible.

43 It Takes Blond Highlights

I decided to take a year off to travel, shortly after moving back to LA. I moved in with Mom to save some money, putting my stuff in storage. There was free Wi-Fi, free cable, free coffee, and she did my laundry and dishes. It was like having a live-in maid. Why did I ever leave? I could hear the murmurs of chirping birds and lawn mowers out my window. It was a wonderful reprieve from honking taxis. The supermarkets were enormous, with only a two-minute wait at the cashier instead of twenty, and I could drive everywhere. I was still paranoid driving, and often wondered if I was being followed, still. Besides that, everything was easy—running errands, going to the gym, seeing friends, seeing movies, at half the price.

I took a leisurely drive around Westlake Village, reacquainting myself with the area. So many old malls and storefronts were gone, with swanky malls with water fountains and valet parking popping up everywhere. I felt lost and had to have Mom use old landmarks when referring to a location. I drove twenty minutes north on the 101 to Newbury Park and drove by our old house. It was painted a fresh bone white color instead of the 1970s brown, so I didn't recognize it at first. I parked against the curb but one house up so the occupants didn't think I was surveilling them. The tree in our front yard that we used to climb was still there. I thought about eating grass and drinking cold water from our garden hose. I heard an ice cream truck coming down the street, and it brought tears to my eyes as I saw the neighborhood kids run up to it. That used to be me. I got an imaginary whiff of Jiffy Pop popcorn, like Mom used to make on the stove for us. I sat in my car for about twenty minutes and just stared, old memories flying through my head. I would have given anything to go back to those days, even for one day.

After I returned home, I told Mom that I drove by our old house. "Why did you do that?" she asked.

"I don't know, I guess I just wanted to reminisce about being a kid, before the strip clubs and Mac's murder." I shrugged my shoulders. Mom was a different person now. She had her own routine with work, church, book club, and bible study. She didn't want to reminisce anymore. Who could blame her? Rachel had remodeled Mom's condo, and it was beautiful, backing up against a creek. Mom fed the birds, squirrels, ducks, and rabbits in her backyard. She had a koi pond for a while, but it ended up being a sushi bar for the raccoons. It was the longest she had ever lived in one place. Her cancer was in remission, and when her hair grew back, she dyed it platinum blond and wore bright pink lipstick.

In 2013, Mom started an online school program to obtain her bachelor's in nursing science. Mom always wanted to get her degree, and I was so proud of her for starting school, especially at 67 years old and still working at the hospital. I helped her with her papers, presentations, and overall technical support.

Ever critical of growth occurring while he was inside, Dad spewed that she was "wasting her time" going back to school and tried to get me to convince her to quit. I was so angry, especially as she was working her ass off day and night. "Laurel, she barely gets any sleep, and is so stressed out when we talk on the phone," Dad whined.

"Yeah, Dad, that's what it's like being a fulltime student, especially taking an online program with little computer experience. You should be proud of her!" I repeated to him every time he brought up her quitting. We just ignored him.

Sometimes she would panic and would be in tears after midnight saying she couldn't find her homework on her desktop. "Maybe your dad's right, maybe I should give up school," she said via Facetime surrounded by piles of homework. "No Mom, remember, you're doing this for you, and you should be proud of yourself." I tried giving her the encouragement my therapist and Anne had given me.

The CDC ("D" for Detention, not Disease) finally transferred Dad to his prison of choice, Chino State Prison. After his conviction, the prison had given him only maximum-security facilities options because of his murder charge. After some time and good behavior, his level-four security, the highest level, was downgraded to a level two, and more possibilities opened to him.

For the family, Chino was great because it was an hour's drive. My prison excursion was now four hours, not thirteen. After a while, Dad hated Chino too. "Lots of keistering going on here, you wouldn't believe it, so many drugs and cell phones." Yep, some of the prisoners had become expert at concealing things in their asses, but I didn't care to ask Dad if he had. He missed Corcoran. But I liked Chino. I could get in and out. I didn't visit with Dad as long as I used to. Now that I saw how he manipulated me, I couldn't handle him talking *at* me for that long anymore. The best part of visiting remained the vending machines boasting flavorful tacos with lots of cilantro, and Red Vines licorice, my favorite.

One day, Dad told me that some guards and inmates thought I was cute and asked Dad who I was. They thought I was a stripper from one of his clubs! Dad corrected them, barking, "That's my daughter." Nonetheless, it felt nice to have options.

After eleven months at home, I had saved enough money. Anne's flight attendant friend, Jill, made me her registered companion on American Airlines, and I traveled around Asia. In Thailand, I discovered scuba diving. It was an entirely different world beneath the ocean's surface, and I loved exploring reefs with their vibrant corals and creatures. Plus, I met like-minded people in the dive community, and we shared our favorite dive sites and fish sightings. It was like an instant bond, both with enjoying the sport, and being concerned about the environment. It felt like underwater yoga, practicing your breath. I remembered when I saw my first manta ray and how quickly I went through my air. Anne had been a scuba diver, and had always wanted me to get certified, but I told her I could see everything I wanted by snorkeling. Why didn't I listen to her?

I spent the summer of 2014 in Europe using London as my base. I hadn't spoken to Henry in four months and thought I could continue holding out. But Anne's loss had weakened me, and Henry and I had such a bond. Barely a week into my time in London, I caved and contacted Henry the Brit, much to the disappointment of my friends and therapist. When Anne died, I lost my life partner. Maybe he could fill her void. We caught each other up with our lives the last few months. We spent the summer together, sneaking around hotels and bars. After all we had been through together, he seemed more confident, which made my attraction grow even stronger.

He was still married and miserable, but he was volunteering, running again, and had a stronger relationship with his children. He bought a new car and had a newly active social life. To me, this meant he had changed. I took it as a sign he was ready to get divorced. I would meet him at work to have lunch or go out for dinner. I had missed his companionship. He still made me laugh. He and Anne had been the two people I spoke to most.

In September 2014, Henry took me to Paddington Station as I waited to board the Heathrow Express to fly back home to Los Angeles. Another pin on the corkboard of so many tearful goodbyes at this train station over the last three years. We embraced and did our usual crying into each other's shoulders. I waved my last goodbye to him as I entered the train to Heathrow. I cried the entire flight home.

That October was Henry's fortieth birthday, and we discussed going to see his favorite band, Underworld, the weekend before in London. I surprised him with $1,000 tickets I purchased on StubHub and forwarded him the email. The next day, he admitted to me that his wife had already made plans with him for that same night. *Of course, she did.* How could I have gotten myself into this place again? Man, I was dumb.

I took the high road and called him on his birthday weekend. I asked him what he did with those tickets. "Oh," he said, "I ended up going with a friend that night.

I'll pay you for half the cost. Again, I'm so sorry." I was so tired of hearing him apologize, and even more tired of feeling like a putz.

I spent the next week looking for apartments in Los Angeles. I was at a loss for where to live after being gone for so long. Back in Los Angeles, it was easier for me to deconstruct my relationship with Henry. Our relationship and the future I believed we had didn't exist. Half-fantasy, it was never truly existent. We weren't going to get married in Vegas or live in the house he picked out. I had come so low as to even stalk his wife on social media. I found a picture of her and couldn't even look it in the eye. I felt covered in a blanket of shame.

I finally saw things from his wife's point of view. I was mortified for what I had done. It wasn't different. It was simply an affair with a married man. I needed to take responsibility for myself and end this.

I texted him to schedule a call. I already knew the lines he would feed my hungry heart—"he can't live without me, I'm the best thing that's ever happened to him, I make him so happy, he needs to go back to couples' therapy and get divorced."

"Are you breaking up with me?" he texted back.

"Yes, for real this time," I responded.

Mom was home downstairs watching the 3:00 p.m. local news, so I called him from my room upstairs. It was warm and sunny out. I couldn't wait to get this over with. Henry was sitting in his car outside of his office. It was 11:00 p.m. in London, dark and raining. He had told his wife he needed to work late that night. I stared at his name in my contacts list for a while, before pushing the green call button.

"Hey," he said, after the first ring.

After we shuffled through the awkward pleasantries, he began regurgitating the same things. Brit Henry pop album. Our conversations had become this time-warped Groundhog Day scenario. However, a newfound clarity triumphed. "Henry, you tell me this every time we talk, but you never follow through." I was done walking on eggshells around him. I could hear Anne saying, "Woods, it's NEVER gonna happen."

I saw through my own eyes what my friends had been telling me the last three years. It was the same feeling as when I had my realization with Dad's murder conviction—total clarity. I was simply a homewrecker and a distraction from his mundane life. Although I hate how in affairs everyone blames the woman, and not the man. Isn't he a homewrecker too? "Please don't give up on me. I *do* want to be with you. I can't imagine my life without you." I could hear him shifting, desperate to keep all the balls in the air.

"Yes, but you don't show me that with your actions. It's been three years, and you're still married, living at home with your wife, and no plan to leave. If you really wanted to be with me, you would. It's that simple." I borrowed some lines from my therapist.

"But why can't we still be together, while I figure things out?" he asked.

"Because if you loved me like you say you do, you wouldn't continue leading me on like this. I don't think you realize how unfair it is to me or your family." I was beginning to get angry.

"No, I do realize how this affects you," he replied. "You're the best thing that's ever happened to me." He sniffled.

"Yes, you've said that, but yet, it still isn't enough for you to get divorced. I've exhausted myself in this relationship." I couldn't believe how well I was keeping myself together this time.

He sobbed into his headset as we said our goodbyes. After we hung up, I laid down in my room and stared at the ceiling. My first impulse was to lie in bed the rest of the day, drowning myself in memories, photos, and Chardonnay. Then I heard Mom scream "Laurel?", which stirred me out of my trance.

I rolled out of bed and put on my favorite yellow and orange Hawaiian sundress. I flopped down the stairs in my sandals and announced to Mom I was going to run some errands. I hopped into my rental car, rolled down the windows, my left hand making waves in the wind, and blasted Lana Del Rey's "Summertime Sadness." It used to make me think of Henry and cry. But this time the song didn't make me sad, it made me happy. Henry wasn't a malicious person; he was weak. I went to Costco and skipped down the aisles, aimlessly. I spent $400 on vitamin supplements, flowers, and wine. I went to the hair salon and got my hair highlighted blond.

My good friend, Susan, my old boss from Playboy, helped me find a quaint, Spanish-style apartment five blocks away from her in Hollywood. As expected, Dad inserted how dangerous my new neighborhood was, and that I needed to reconsider. I just laughed and told him his neighborhood was even more dangerous. It took me a few days to unpack and go through everything, but in the end, in my sunny place surrounded by my things, I was home. Lita, also from my Playboy days, lived ten minutes away, and she and Susan became my new besties. It was hard to believe that we had worked together twenty-five years before; time passing never ceased to boggle my mind. It was already two years since Anne had died.

I took pleasure in rediscovering my hometown, getting lost, trying new restaurants and bars, and finding a great gym. Rachel drove a Volkswagen, and as I knew she embarked on endless research on purchasing the right car, I bought the same one in the same color. I thought when I left New York that I would miss the seasons and get sick of sunny days, but driving around Los Angeles with my sunroof open, as the warm wind blew through my blond hair, I knew I had made the right decision at this point in my life. I woke up each day, made a protein smoothie or green juice, and hit the gym. On weekends, I went to farmers' markets.

It didn't take long before Dad began calling me several times a day, asking me to research parole attorneys, gather legal documents, and contact people to write letters of support for him.

"Dad, you don't even know when your parole hearing is yet," I said.

"I need to start preparing now, and I know you're the only one I can rely on. Rachel is working, and your mother is too busy with school."

He was still trying to get Mom to quit her bachelor's program in nursing science. "I mean, she doesn't need that degree for work, and she won't get a raise because of it," he said.

"Dad, she's doing it for *herself*."

Even though Mom had become her own person, she still made excuses for him. "Remember that's all he did when he ran the clubs, Laurel, call up people and tell them what to do all day."

I ignored Dad and started a new job helping a friend's husband open up and manage his boutique law firm in downtown Los Angeles. I enjoyed having new challenges and the process of starting a business from the ground up. I explored downtown at lunch and after work, thinking about how Dad took us to the Bonaventure hotel on weekends for brunch. The hotel was still there, but all the new modern construction towered over it, making the Bonaventure seem dated.

I thought getting a job would put a barrier between Dad and me, but he still called me during work hours, about a half dozen times daily. One day, after his fourth call, I finally picked up. "Where have you been? I've been trying to call you all day," he said.

"Dad, I have a job. I can't take all your calls while I'm working."

"No, Lip, even if you can't talk, you still need to answer. Don't you know how long I wait in the phone line to make calls?"

When I did talk to Dad and listened to him rant about "what I need to do," I ignored his requests; most times he didn't even notice. I talked to Rachel about it. "No, he doesn't call me and tell me what to do. He knows better. *You* let him talk to you that way."

Not long after, I emailed my New York City therapist to ask if she would consider Skype sessions. "I was wondering how long it would take to hear from you," she responded.

With a little encouragement from my therapist, I was able to iron out my current dad situation by creating even more boundaries, now that I was closer to him in California. I practiced saying "no" a lot, I didn't answer the phone, I didn't run around LA for him doing his errands like collecting legal paperwork for his parole. I only visited when *I* wanted to, not when *he* guilted me to. Instead, in my free time, I took road trips to San Francisco, visiting all my Lucasfilm friends, camped in Big Sur, enjoyed the desert out in Palm Springs, and took Amtrak along the coast to San Diego. Rachel took me hiking along the mountain ridges of Malibu, and we gazed at the glittering ocean, with the pink sun hitting the water, seagulls flying by in the salty air.

In May 2015, Rachel, Mom, and I drove to Phoenix for Mom's college graduation, and no, not the University of Phoenix. God, it had been twenty-six years since I had graduated from UCSB, and eleven since my MBA at Mills, and I'd forgotten what a big deal graduation was. We bought Mom flowers, took pictures of her with her cap and gown, and hosted a graduation party for her in our hotel room. Aunt Deanie and Aunt Martha also came, and we toasted to all of Mom's hard work and dedication. I only wished her mom were there to see the day; I wanted to hug Mom and never let her go. During the ceremony, when she threw her cap up in the air, screaming, Rachel and I looked at each other through glassy eyes and gave each other a high five.

PART SIX

OUT OF THE CAGE, INTO THE WILD

44 Panic and Parole

I woke up Thursday morning, June 2, 2016, remembering that Dad's first parole hearing was taking place. We had been preparing for over two years—hiring new parole attorneys for Dad, gathering boxes of legal paperwork, organizing letters of support for his release, and coaching him on the IRRs (insight, responsibility, and remorse), a document Dad's attorney provided us with, and the parole board would scrutinize Dad for. Dad still maintained his innocence throughout his sentence. And even though he'd done his time in the slammer, he wasn't guaranteed parole. He still needed to prove why he should be released back into society. The parole board looked for inmates who admitted their crime, gained insight and learning in prison to avoid a repeat offense, and showed genuine remorse for the victim's family. He had yet to do any of this. I reminisced about Dad's first phone call after his conviction, when he blamed me for not getting him better attorneys. I didn't expect Dad to be released this first time around. The only reference I had for parole hearings was in the movie *Shawshank Redemption*.

As part of his parole hearing report, the prison psychiatrist evaluated Dad, and diagnosed him with narcissistic behavioral disorder. I laughed so hard when he told me, as if this was some hugely surprising revelation. This news concerned Dad's attorney, Jared, who instructed us to drill the IRRs into Dad daily, but Dad didn't listen. After his evaluation, the next time I visited prison, Dad spent two hours explaining to me why he wasn't a narcissist. Like nonstop two hours, finger pointing and all. He said, "I'm not narcissistic, Laurel, I'm proud." What the hell did he think he had to be proud of these last sixteen years? I had a gut feeling his hearing would not go well.

I was in San Francisco visiting my friend, Melody. We drank coffee as we planned our day together in the city. She left for work, and I packed my things for the gym when Mom texted me, "NEXT JUNE!"

I stared at my phone in silence. For thirty seconds, I smiled, envisioning Dad hi-fiving his cellmate and buying his buddies hot chocolate at the canteen. He deserved to get out, having served the time given for his conviction and as a model inmate. He maintained a job in prison, stayed out of fights, and got along with guards and inmates. But as the day unraveled, flashbacks of my life with Dad filled my mind. I thought about how things were before Dad's arrest, then during his trial and conviction. I thought about sixteen years of seeing Dad in orange jumpsuits, double denim, and shackles, of Christmases in prison, and collect phone calls. I had become accustomed to this new life, which once had seemed horrific, but now comforted me.

Now everything was about to change all over again.

My body tensed and my jaw locked. I felt nervous adrenaline coursing through me. I wanted to chug a bottle of wine. Instead, I took a yoga class, and got a migraine halfway through. The teacher came over and said she could see me holding my breath. What was happening to me?

I spoke to Dad later that day, and he told me about the hearing, but he didn't share many details. After all these years, talking on the phone finally made him paranoid. The parole board granted his release "all due to me and how I presented myself." He told me what a great job his attorney did.

"What about the fifty plus letters of support I organized for you?" I inquired.

"Oh yeah, yeah, that was great," he said.

Over the next week, my mind wandered as I thought about how my life would change. I had fought so hard for my independence from Dad and the family guilt. Would he expect dinners at home once a week? Holidays with the family? Did he think he would manage our finances? He told Mom from prison what car to buy and fumed when she bought what she wanted instead.

How would he reintegrate into the family?

Dad called me the following week from prison.

"Mom told me about your bar in New York City." I recently invested in a craft beer bar in New York with a bartender I knew from my many late nights out in Times Square with MTV cohorts.

"I *cannot* believe you wouldn't ask my advice about that, that's what I do for a living! I mean Laurel, come on!" He was legit hysterical.

"I *did* ask for advice, just not yours," I told him. I was sitting at home on the same green fleece couch I sat on when Mom first told me about Dad's arrest. I had a bowl of popcorn in my lap, and was settled in and comfy for the evening, flipping through Netflix as Dad rambled on.

"I'm still the head of this household!" he screamed. As if? "I have knowledge and wisdom that you lack. I'm not saying you have to do what I say, but you need to listen to me before making any big decisions." This was a recurring one-way conversation we had, once his release date was set.

Dad confided in Mom that he thought his biggest hurdle once released would be learning how to use new technology. I thought maybe it would be assimilating into a family unit that had long since changed! The only possession of his we kept was his leather jacket with a lamb's wool collar that he had worn in the 1970s, along with his blue bathrobe with nautical flags on it. I thought about the "Mork and Mindy" episode, where "Mearth," played by Jonathan Winters, bursts out of a giant egg as their adult child. That's how I imagined Dad's release. No clothes, no car, no driver's license, no credit cards, and three friends. He was a convicted felon and couldn't vote or leave the county, or state, without permission. He needed to learn about veganism, gluten-free diets, the return of froyo, venti half-caf-no-foam-soy milk lattes, Uber, Amazon, Google, emojis, iPhones, on-demand TV, Wi-Fi, Bluetooth, email, and "Game of Thrones."

I did want Dad to be in the loop about at least one viral video, so I told him about "Christian the Lion," the baby lion an Australian couple had bought at Harrods in London in 1969. After realizing that Christian was too big for their apartment, they finally decided to release him back into the wild in Kenya. It was a tearjerker viral video that circulated. I bought Dad the book so he could read the story. I told him these are the kind of things people watch on YouTube.

Dad called me a week later, while I was at Trader Joe's. "Hello love," he said. There was silence on the phone.

"Are you crying?" I asked him. I could hear sniffling as I perused the seltzer section.

"Yes," he said softly.

"Why?" I said, reaching for my favorite raspberry lime seltzer pack. I felt numb when we spoke now; it was like a chore that I couldn't wait to be over with.

"Because I love you and I want to spend time with you." I stopped loading my cart.

"Dad, it's going to be weird. I'm not used to having you around. It's not going to happen overnight." It was like the ex-boyfriend who wants you back and pretends nothing's happened.

"I know." Then the prison phone cut us off.

I stared at the wine section. All I wanted to do was go home, lie on my green couch, and swig Chardonnay while watching Netflix. I fought the urge. It was the first time he mentioned me in his plans for release that didn't involve me helping him out with technology. Was he morphing back to the dad I remembered and loved from my childhood? Suddenly, I felt guilty about the way I spoke to him. I checked out at Trader Joe's wearing my sunglasses with the cashier. I drove home, leaving my stuff in the car. I opened the door to my sunny apartment, laid down on my couch, and covered my face in my hands so no other tenants in my building could hear me thrashing about and wrestling with my emotions.

After Dad's parole hearing, the anxiety attacks began. I would be at work or at the gym, and suddenly I would get this overwhelming jittery feeling, dry mouth, lack of focus, followed by complete physical exhaustion. I couldn't sleep unless I popped a Valium I had bought while traveling through Thailand. It didn't help that I received a piece of hate mail by "Angel" on my blog after writing about missing Anne, who had now been gone for four agonizing years. Unedited to show you the depravity of an illiterate wench.

> Boohoo. Karma was served it seems in this story. Your friend doesn't need to be alive to have a lover of murderers in her life. How unsafe to have her around your father? You would've. You did. So glad your POS murderer father suffered many years in his cage. Can't get those years back. All you care about is exploiting a victim and his family so you can write how cool it is to have a murderer father. Pathetic. Typical Californian too. You're shallow. You are manipulative and you want daddy's dirty money for inheritance. Not everyone is as stupid as you think. Bye creepy lady. Bye Mike the Dickhead. No wonder Bruce committed suicide long ago. He had guilt. Your father has zero remorse. He's a psycho and in these recent pics you posted and boasted of him. It's so clear he's Evil. You lack basic intuition. I do not feel sorry for you or your family and no police officers do either. I'm on the right side of the law, you're a lover of murderers and men that profit from women with low self esteem from DV and or Child abuse. Enjoy your Evil inheritance. Facts. Truth.

Angel's spelling and grammatical errors were more disturbing to me than his fucking nonsensical message.

Truth: I started drinking heavily again—four glasses of wine a night (not because of Angel), and after two months, I realized I needed a change. I was out one night in Los Angeles with an old MTV coworker, discussing my current situation.

"You should try weed," he suggested. "It's the best, it totally mellows you out."

"No way man, I did that stuff in the eighties, and I never liked it," I laughed.

"It's changed a lot since then. They have tons of strains. I just come home and vape and don't even drink anymore. I lost weight within the first month." That perked me up.

"Really? What do they ask you? How does it work?" I leaned into my glass of wine. I remembered trying to buy pot in high school and how taboo it was.

"The doc shows you a laminated sheet with eight symptoms and asks you which two best describe you. Literally, the appointment is like two minutes. The doc doesn't even look you in the eye and just hands you your paperwork."

I had nothing to lose. I took his doctor's information and made an appointment at the local cannabis clinic in Hollywood. I showed up on time, a little nervous. I felt out of place in the waiting room. Everyone was covered in tattoos, and had wildly dyed hair, while I looked more like I was picking up my kid from soccer.

The doctor called me in, and I followed him to his office.

"What do you use marijuana for?" he asked while taking notes.

"I don't, that's why I'm here."

He looked up at me, perplexed, "You *don't* smoke?"

"No," I repeated. "I was referred to you by a friend for treating anxiety and insomnia. That's why I'm here." The doctor set down his pen and shot me a steady stare.

"Have you ever used weed? Do you even know what it looks like?" *Dude, I'm not that stupid*, I felt like staying.

"Yes, but not in like twenty years or so. How does it work now?" When I smoked pot before, you got a bag of pot from a guy named Chippy and hoped it wasn't laced with heroin or oregano. There was none of this varietal hybrid bullshit, crank, tramp, trank, and deadly fentanyl.

I told him I didn't like smoking pot, weed, Indica, sativa—whatever it was called now. He'd written out my paperwork to get a medical marijuana card for a year but changed it to one month. "I'm going to give you a temporary card for thirty days to see if you like it, and I need you to come back in for a check-up."

When I told my friends, they laughed at me. No one had ever heard of only getting a card for thirty days. "What did you tell him?"

The doctor gave me his recommendation for what to buy—Indica. He said they called it "In-da-couch" because that's all you wanted to do. He also warned me about taking edibles, saying that people overdose on them because it takes a while to hit, and, when it does, it hits hard. I couldn't believe I was having a conversation with a medical professional about ingesting dope.

I left the clinic, feeling less dirty than I did when I went in there, and looked up which dispensary was closest to me. I found one not far from Pink's on La Brea, so I pulled over and parked. After a large, armed guard checked my ID and medical marijuana card, I was buzzed into the back. It felt like *Charlie and the Chocolate Factory* with a small room of counters full of beautifully packaged candies, gummies, lollipops, and a fridge full of sodas and brownies, all containing cannabis. The choices overwhelmed me, so the woman behind the counter helped. She took things seriously, just like salespeople in sex toy stores.

That night, Dad called me collect to let me know he knew about my card, thanks to Aunt Martha spying on my social media. He warned me of the dangers of "grass," as he called it.

"You know, there are studies out there saying people are less productive when they use it, Lip."

"Oh really? Good for them!"

I tried to explain I got it because of him and his fucked-up situation in the first place. He didn't want to hear it.

In the fall of 2016, Westlake High School hosted a thirtieth class reunion. I was still friends with many classmates and couldn't wait to reconnect once again in the same place. I stayed in a hotel in Westlake with Nicki and two other high school friends. I could have stayed with Mom but didn't want the judgment of coming home late and drunk. I was now 48 years old, by the way!

When we arrived at the venue, they had a memorial table with photos of all the classmates who had died since graduation—thirty classmates, including Anne. I had brought some bookmarks with Anne's picture and obituary on them, that her parents had made for her memorial. I laid them next to her high school picture, my lip trembling. People came up to me offering their condolences, asking how exactly she died. I was proud to represent her. I felt like her widow. I wiped away my tears and swaggered over to the bar, eyeing people I recognized and some I didn't. I remembered looking at the calendar in high school, crossing off days until I turned sixteen so I could drive. I thought that day would never come. And now I was 48 years old. It was bizarre being in a room where everyone was exactly the same age. We all looked so different now—hair loss, weight gain, wrinkles ... Where had the time gone?

Several people came up to me and asked how my father was doing. Most had heard about it in the papers or seen it on the news. "I never knew your dad owned strip clubs, that's so cool!" one guy said to me. "I always wondered how you were able to drive all those exotic cars to school," he added.

I ran into Doug, one of our neighbors from Cheswick Place, and gave him a big hug. He asked how my family was. "Oh, Dad's getting out next year, so that should be interesting," I sighed. Many people asked me about Dad's clubs, his murder conviction, and his time in prison, and it felt so freeing talking about it openly. "Wow, that's going to be so crazy when he gets out. Are your parents still married?" they mostly asked. "Amazingly, yes," I replied.

The next day, I went out to sushi with Mom and gave her the scoop. "I couldn't believe how many people asked about Dad!"

"Oh no," she said, "Are people still talking about him after all this time?"

Mom still hadn't told her new neighbors about him, even though she had pictures of the two of them up in her condo. She had that way of making someone feel too uncomfortable to ask personal questions. Mom had started hanging up Thanksgiving decorations around her fireplace.

At lunch, we discussed our upcoming Christmas trip together—Mom, Rachel, and I were taking a cruise to Antarctica. It was our last hurrah.

"I'm worried I won't be able to travel once your father's out," she said, eating edamame.

"I can't believe you would even say that. Why should that matter?" I felt my cheeks get hot.

"Your dad's parole is going to be pretty tight when he gets out. His parole officer said it's a fifty-mile radius from my condo."

"Well, that's *his* parole, not yours. Why should you suffer?"

"I just hope I can still go out with my girlfriends," she said, shrugging her shoulders.

"What do you mean? Of course, you can. Why would you even think that?" I could see Mom's sense of independence melting away before my eyes.

"Well, your father won't have any friends, and I feel bad leaving him alone while I'm out living my life."

"Mom, he left you alone for seventeen years and before that, he was always out late with David or having dinner with his 25-year-old blond massage therapist. Don't you remember when Dad said if the tables were turned, he'd never wait for you?" It reminded me of all my discussions with Henry that went nowhere.

"Well, we'll see." She gazed into her salad bowl and sighed.

I leaned back into the booth and stared at her in silence. I was shocked to see how quickly Mom was regressing to the way she was when Dad was a free man. She had already given up.

45 Hungry for Seven Carts of Groceries

Dad's parole date was set for June 28, 2017. Jeezus, how did that creep up on us so quickly? Rachel and Mom were sure Dad would die in prison. My therapist tried to calm me down each week, as the date approached.

"Just practice saying *no*," she kept telling me in our therapy sessions. Dad informed me that I would be his buddy when he got out. He reiterated that he needed me to help him out with stuff, like technology, buying clothes, and a new car. I imagined having a large foster child living with me. I didn't chat with Mom and Dad too often on the phone. I had boundaries. Scuba diving and traveling the world brought me so much joy and purpose.

Dad continued to blame David, Johnny, and his attorneys for his conviction, and planned on hiring an attorney to sue "everyone" when he got out. I just wanted to slap some sense into him, but knew it was a wasted effort. Whenever he went down the path, I quickly changed the subject or told him I needed to go.

He told the family how we were all moving to Nevada to save on taxes. This was brought up repeatedly as if we said yes to him, when in fact we all told him none of us were interested. He told me when he got out that we were going into business together, possibly boat charters where he could be the captain and I could be the dive master. Not once were any of us asked what we wished for after his release.

Half of my friends urged me to move out of California. My friend, Nicki, researched cities including Nashville and Portland, two places I could jive with. In contrast, my therapist urged me to stay in Los Angeles. "The best way to build boundaries, Laurel, is by saying no to your dad!"

I visited Dad at Chino, a week before our Antarctica cruise trip. By the time I got there, all the inside tables were taken, so we sat outside in the sun on one of the picnic tables. We sat across from each other, and he reached across the table to hold my hands. Dad wore a large straw hat due to skin cancers being removed from his balding head.

I told Dad I thought he and Mom needed couples' counseling and that he needed individual therapy.

"Oh yeah, your mom definitely needs therapy," he said.

"No, Dad, *you* need therapy," I repeated.

"Me? I don't need any therapy. I'm pretty well adjusted," he said, letting go of my hands.

I asked Mom several times if she found a couples' counselor for her and Dad to go to. "Oh yeah, I'm working on it." After asking for the fifth time with the same response, I gave up. I felt like I was the only person panicking about Dad's parole. It didn't even occur to me that it wasn't my problem. I just wanted to protect Mom more than anything.

Now with a confirmed parole date, Dad would start each call from prison with a countdown. "One hundred and seven days and counting!" he announced. He was restless now that he could almost taste freedom.

"I mean, in here, you never know what's going to happen from day to day. I don't understand why they don't release me now. They have all the paperwork and it costs the state more money to keep me here. The problem, Laurel, is I'm surrounded by a bunch of idiots."

That comment made me laugh out loud as I covered my mouth.

"Just try to remain calm. You don't want to jeopardize your release." He was finally getting released and *still* complaining.

"You know, Lip, I already know what my priority is when I get out." I stopped washing dishes and sat down at my kitchen table, pressing the phone hard to my ear. "I'm going to get a hair transplant." Unbelievable. I put him back on speakerphone and loaded the dishwasher.

Dad continued, saying he didn't want a felony on his record and might take action to get it erased. He also didn't think he should be on parole, due to maintaining his innocence. I was reminded again about *Shawshank Redemption* when Red says to Andy Dufresne upon his arrival to prison, "You're gonna fit right in. Everyone in here's innocent," he says, chuckling. Seventeen years in prison for a murder conviction, every appeal denied, and this was Dad's focus—his hairline. You could not make this shit up.

I began to realize how much my father's prison time had become a part of my identity. Normally, people identified themselves through their jobs. But when I met people, my value add would be, "Oh, my Dad's in prison for murder, and I help out with his needs."

One night, I started reading through my old journals. I couldn't believe I had survived it all.

> 12.13.2000: Sunday Mom and I went to the jail to visit Dad. We took a number and waited for four hours. When they finally called our number, we went to the window and they wouldn't let us see Dad because his area had already seen the max number of visitors, we both started crying.

> 12.29.2000: We have all gotten so much stronger. In the beginning we didn't know who to trust, whom to talk to, we don't talk on the phone or say too much in the house. We have found out the wildest shit about people. Johnny confessed and he's a nutcase. He said he and David have been lovers for years. He finally got religion and informed on everyone at the clubs.
>
> 4.7.2001: Dad had another hearing yesterday and it was all over the news and radio. I saw him on TV when I was at the gym. Then when mom and I were driving to the jail this morning we heard it on the radio again.

Man, I was just a kid then, a 32-year-old sheltered kid. I wasn't used to having a parental unit anymore. My parents were still married, fifty-two years, but I couldn't imagine my parents living in the same house again. Dad mentioned spending some nights at my apartment to get away from Mom, but I stopped him. "You can stay at a hotel nearby if you need to." My therapist was proud.

I wanted to stop feeling panicked. But I found myself going through possible scenarios of us moving to Nevada, Dad telling us what cars to buy, firing our family attorney, and worrying about Mom. I somehow couldn't remember that I had control over my own life, wherever my Dad was.

"One day at a time," my therapist said, "enjoy the free time you have left." Even she admitted to me that there would be an adjustment period after he got out. "You'll get back to where you are now, don't worry," she assured me.

As my panic lessened, I felt depleted of any emotion, like in the old days, when I went through jail and court visits like a robot on caffeine. And for the last prison visit on April 22, 2017, the most indulgent $16 latte would get me through. I hadn't seen him in five months and felt no guilt about it anymore. I wore the same brown travel pants with a striped shirt, my uniform for the previous year. It would go to Goodwill soon like the rest of the prison garb.

I arrived at the prison at 8:48 a.m. The visitor line stretched outside a makeshift reception center. Between now and my last visit, the old reception center's roof had collapsed. The prison was built in 1940 and had undergone minimal upkeep and maintenance. The paint peeled off the walls, the toilets barely flushed, the porta-potties outside had flies and no toilet paper or soap, and the air conditioning was usually broken. Even though I had a 9:00 a.m. appointment, I waited in line for thirty-five minutes, standing in the sun, staring at other visitors, watching as some were turned away for outfits or not having an appointment. They had a button that you push that randomly turned red or green. If it turned red, you were in the clear; if it turned green, you were to be searched for drugs or other contraband. They pulled me into another room of guards with blue latex gloves on, swiped my hands down with a cloth, and put it in their machine. Then they made me spread my arms and legs and ran a security wand over me.

I watched one guard send this poor woman back twice to the clothing trailer to change her clothes because they were too tight and might arouse the inmates. She teared up, but all I could think was, *this is almost over. I'll never ever have to do this again or see other women humiliated.*

I retrieved my pass and walked over toward the dilapidated reception center where more guards waited outside the closed-down building under a blue tarp, with the x-ray machine and wand to check in the visitors again. That same poor woman was there, now being told she couldn't bring in five-dollar bills, only singles and quarters. The guards informed her she had to go back to the other reception center and get quarters from the change machine. She sat down and cried into her hands. I wanted to give her a hug, but I knew better. I didn't want the guards to think that I was siding with her. I watched her and couldn't believe that was me seventeen years ago, a clueless prison newbie with an underwired bra on.

I walked to Dad's yard and presented my pass to the guards, who gave me table number twenty. While I waited for Dad, I grabbed a water and a Diet Coke from the vending machine. Dad came out of the door attached to the prison housing area. I waved him over to our table. He appeared more fragile, pale, and gaunt. He gave me a big hug and kiss and told me how great I looked. I still felt self-conscious around him. "It's a prison outfit. I dress nicer outside of this place," I replied.

I looked him up and down. I couldn't believe in two months he'd be a free man. This guy in prison I called DAD! "What's the first stop you want to make when we pick you up?" I asked.

"McDonald's. I want a real breakfast. It's all I think about," he laughed.

Funny, O.J. Simpson wanted the same thing when he got out, I thought.

Dad talked about what car he was going to buy—a convertible Mustang.

"Your mom doesn't want me to get a convertible because of the sun, but I told her that I'll only put the top down in the late afternoon or the evening. I'm going to take a driving course when I get out. Some of the guys say I'll need the practice. All I think about is driving, I think about it every day."

"You know Dad, I think you're going be depressed when you get out and I'm worried about you. Mom's place is a mess, and two of the three bedrooms aren't useable—they're full of junk. Mom can barely get her car into the two-car garage because it's so full of crap." I leaned back and folded my arms. Dad snickered.

"Laurel, you don't understand what it's like in here. I have a bunk bed and a locker about 2×2 feet with all my belongings. I'll be fine. At least I'll be able to step outside and away from all the inmates and guards." He then pointed out some of the people he wasn't going to miss, in his unsubtle way. God, he was so clueless!

"I still think you're going to need counseling once you get out, to adjust to everything." I was truly worried about him. He acted like this eager child who knew he was going to visit Disneyland. Again, I thought more along the lines of my main reference, *Shawshank Redemption*. One of the characters, Brooks, is released from prison, and a short time after he's released, he decides to hang himself, unable to adapt to the outside world. I suddenly got chills, thinking about Dad feeling like an alien fitting into society.

"Laurel, honestly, I want to take one day at a time. We'll see how it goes." He leaned over, patting me on the head.

I reminded Dad that a lot had changed since October 2000.

"I know the family is fractured and scattered, but things are going to be better when I get out," he assured me.

"Don't expect things to change overnight," I said, letting out a deep sigh and slouching in my chair.

But Dad was confident. I sensed calmness in Dad that I hadn't witnessed before. He focused on what he wanted with his own life, not in controlling ours.

"I can't wait to go to the grocery store. I'm going to fill seven carts full of food." He laughed, smiling like a little kid. Suddenly, I didn't feel so numb. I wiped a tear from my eye. His eyes lit up, the gaunt expression faded, and he squeezed my knee.

We took a photo together, my last prison photo with Dad. At 11:30 a.m., I told Dad that I was ready to leave, so we got up, and he walked me toward the exit.

"Next time I see you, we'll be taking you home. I can't believe it." I punched him in the arm.

"You and me both, kid."

"I'm going pick you up in my Wookie onesie, okay?"

"What is that?"

"My Wookie onesie, you know, Chewbacca!"

He laughed. I reminded him of the time he scared Rachel and me at Halloween with the Darth Vader mask—he'd forgotten about it. I wanted him to see me as his daughter, not as his confidant or assistant, scurrying around getting shit done for him.

I took my last look around the visiting room, with everyone sitting at their tables, the prisoners, and guards I knew well, and realized that this chapter of my life was closing. I was going to be free too. I wasn't going back to jail, prison, courthouses, or attorneys' offices. Dad expected to be off parole within six months of being released.

"Parole isn't a suggestion," I said.

"No, Laurel, I'm different. I've maintained my innocence," he responded.

I stood up, and Dad and I kissed and hugged each other goodbye. I said bye to the guards. I didn't bother telling the flirty, ogling ones this was my last visit.

46 The Homecoming

On June 28, 2017, my alarm went off at 7:00 a.m., but I had been awake since 5:00 a.m. with that first-day-of-work feeling. The prison would drop off the released inmates at the Montclair Transit Center sometime in the morning. Rachel met me at my house in Hollywood at 7:30 a.m. and we drove down together. "Ventura Highway" by America came on the radio, and we sang at the top of our lungs with the sunroof open—it calmed our nerves. We boasted about the outfits we were wearing—things we were never allowed to wear at prison. Rachel wore khakis and an orange bra with a sheer white tee shirt. I wore a sleeveless sundress with no bra and lots of metal jewelry. Both outfits were considered contraband for prison visiting. They could suck it.

We arrived at the bus station at 8:35 a.m., while Mom and Aunt Martha cruised in forty-five minutes later. We stood under the trees in the parking lot to avoid the dry heat, holding balloons and flowers. Rachel and I laughed about something stupid, just when we noticed this large Black woman across a bus platform yelling at us. She turned and pulled down her worn jeans to her knees, mooning us, slapping her large black ass as she continued yelling obscenities. It took us a few moments to process it, but I realized she thought that Rachel and I had been laughing at her. It was the icing on the cake for our last day of anything to do with prison. The woman pulled her pants up, flipped us the bird, and walked to another bus platform.

An hour later, an all-white van with a sheriff logo on the side arrived. A prison guard got out of the passenger side and told us to stay back. We stood across from him, with a "Welcome Home" balloon and a bouquet of flowers, snapping pictures and waiting for Dad to come out. The guard unloaded prisoners from the back of the van. Dad was the last to get out. The other prisoners, Dad told us, were all short-term prison drug dealers. Dad wore a baseball cap, white tee shirt, and gray sweatpants and walked with his cane. He looked so old and skinny. He had lost forty pounds since his arrest. He carried a purple mesh bag with his belongings.

The guard passed out envelopes containing ATM cards for each prisoner with $200 on the card. It was official—Dad was no longer California Detention Center number T-47887! He was just Michael Woods. He walked toward us, glowing with a gigantic smile not formed in almost twenty years.

Aunt Martha hugged him and cried. Dad walked over to Mom next, and her face lit up as they hugged. We walked Dad back to our car and gave him a nice blue collared shirt and jeans Mom had bought for him to change into. Dad reached into his mesh bag and handed us presents—a bag of peanut M&M's for each of us. On the drive, Dad commented on the new cars he hadn't seen and how fast everyone drove on the freeway.

As we arrived at the restaurant, Dad looked at me and asked if he could use the restroom. He wasn't accustomed to doing things without asking permission. I walked Dad to the men's room and waited outside. It was the first time using a private bathroom without armed prison guards or inmates present. Back at the table, the waiter came to take our order. The nice waiter stunned Dad with his polite demeanor, as he jumped a little in his chair, and he was timidly asking for coffee.

Dad was antsy and kept looking around. "I feel like I'm in a dream," he said skittishly, holding my hand.

The waiter returned with coffee for everyone and took our food order. Dad ordered pancakes, two eggs over easy, and a side of Polish sausages. The waiter asked if he could refill our coffee, and Dad commented on how good and hot it was. He picked up the silverware, calling the knife a *shiv*, because he used only a plastic spork to eat his food in the mess hall.

As we waited for our food, I looked up and realized that we were on our phones, texting away, sending pictures, uploading to Facebook and Instagram. "I'm sorry, Dad, we're all on our phones. This is the way it is now, on the outside."

"Yes, I can see that." He looked around the restaurant, squinting his eyes and absorbing the lively atmosphere.

"We're just texting our friends who are asking how you're doing." I showed him my phone so he could see what texts looked like.

I felt bad that we were all ignoring him, so I put my phone down. Dad glanced around the restaurant, watching peoples' meals being served, pointing and asking me what they were eating. Finally, our food arrived. Dad wolfed down his entire meal in five minutes. No, really, I timed it.

"How was your first real breakfast?"

"Great!" he had tears in his eyes. "Normally at chow, we'd be having this dry coffee cake and instant coffee with powdered milk. Sometimes I don't even eat it, it's so bad."

We continued our drive out to Mom's house. We entered her place, now Mom and Dad's place. Dad walked in, eyes darting and squinting, "I'm not used to so much natural light." Mom's three cats approached Dad, sniffing him out. The animals rubbing against his legs captivated him like they would a child. Mom and Rachel had Dad try on the clothes we bought for him. He tried shorts on, and I saw Dad's scar on his left knee from his motorcycle accident as a CHP officer. I had forgotten about that scar.

Dad rummaged through his purple mesh bag and pulled out his parole papers. He wanted to call his parole officer right away to make the required next-day appointment. I handed him my iPhone, but he couldn't figure out how to use it, so I grabbed Mom's house phone instead. The parole officer was polite and told Dad to come in the next day, in the early afternoon.

Dad continued going through his belongings of the last seventeen years—books, medication, pictures of his inmate friends like Catfish and Terry, and two file folders full of cards and letters he had received over the years. He had saved a crime novel he wanted me to read and showed us his parole letters of support.

I went out to my car and grabbed Dad's brown leather jacket from the 1970s.

"Oh my God, that jacket. I had forgotten about it. I used to love that. I wore it when your mother and I went to England." He tried it on, and it was big on him. His eyes welled up with tears. "Wow Lip I can't believe you kept this." It was the only possession he had left from his former life, except for his blue bathrobe Mom had hanging on the back of her bathroom door, all these years.

"Oh, yeah, I remember that," he said.

He sat down and gazed around Mom's living room, at their grandfather clock and an old phone from the 1930s hanging on a wall.

"Remember that time, Lip, when I was carrying you around on my back, and you accidentally kicked the phone off the wall? Your mom was so pissed at us."

"I do remember that!" I cackled.

It was like he was incapable of remembering while in prison, and everything was coming back to him now. He looked at me and asked if he could take a nap.

Mom told him to take a nap in the guest room upstairs. Dad looked like one of those dogs on YouTube climbing stairs for the first time. "I haven't gone upstairs since my old prison in Corcoran over six years ago." He clung to the side railing the whole way up, taking one step at a time. Dad had arthroscopic surgery on his bad knee in prison, but now he needed knee replacement surgery. I'd only seen him walk a little bit at prison. Now I saw how much pain he was in.

While Dad napped upstairs, Mom made a nice meal for dinner—pork chops, salad, mashed potatoes, and corn on the cob. Dad came down after twenty minutes and helped out in the kitchen by shucking corn, carrying food over to the table, and taking out the trash. I was melted by watching him help out. He didn't know where anything was, but he tried his hardest and it crushed me. During our prison visits, we had to do everything for him while he sat down, facing the guards.

Once dinner was ready, we sat down at the table. Mom said grace as we held hands, thanking God for Dad's release. We dug in and watched Dad quietly devour his meal, as if it were his last. We reminisced about all the prisons, the long drives, and the visiting procedures. Mom didn't want Dad to talk about prison life now that he was released. But what else did he have to talk about?

After dinner, Aunt Martha, Rachel, and I said our goodbyes.

"It's great to see you, Dad, and in normal clothes."

"I'm just so happy to be back with my family." Tears streamed down his pale cheeks. Rachel and I hugged him and got into my car. He stood there as we drove away, waving goodbye.

I drove Rachel back to my place to retrieve her car, and we let the day sink in.

"I still can't believe he's out. I never thought he'd get out of there … alive," Rachel's voice trailed off to a faraway place as if allowing enough time for all the years to catch up to her.

"He seems so old and fragile," I said.

"He *is* old and fragile, Laurel!" It was nighttime, and we drove with the sunroof open as Rachel played DJ on my car stereo. The wind whipped around our hair.

I walked into my apartment and called my parents. I needed to change Mom's number in my iPhone to "Mom and Dad". Dad answered the phone.

"Hey Lip, you made it home okay?"

"Yeah, traffic was light. What are you guys doing?" I was so curious about his every movement.

"Oh, watching the news and getting ready for bed."

"It's great to have you out Dad, and it's great to talk to you on a phone line that's not being recorded."

"Well," he chuckled, "that's what you think. You never know …"

"Good night, Dad. I love you."

"Good night, Lip, really good to see you, talk to you tomorrow."

Maybe things weren't going to be so bad, after all.

It felt anticlimactic having Dad released from prison. All those years reduced to one pickup in a bus station. I called my parents the next day to see how things were going. I felt the need to monitor them. Even stranger, there was no prison recording every sixty seconds announcing that I was speaking with a "California inmate."

"How did you sleep, Dad?" I was in my pajamas, pouring myself coffee in my kitchen. KCRW played in the background.

"Oh, pretty good. I tossed and turned some and Milo," one of Mom's three cats, "started howling at 4:00 a.m."

"Yeah, he does that all the time. You better get used to it." Milo, a rescue Himalayan, was 17 years old and a bit senile these days.

"I'm having Cheerios and blueberries for breakfast, and your Mom and I are watching the news. Your mother made me a DMV appointment at 9:00 a.m., so we're going to hit the road soon."

"Good luck. Will you have a stamp on your license that you're a felon?"

"I hope not, but we'll see!" he laughed.

Mom had been renewing Dad's license in the mail since his conviction, so all he needed to do was go to the DMV and take the written test with an updated photo. They administered the test on a computer, which he didn't know how to use, and Mom couldn't help him. Mom said he struggled but passed, receiving his license, which meant that he didn't need to use his prison ID to get around. He'd been wearing his prison ID around his neck on a lanyard since we picked him up. Mom kept telling him to tuck it underneath his shirt.

Three days later, I drove an hour north to Mom's house, err, Mom and Dad's. Mom was at the gym. I walked in and Dad cornered me in the doorway, complaining about how messy Mom's place was.

"Lip, you can't even walk in the garage because there's so much stuff on the floor. And there's nowhere for me to put my things. All of the closets are full of Mom's stuff! There's even clothes with tags still on them on the floor!" He pointed at a pile of clothes spilling off a chair.

"I warned you, and so did Rachel, Aunt Martha, and Aunt Deanie. You said you didn't care, all you wanted was out of prison and some solitude." I walked around him, toward the kitchen. Milo followed me looking for food.

"Yeah, but I can't live like this, Lip. I just can't believe how much stuff your Mom has, and every time I go to look for something or help tidy up, she yells at me."

It only took three days of freedom before Dad started complaining about something. Those seventeen years of prison were a distant memory.

Mom came home from the gym, and Dad went upstairs to shower.

"How's it going?" I asked her.

"Laurel, he follows me *everywhere*. He needs to make some friends and find a hobby. I have no privacy. He controls the TV, he looks at my phone whenever I get a call or a text, and he goes through my mail."

I fought the urge to shout, "I told you so!"

Then Dad came downstairs dressed for the day, wearing khaki pants and a blue collared shirt. I asked him if he wanted to go to Costco with me, and his whole face lit up as he said, "Yeah, let's go, Lip!" I remembered how Dad used to have panic attacks from sitting around too much. Even when we visited family in Wyoming, with a direct view of the snowcapped Tetons, Dad had to be on the phone calling the clubs several times a day.

I let him drive my car so that he could practice driving. He hopped in and began scanning the dashboard, pressing buttons. He hesitated before putting his hands on the steering wheel. My car was a stick shift, and he fumbled with the pedals, as he practiced shifting while parked. I flinched every time I heard my gears grinding. After a few failed attempts of driving forward, I could see his frustration and stopped joking about my whiplash. "Wow, I haven't driven a stick shift in a long time," he said. He stalled a few times in the driveway before he got us on the main road. I didn't dare take my eyes off him. He was easily distracted by the other cars and my satellite radio.

As soon as we got on the road, he started complaining again about Mom.

"You know, your mother doesn't want me talking about prison anymore. But it's all I've got to talk about. It's been my life." My car continued to chug along.

"Dad, I told you things would be hard when you got out. I really think you two need couples' therapy." I opened up the sunroof and let the windows down.

"I agree with you one hundred percent, Laurel." He had just shifted into fifth gear instead of third, but I didn't correct him.

"Really? I'm glad to hear that, because last time we spoke about this, you didn't believe in therapy." Wow, he *was* open to listening and changing.

"Oh, I don't need therapy. I'm perfectly well-adjusted. I want to go to couples' therapy so I can tell the therapist what's wrong with your mother!"

"It doesn't really work that way." I turned up the radio.

I knew this would happen. I just didn't expect it so soon.

At Costco, I watched Dad enter the warehouse like that same kid going to Disneyland. He loaded our cart up with all kinds of stuff—Cheerios, blueberries, pastries, bread rolls, cheese, and vitamin supplements. In prison, staying healthy was key, and as the medical care was so bad, Dad took supplements and herbal remedies. He walked down each aisle, exploring everything and taking it in like a magical grocery universe. I thought he would legit fill the seven carts of his dreams.

"I remember when you wanted aspirin, you just bought the one type of aspirin." His breath was ragged.

At checkout, Dad tried to pay with his prison ATM, but they declined it. "I'm so frustrated by all these things, Lip. I'm still waiting for Mom to add me onto her American Express account." Dad had a hard time getting a credit card because he had no credit history, and banks refused him as a client, saying he was a felon with funds from "questionable resources." I had to practice patience. Four days ago, he was still in a prison cell and shackled. Now he was in swanky Westlake Village at a Costco offering anything you could possibly want. Yet, complaints about not having a platinum Amex card abounded.

A couple of days later, Mom took Dad to the local AT+T store to buy an iPhone. When Dad was in prison, he insisted he had no interest in a smartphone, but once he saw the whole world on their phones, he wanted one too. He called me at home from his new phone.

"Hey Lip, I'm on my new phone, and now you have my number."

"Wow, that's so weird that you have your own phone. Do you like it?"

"Honestly, Laurel, I'm overloaded. Not just the phone, but by everything. The credit cards have chips now, security codes, everything is so expensive I can't believe it."

"Do you know how to text yet?"

"Oh yeah, I wanna ask you about that, I think something's wrong with my phone. I tried texting Rachel, and each text sends as invisible ink. I don't know what I'm doing wrong." That was one of iPhone's texting options, which he'd obviously found by mistake.

"I'm sure there's an *iPhone for Dummies* book I can find you."

"Oh yeah? That would be great."

I sensed his frustration and lack of control. Just like that, he went back to his old self. I had such high hopes of him simply enjoying his freedom, eating good food, taking walks, asking us about ourselves and how our lives had been, wanting to see photos from all the trips we'd been on. My friends were curious about Dad's readjustment back into society. "He must be so happy to be out!" I heard it over and over. What could I say? That he complained about not having a platinum Amex card, his iPhone woes, and Mom's beautiful Westlake Village condo being too cluttered? I saw what my therapist meant now, her words "enjoy it while you can," still ringing in my ears. I called her immediately. I didn't tell her about the latest achingly illiterate hate comment on my blog from "Angel":

> I worked for your father in the 80s and he was a mean son of a bitch. How can you act like everything is ok when he fckin had a man killed? I worked at Bare Elegance back then and everyone knew he did it. I worked for Dave too. He was my Manager. It's sickening to see your Evil father is free. He will meet his little buddy Satan in Hell. I'm praying anyway. You are a shallow despicable woman and the apple doesn't fall far from the tree. Enjoy your Evil DNA. My own brother murdered someone I never met and guess what dipshit? I do not have a relationship with him. Because I do not associate with MURDERERS. MIKE THE UGLY WIMP WOODS deserves LIFE in jail or the Death Penalty if it was an option. I CAN STILL PICTURE YOUR DAD'S STUPID ASSHOLE FACE WHILE I HAD TO DEAL WITH HIM AT WORK AT THE CLUB. YOU NEVER FORGET EVIL. TRUE NARCISSIST.

A week after Dad's release, Mom had neck surgery. She had been having back and neck problems for the last several months and couldn't understand why. "Stress, that's why," I said to her. Luckily, she was still cancer free, getting checkups every six months at City of Hope.

We were at Ventura County Hospital, thirty-five miles north of Mom and Dad's house. Mom was still in recovery after a successful operation, and some of her nursing friends stopped by to check up on her. It was the first time any of them met

Dad, and the whole exchange seemed so awkward. Mom's friends shook hands with Dad, one by one, as Dad said, "Nice to meet you, I'm Diane's husband." After getting uncomfortable pleasantries out of the way, I suggested that Dad and I leave them and get lunch.

Dad insisted on driving Mom's car. I took him to this local seafood spot on the beach, by Ventura Pier. We both ordered fish burritos. While waiting for our food, I showed him the "Christian the Lion" video on YouTube, and he got teary-eyed. "You know, Harrod's should never have been selling wild animals." I was only a quarter into my burrito when I looked at Dad and saw his plate was already empty.

After lunch, I asked Dad if he wanted to walk on the beach before going back to the hospital. We took a short stroll, as Dad inhaled the salty air and watched the waves crash, just like taking a dog to the beach for the first time. Then Dad saw some young women lying on their towels, sunning themselves in string bikinis.

"Oh my God, Lip, look at those women—practically naked! I haven't seen women like that in years!" He turned away, then back around for another peep. "It's so nice to see women again," Dad looked at me. "Those female prison guards were not lookers."

After lunch, we came back to Mom's hospital room. The doctor was filling in Mom on how her surgery went. Dad kept interjecting with his medical expertise as Mom and I shook our heads. Dad's phone rang mid-conversation, and he opened the door and took it out in the hallway. Mom was able to ask her doctor her own questions before Dad came back in with a sense of urgency. "Lip, that was my new parole officer. He wants to meet me in an hour at the house. Can you drive me there?" Dad couldn't dare get even a speeding ticket at this point in his parole. The doctor's eyes widened as we excused ourselves.

After an hour of speeding south on Highway 101, we arrived at the condo, just before Dad's new PO rang the doorbell. Dad answered the door, and Jay introduced himself to both of us as he came in. I caught my breath as I scanned Jay up and down. The resemblance was uncanny—just like Dad's partner, Mac—tall guy, dark features, muscular, wearing an officer badge and carrying a gun. He looked like a bounty hunter you would see on a TV show. Dad asked him if he was Samoan, and I just shook my head. Jay was Dad's third parole officer, as they kept getting transferred around the county. I had no idea Ventura County was hopping with so many criminals. Jay explained that he needed to examine the house, to ensure that Dad lived there, and to look for any contraband like knives or guns.

He began his physical inspection and walked upstairs. "This is a nice place you have here. I don't see this that often with parolees," Jay said in his deep voice. We watched him go upstairs and examine all three bedrooms. We could hear his keys jingle as the closet doors opened and closed. Dad looked at me with wide eyes, and we shrugged our shoulders in silence. After a few minutes, Jay came out of the master bedroom toward the staircase, glancing back down at the living room. Dad said, "Oh all this junk in here is my wife's, not mine." Why did he have to say that? The parole officer remained silent, as he walked back downstairs.

"I don't know how much you know about my case," Dad started, "but I've maintained my innocence since my arrest." Dad began telling Jay his life story, how David and Johnny had framed him, and discussed all the appeals he'd filed. Dad and Jay stood in the living room while I played Words with Friends on my phone in the kitchen. After twenty-five minutes of Dad rambling while Jay remained silent, I walked back into the living room. "Dad," I said, "he knows about your case. Just stop talking and let him do what he came here for." He legitimately didn't know when to shut up, after all this time. "Loose lips sync ships" all over again.

"Yes, this is a very serious case, Mr. Woods," Jay said. "Your case is different from the other parole cases I have. Most parolees don't have a nice home and family to come home to. Do you plan on working?"

"Oh no," Dad chucked, "let's just say I'm set for life," he responded with that Cheshire cat grin. Dad still had his money from the strip clubs waiting for him in Mom's name. He was still on the hunt for a financial institution to take him on as a client. He hated that everything was in Mom's name.

Dad thought his parole would only last six months, claiming innocence and all. He filled in Jay about his travel plans to Arizona for Aunt Deanie's eightieth birthday party the following March, as if it was no big deal. Jay stoically explained that Dad was on parole for LIFE, with a chance for adjustment after seven years. Dad couldn't go further than a fifty-mile radius from their house, and he couldn't travel anywhere for at least the first six months and a reevaluation by his supervisor. Jay continued, explaining that he could come to the house anytime he wanted, unannounced, and Dad had to sign up for a lifer's group meeting, once a month in Ventura, which his parole officer also attended.

Jay basically regurgitated everything that Dad's first PO had told Mom four months before Dad's release, when she would come out to the house to meet with Mom. Mom had relayed all the information to Dad, but he insisted his PO was wrong.

After Jay left, Dad looked at me. "See? He said my case is special. I'm different." He put his hands in his pockets and jingled his change.

"Yeah Dad, I think he meant more like 'what rags-to-riches white guy who had it all would get involved in something so stupid' kind of special."

It was August 2017, six weeks after Dad's release. Mom, Rachel, Aunt Martha, and I continued helping him adjust back to life on the "outside." He wanted everything done, immediately. He called *and* texted now.

I came out to the house and Dad had pinstriped his new car, a VW Passat. Then he pinstriped mine, then Rachel's. "Looks great, doesn't it?" he chirped proudly, pointing at the red stripes on my front grill. I could tell he was trying to gain some type of control and meaning back in our lives. I felt sorry for him. I reminded him of the time he pinstriped my pink and green Schwinn bike, before I took off for UCSB. "Oh yeah, I forgot about that bike."

Things we took for granted were still new to Dad and seeing things through his eyes was refreshing. This was my most favorite part of his journey. When using a paper towel in the kitchen, he would fold it into perfect quarters, using one quarter at a time. He used milk sparingly, always washing his glass after, and planned his days around mealtimes. Mom was used to having instant oatmeal for dinner in front of the TV, but Dad insisted on traditional meals at the table. He still gazed at his dinner knife in awe.

Mom tried signing Dad up for Medicare before he was released but found out she was supposed to do it earlier, like nine years earlier. Dad visited the Social Security office several times to figure it out, but they wouldn't enroll him for another year. He was fuming when he called from his car to complain, "Can you believe your mother waited so long?"

"Dad just be thankful you have the freedom to go to a doctor, even if you have to pay out of pocket for now. Remember how much you complained about the health care in prison?" I laughed that Dad was so shocked at Mom's behavior as if he didn't know the woman's operations mode. She had consistently been a procrastinator for years.

It was both endearing and terrifying watching Dad adjust back into society—a legit social experiment. I wondered mostly what he would say to people. He had his narrative down to discussing his horrendous childhood (okay, fair enough), his time in the Army, being a retired CHP officer, and what a great father he is. When he referred to his time in prison with family and friends, he talked about how highly regarded he was by the other inmates and guards. "You know, they always referred to me as Mr. Woods," he would say, standing up straight with his chin high and shoulders back. "I was considered a celebrity, once they saw me on TV in one of those true crime shows," he said proudly.

Realizing I needed to circle in some boundaries before he bled me to death, I began dialing back what I did for him. I answered his phone calls less often, so he began texting me more. But as soon as I responded to his text, he called me. It was like that one needy friend that you just could not shake and didn't take the hint. Even though I had worked with my therapist on so much, putting this all into practice with my new reality was a daily struggle. I felt obliged to get him up to speed on life. I mean, he did raise me as a child, didn't I owe him? "Remember," my therapist said, "you don't *have* to do anything." Instead of continuing to drop everything for him, I set up my own schedule with working, workouts, and visits with friends.

Two months after Dad's release, I talked to Rachel on her way to work. "I mean it's so weird, it's as if the last seventeen years didn't happen, and he's pretending we're all one big happy family," I said while making coffee in my kitchen.

"I know Laurel, but what did you expect?" As usual, Rachel then honked at someone on the freeway.

"Some sense of responsibility or sympathy, or at least asking me anything about *my* life since October 2000?"

"Yeah, good luck with that!" she laughed.

My high school friend, Olivia, who came to several of Dad's court hearings, even when pregnant, was visiting from Seattle and wanted to see Dad, so we made plans for lunch. I drove out to my parents' house to pick up Dad. He peppered me with his usual tech questions about his car, iPhone, and TV, but I was short with him. I felt him stare at me while I talked to Mom. After Mom went upstairs, he walked over to me, put his arms around my neck, and looked at me with his bright blue eyes.

"I love you Lip, and I'm sorry for what happened."

THIS IS IT, I told myself. I'm finally going to get the apology, the acknowledgment, the sympathy—*something*.

"But you're bitter, and you need to get over it."

At lunch, Dad dominated the conversation, as he talked about his recent lunch with his old strip-club managers, Ricky and Cliff, now both in their eighties. Ricky still worked at the Jet Strip for David, and Dad loved hearing all the gossip about David, Johnny, and the club. As Dad rattled on and on about how poorly the Jet was doing financially, Olivia and I stared at each other.

I spoke to my therapist about Dad's callous brushoff. "Honestly Laurel," she sighed, "your family will never change. I don't think you should waste time discussing them anymore with me. You can't make someone go there if they don't want to. I'd like you to start focusing on finding a job and a man." She was right. Dad would never see things he didn't want to, no matter how much I forced the situation. But I had no energy left to focus on myself either. A week later, I broke up with my therapist.

47 Still Bionic

At the end of August, Lindsay Wagner, aka *The Bionic Woman*, appeared at the Palm Springs Comic Con to sign autographs and take pictures with fans. I told my high school friend, Nancy, about it, and we made a weekend out of it in the desert. We looked at the Comic Con program to find Lindsay Wagner, and after meandering through the comic book and toy stalls, found the autograph hall against the far wall of the Palm Springs Convention Center. I saw Lindsay just hanging out there with her assistant; no one was even in line to meet her. I felt like a little girl and looked at Nancy.

"I'm too nervous to go up to her."

Nancy laughed, "Why? She'll probably love it!"

I cautiously approached her booth. I think the whole Carrie Fisher stalker thing still affected me as I half-waited for security to escort predatorial me outside. But this was my first idol ever! Lindsay sat there calmly, as I walked up and I couldn't even speak.

"Uhm, my name's Laurel, and I bought an autograph with you on the Comic Con site?"

"Hi, yeah you should actually speak to this woman next to me. She takes care of all that stuff, I don't know anything here," she said, smiling at me. She still looked so beautiful, and taller than I imagined.

Her assistant, Regina, asked to see my receipt, so I showed her my phone. Then Lindsay asked me which one of her photos I wanted her to autograph. She had stacks of 8 × 10 black-and-white and color photos, ranging from *The Bionic Woman* era, up to the present. She watched me scrutinize the photos, trying to select one. "I'm so sorry, Lindsay, I'm such a huge fan, and I'm so nervous right now." Sweat dripped down my temples. *Get a fucking grip, Laurel, be Bionic!*

She tilted her head and smiled. "That's okay. What does your tee shirt say?" she asked. I was still so hyped up that I couldn't speak, so I held my tee shirt up for her to read, "Oh, it says *Adventure Is Waiting*, that's nice." She smiled at me. I selected a more recent still photo and handed it to her, as she asked me to spell my name. My heart pounded and I watched her as she autographed it, "To Laurel, Blessings … Lindsay Wagner." She gave it to me and smiled.

I said, "It is an honor to meet you. Thank you so much, Lindsay." OMG HONOR TO MEET YOU? I was almost 49 years old and was acting like a 6-year-old. I walked away and hit myself on the head.

I told Dad about Lindsay, "Oh yeah, you used to love her as a kid. I remember you sent in for her autograph when you were 8 years old." I scanned Dad like a foreign alien, and took a deep breath in, observing him. I was lucky to still have a father in my life. Half of my friends' parents had died or lived with illnesses like Parkinson's or Alzheimer's. Mine just had a strange case of narcissism with a tad of denial and delusion.

Seven months into Dad's release, I took him shopping again at Costco. This time, he mastered every aisle, knowing exactly where to go for his stash. I still loved observing him adjust back into society. He still couldn't get over all the consumerism, although he never missed out on a jumbo box of Cheerios. He had more clothes in his wardrobe now and wanted to send out his slacks to be pressed. "In prison, I paid this guy, Speedy, to press my uniforms."

I was slowly learning to appreciate and love Dad for who he was, instead of dwelling on what he was incapable of, or who he murdered, anymore. My friends laughed at me. "If he hasn't changed yet, he's *never* going to change," Olivia said.

I didn't know anyone else who had a dad released from prison, besides Rachel who didn't want to speak about it, so I had no benchmarks. We never talked about it as a family. Mom kept telling Dad not to talk about prison, Dad kept referring to himself as a retired CHP officer, and Rachel told me to stop dwelling on the past. Whenever Mom, Rachel, and I mentioned all those long prison drives, Dad cut us off saying, "I don't want to talk about the past anymore." But we hadn't talked about the past *yet*, together as a family.

I began changing my tune about Dad. It wasn't that he didn't want to talk about it, he *couldn't* talk about it. It was too painful for him to acknowledge. With all my years of therapy, how had I not seen this earlier? I actually began to feel sorry for him. He wanted to erase reality and replace it with his carefully constructed narratives. I couldn't tell if he lacked self-awareness or was overly self-aware.

Once I began letting go of my anger and expectations of him, my life became easier, and I was happier. All those restless thoughts swarming around in my head settled down. I was less stressed and slept better at night. For better or worse, he *was* my father—he raised me, protected me, then didn't, wanted a good life for me, then turned it upside down, and loved me. I was slowly starting to accept the sweet with the sour. I felt more relaxed around him, and truly enjoyed his company. We both had a sick sense of humor and talked about classic cars. I enjoyed his prison stories more now, which he told when Mom wasn't around, because it made me appreciate being free on the outside. I'd told him I wanted to get an El Camino, so he searched on Craigslist for one with his recently purchased iPad.

He texted me every morning to say he loved me, and even learned how to send emoticons like roses and hearts. A part of him seemed to miss prison—he had people to talk to, and a routine. He kept in touch with a couple of inmates and sent them pictures of himself dressed up with a sports coat and slacks on. His old cellie, Rob, called him a couple of times a week, and they gabbed away like two teenage girls.

At the end of his first year of freedom, I took Mom and Dad to see *The Last Jedi* at The Chinese Theatre in Hollywood. I dressed up like a storm trooper, and Dad dressed up like the emperor. Dad hadn't seen a *Star Wars* movie since I took them to see a screening of *The Phantom Menace*, the first film I worked on in 1999. We waited in line and took photos with other people who were dressed up. Dad reminisced about the first time he took Rachel and me to see the original *Star Wars* in Ventura. "I remember you guys didn't want to go!" he bellowed.

"Well, look at me now and the superfan you created!" I beamed with excitement. Dad bought me a commemorative *Star Wars* popcorn bowl, with his own money.

48 Freebird

After seven months of good behavior, Dad's parole officer granted him permission to go on his first trip to Arizona, for Aunt Deanie's eightieth birthday. Dad was afraid airport security would flag him for being a felon, so he insisted on driving. I offered to be his co-pilot, while Rachel and Mom flew. I didn't tell him I had brought a handful of weed.

Dad drove so slowly and was so busy trying to figure out the buttons on his dashboard that he swerved into cars. He even made a left turn and drove down the wrong side of the road, and I screamed. He kept referring to Bluetooth as Wi-Fi, so I schooled him on the difference. I helped him with his dashboard as I gripped my seatbelt. We passed a road sign—STATE PRISON NEXT RIGHT, DO NOT PICK UP HITCHHIKERS. I asked Dad to keep his eyes open for any prison buddies of his. Well ... *I* thought it was funny.

We crossed the state line into Arizona. It was Dad's first time leaving California in eighteen years. He was silent, taking it all in, checking out other cars, roadside stops, and the desert scenery, peppered with saguaro cacti. "You forget how much space there is out here," he said in awe. I kept my eyes on the road.

I asked about Bobby, Dad's old car buddy/baccarat dealer who was once a club manager. "Oh, I talked to him last week, his Parkinson's is advancing so he's going to move into an assisted living place in Vegas."

"That makes me so sad," I said. "We really need to go visit him. Maybe after this trip, you can ask your PO if you can drive to Vegas with me and we can visit him. He was so good to us when you went away. He always called to check in on us and came to visit you many times." I felt the need to remind Dad of so many things.

"Oh yeah, Laurel, I know. I gotta put that on my list, I don't want to push it with my PO."

We picked up Mom and Rachel at the airport in Tucson later that day and drove to our hotel. Dad went to check in, and I helped Mom unload the luggage. "Dude, what did you bring?" I asked Mom. In the trunk were two enormous suitcases, and a smaller weekend bag in the back seat.

"Those aren't mine," Mom pointed in the trunk. "Those are your father's." It was like Britney Spears had packed for a weekend show in Vegas.

"What the hell is in there?" I asked Dad.

"My clothes and shoes!" He crossed his arms. Then it hit me. He was used to packing up all his belongings in his cell whenever he transferred to new prisons or cells. I stopped busting his chops.

Aunt Deanie's birthday was like a family reunion. We ate, drank, took photos, reminisced about the good old days, and met some of her friends. I watched Dad working the room, giving every ear that would listen his curated narrative—army, CHP officer, maintaining his innocence—the usual. I went over to Mom. "Dad has got to stop talking so much about himself. I can't take it!"

"Laurel, just remember, your father absolutely worships you. Try to go easy on him." Wow, that hit me by surprise. Then I really felt like an ass. I just wish he showed it more.

At the hotel, Dad paced around, complaining about his shortness of breath and lack of sleep. We went shopping, and after a few minutes, Dad walked toward his car, saying he was ready to leave.

"What is up with Dad?" I asked Mom. "He can't wait a few minutes for us to window shop, after we waited for hours in all those damn prison visiting lines?"

"Laurel, your dad's having panic attacks. He does this same thing at home."

Just as I'd predicted, Dad was having reentry anxiety.

When we arrived back home to Westlake, I sat down with Dad on the couch. "Dad, I still think you need to see a therapist. I mean it can't hurt, right?" His eyes widened.

"Yeah, I think that's a great idea." He let out a deep sigh. "I'm so overwhelmed."

"By what?" I was curious. I looked into his blue eyes darting back and forth.

"By everything!" he raised his hands in the air. "There's so much information on the Internet. Before, I could only get access to the local *Auto Trader Magazine*, and now I can Google cars worldwide. Amazon is the Sears of their time and there's so much for sale, too much! And I can't believe all the paperwork you have to fill out for things, and all the bills we get! And what's with all these service charges when we go out to eat? Am I supposed to tip on that too?"

Dad hadn't taken care of anything financial or health-wise or tax-wise or, really *anything* life-wise for almost twenty years. I stood up from the couch and gave him a hug.

"Dad, it's nothing to be ashamed of. I've watched documentaries on inmates being released back into society, and the ones who had more to come home to actually had a harder time adjusting, because they failed to see there would be a process for re-entry. I really think they should have placed you in a half-way house for a few months to help you assimilate."

"*What?* Are you crazy? I don't need a half-way house. Those are for people with drug problems. How could you say that?"

"Well, anyway," I said, "let's find someone for you to talk to you right away."

"Okay, Lip." I stood up and kissed him goodbye before leaving.

Dad asked around and got a referral to a counselor in Westlake and began seeing her weekly. After a couple of months into Dad's therapy sessions, I could already see a change. First off, he had someplace to go and part of a routine. He was also trying to figure out more things on his own first, before asking.

One day, while visiting Mom and Dad, Dad suggested that I go with him to therapy. "Sally thinks it's important for family members to come with me for support," he said. Mom had been once with him. That was all she could handle. "I'm just not a talker," she said. I felt bad for Dad. "Sure," I said, "but I'm going to meet with her first, before we go in together."

"You'll like her," he said, "she used to be a bartender in Brooklyn."

Dad drove us to his therapy session. As he opened Sally's door, she seemed startled and wasn't expecting me, as I assumed. "Hi, I'm Laurel, Michael's oldest daughter," I said, following her into her office, and sitting down on the couch, while Dad sat in the waiting area outside. "So, how does this work? I'm not sure where to start," I asked, having sudden flashbacks of couples' therapy with Mom.

"I'm surprised to see you here," she said, settling into her velvet burgundy armchair.

"Oh, I thought Dad said you were expecting to see me today." I sat on the edge of the sofa.

"Oh no, it doesn't matter. I'm happy to meet you, your dad has mentioned you quite a bit. What are you expecting from today's session with your father?" she asked, flinging back her long, blond, and permed hair.

"Honestly, nothing. I don't have any expectations of him anymore." I mean, of course I did, but I was still retraining myself not to have any, and I wasn't about to commit to seeing Dad's therapist with him on a regular basis.

"I've been in therapy half my life, and I'm slowly learning to accept him for who he is. Whenever I mention anything about how his incarceration affected us, he turns the conversation back to him and how hard it was on him, so I have no hope," I said, leaning back and crossing my legs.

"Well, Laurel, you can't change his narcissism, because that's a behavioral disorder. But we can definitely work on empathy," she said folding her hands together.

"Yeah, sure, whatever. I'm just here to support him." I smiled and inhaled deeply.

After about twenty minutes of me giving her my version of the "situation," Dad came back into the room. He sat down next to me on the couch, squeezing my left knee and smiling, as Sally said she wanted to discuss empathy. Dad said, "Oh, well, okay then."

She asked me to look at Dad and tell him how his years in prison were for me. I took a deep breath and paused. Then I turned to him and told him how depressed and paranoid I was, how I cried all the time, how overwhelmed I was running the clubs and organizing attorneys, and how I'd put my life on hold. I told him I was suicidal in the beginning but couldn't leave Mom and Rachel alone to deal with it all. I could have gone on, but I knew he was a delicate flower, so I left it at that. I was overcome with a massive wave of drowsiness.

"Okay, Laurel," she exhaled. "That's a big statement to make, and I'd like to pause right there. Michael, what do you think about what your daughter just said?" Sally asked, gesturing to Dad with her hand.

"Oh, I agree!" Dad leaned up on the couch, "I mean *I* was suicidal *too*! I didn't know whom to trust, I was afraid to talk to anyone on the phones, and I was worried my cellmates were informants!" He went on about his situation while I sat there, arms crossed, looking down at the peach carpeting.

"Have you and your family discussed what it was like for them during this whole period?" she asked Dad.

"Oh yeah, for sure we have." He glanced at me, and I gave him a blank stare. "I mean, I'm sure we could talk about it more, but we've definitely talked about it," he said, fumbling his words.

Then our time was up.

After the session, Dad and I walked out to his car. "That was great!" he said, patting me on the back. "I just need to get your mother back here again."

"Well, Dad, you can only lead a horse to water," I said, putting my seatbelt on tight. I stared out the window in silence on the ride home. I couldn't decide if I wanted to laugh or cry after the session. Not even in therapy could Dad look at someone else besides himself. Why had he wanted me to go? One thing I knew for sure was that this session gave me the answer once and for all. For my own sanity, I needed to let this go and move on. I had already tortured myself with the most oppressive device from the Inquisition I could, waiting for some apology or remorse from Dad. Pure torment.

My therapist was right again—he'd never change how I wanted him to, not even with therapy, like Henry the Brit, or the orange Smurf, or Forest, the selfish and Cheap Guy from Atlanta. Basically, everyone I had dated so far. Except I didn't know their diagnosis other than not being suitable for me. However, I had one for my beloved dad: narcissism.

I recently turned 56, ten years older than Mac was when he was murdered, and two years younger than Dad when he was arrested. I've outlived Anne now by twelve years. My identity for so long was the daughter of a strip club owner, then of a convicted murderer. After taking that hike in the woods the day Dad was arrested, searching for a meaningful career, I finally found one. I start nursing school in the spring and am excited to be giving back to my community, helping those in need. Who knows, I might even work at a prison.

When I hear "Rhinestone Cowboy" by Glen Campbell on the radio, I smile and think about how much I've overcome since those first dark days. At night, sometimes I watch those true crime documentaries. There's even a new one on Mac and Dad. I watch the defendants, like Ted Bundy, O.J. Simpson, or Scott Peterson, for example, sit there and passionately deny to the interviewer any wrongdoing, like it's all some huge misunderstanding. It's alarming to see how they've convinced themselves they are innocent.

Dad told me he's working in therapy on not being so negative and critical. I told him that was a good thing, because only unhappy people criticize others, and it just makes him look bad. He still comments on my weight, and I asked Rachel if he does that to her too. "Yeah, he does, he just can't help himself, I ignore him," she said shrugging her shoulders.

Once I accepted Dad's guilt, it was somehow easier to listen to his rants more. I thought he would die in prison, and I'm happy to have him back. Dad and I were having a heart-to-heart one time in their kitchen, and I just blurted it out, "Dad, just so you know, I think you did it." He looked at me and let out a deep sigh, "OK," he said. That was all we said about it. Mom and Dad are still ironing out the kinks in their relationship. They finally moved into the house Dad bought. Dad has his big garage again and put up posters of the cars he used to own in his previous life.

Mom has a picture of Dad on her wall that I like to look at. It's a weathered black-and-white picture of him at 4 years old, taken by his father at their apartment in New Jersey. Dad is sitting on a stool, smiling, with all his front teeth missing, wearing a newsboy cap, knickers with suspenders, and no idea what horrors were in store for him throughout his childhood. I see my father still as that insecure little boy, longing for parental love, affection, and attention. The rejection from his parents selling him still haunts him. He mentions it often, as if it happened recently. I see so clearly how there is so much that has happened to him that he'll never be capable of processing, and I feel sorry for him. Once I was able to accept him for who he is and see his emotional parameters, it made it easier for me to love him, to choose to love him. Dad was set free by the prison system, and I am set free by forgiving him.

ABOUT THE AUTHOR

Laurel Woods is a proud Los Angeles native. She has been featured on KCRW's radio show UnFictional, as well as published in Chicken Soup for the Soul, Thrillist.com, and The Nervous Breakdown, and was a regular contributor for MTV Geek franchise covering all things Star Wars. When she's not helping her dad out with technology, she scuba dives in exotic locations with sharks. She also enjoys spending time on eBay buying Moonlighting, Mork and Mindy and Bionic Woman memorabilia. Strip Club Heiress: The Jet Strip, My Father's Conviction and the Murder of Mac McKenna is her first memoir.

Laurel Woods, photo courtesy John Davis, https://jdph.com/.